Database Directions

From Relational to Distributed, Multimedia, and Object-Oriented Database Systems

James A. Larson
Illustrations by Carol and Michael Larson

For book and bookstore information

http://www.prenhall.com

Prentice Hall PTR
Upper Saddle River, New Jersey 07458

Larson, James A.
    Database directions : from relational to distributed,
  multimedia, and object-oriented database system / James A. Larson.
        p. cm.
    includes index.
    ISBN 0-13-290867-0
    1. Database management.   2. Data bases.   I. Title.
  QA76.9.D3L368 1995
  005.75--dc20   95-7043
                                                           CIP

Editorial/production supervision
  and interior design: **Ann Sullivan**
Cover designer: **Wanda Lubelska**
Manufacturing manager: **Alexis R. Heydt**
Acquisitions editor: **Paul Becker**
Editorial assistant: **Maureen Diana**

 ©1995 by Prentice Hall PTR
Prentice-Hall, Inc.
A Simon and Schuster Company
Upper Saddle River, NJ 07458

The publisher offers discounts on this book when ordered in bulk quantities.
For more information, contact:
            Corporate Sales Department
            Prentice Hall PTR
            One Lake Street
            Upper Saddle River, NJ 07458

            Phone: 800-382-3419
            Fax: 201-236-7141
            email: corpsales@prenhall.com

Printed in the United States of America

10 9 8 7 6 5 4 3 2 1

ISBN: 0-13-290867-0

Prentice-Hall International (UK) Limited, *London*
Prentice-Hall of Australia Pty. Limited, *Sydney*
Prentice-Hall Canada Inc., *Toronto*
Prentice-Hall Hispanoamericana, S.A., *Mexico*
Prentice-Hall of India Private Limited, *New Delhi*
Prentice-Hall of Japan, Inc., *Tokyo*
Simon & Schuster Asia Pte. Ltd., *Singapore*
Editora Prentice-Hall do Brasil, Ltda., *Rio de Janeiro*

to Carol and Mike

Contents

Preface

Relational database systems are widely used today. They have solved many database management problems, including data persistence, easy and efficient access by multiple users, and isolation of data structures from application code (often referred to as data independence). However, today's relational database management systems are generally limited to centralized systems that support only structured data consisting of digits and short character strings. This book introduces database management technologies and techniques that go beyond the limitations of today's relational database management systems.

The accompanying figure illustrates the space of database management systems (DBMSs) described in this book. Today's widely used centralized relational database management systems are positioned in the lower-left corner. The two axis represents two types of enhancements to today's centralized relational DBMSs. The vertical axes represent the extension of centralized DBMSs into distributed DBMSs. The horizontal axis represents the incorporation of new types of data, including text, images, audio, video, and object-oriented data. The upper-right corner represents the integration of data distribution and multiple data types.

This book describes various types of DBMSs that break the limitations of current centralized relational DBMSs, beginning with distributed DBMSs.

Distributed DBMS

A distributed relational DBMS is software that manages structured data consisting of digits and short character strings stored in multiple databases, possibly on multiple computers connected by a communication system. A distributed DBMS enables users to locate, access, and integrate data in multiple databases. This book presents several alternative solutions to the problem of how to access data in multiple databases residing on different computers. The first part of this book characterizes distributed relational DBMSs, what they are, and why we need them. This book describes the concepts and strategies of distributed DBMSs. It will help you to determine if and when you should migrate to a distributed relational DBMS. It will help you to select the type of distributed relational DBMS that meets the needs of your enterprise. It discusses the major technical problems associated with distributed relational DBMSs and presents alternative solutions to these problems. It points out the major pitfalls of distributed relational DBMSs and offers suggestions for avoiding them.

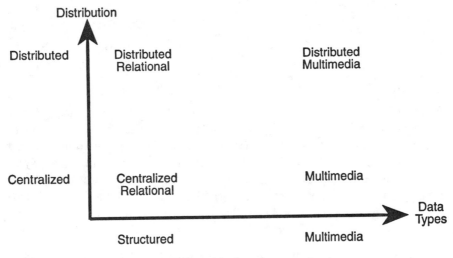

Figure P.1   Distributed database management systems

Chapter 1 introduces the basic types of distributed DBMSs. It also explains the two major paths to distributed DBMSs: integration and distribution. Chapter 2 overviews software architecture for sharing data. It presents the major software components in a distributed DBMS and briefly explains how each component works. Chapter 3 discusses federated DBMS, a special type of loosely-coupled distributed DBMS. Chapter 4 addresses the problems of designing distributed databases. Chapter 5 addresses the problems of specifying distributed execution plans. Chapter 6 discusses distributed transaction processing. Chapter 7 discusses a major trend: client–server architectures.

The chapters in the second part of this book examine other types of data that can be managed by a DBMS and how those data types can be distributed.

Textual DBMS

Users need access to textual documents stored as files. While a file system enables users to access a file or document by its name and location within a hierarchical directory, a textual DBMS enables users to retrieve documents by formulating queries describing the desired content. Chapter 8 discusses solutions to the problems of storing, indexing, and retrieving textual information.

Multimedia DBMS

DBMSs also need to manage a variety of new data types, including text, image, audio, and video data types. These new media types introduce special problems, including large data objects, continuous temporal data objects, and the problems of synchronization of multiple streams of temporal data such as audio and video. Chapter 9 discusses solutions to the problems of storing, organizing, retrieving, and synchronizing multimedia information.

Object-oriented DBMS

Object-oriented design, object-oriented analysis techniques, and object-oriented programming languages are invading software engineering and development. This chapter describes another piece of the software industry trend toward object orientation—object-oriented DBMS. This chapter describes the basic principles of object-oriented data and the problems of storing and retrieving objects. Chapter 10 also summarizes new types of applications made possible by object-oriented DBMS.

Textual, multimedia, and object-oriented data types present special problems in a distributed DBMS. This book describes solutions to the new problems introduced by distributed textual, multimedia, and object-oriented DBMSs.

This book contains two useful appendixes. Every distributed DBMS needs a communication subsystem to transport requests and responses among local DBMSs. Appendix A presents a high-level overview of communication systems. Appendix B presents a methodology for evaluating distributed DBMSs and suggests some questions that should be answered before a decision to purchase is made.

Target Audience

This book is written for data-processing managers, systems managers, systems analysts, database administrators, and others who are considering venturing beyond centralized relational DBMSs. This book outlines the basic principles of these new types of DBMSs without drowning the reader in the details and complexities of specific commercial products. This book assumes that the reader is familiar with a relational DBMS. This book will help you to see beyond today's relational database systems and prepare you for the next generation of data management technologies and techniques.

James Larson

Trademarks Used

Acrobat is registered trademark of Adobe Systems Incorporated

DB2 is a registered trademark of IBM Corporation

FoxBase is a registered trademark of Fox Holdings, Inc.

Gemstone is a registered trademark of Servio Logic Development Corp.

HyperCard is a registered trademark of Apple Computer, Inc.

HyperTalk is a trademark of Apple Computer, Inc.

IDMS is a registered trademark of Cullinane Database Systems, Inc.

Imara is a registered trademark of Imara Research Corporation

IMS is a registered trademark of IBM

Indeo is registered trademark of Intel Corporation

Ingres is a registered trademark of Ingres Corporation

KeyFile is a registered trademark of KeyFile Corporation

KeyFile is a registered trademark of KeyFile Corporation

Lotus Notes is a registered trademark of Lotus Development Corporation

MacroMind Director is a registered trademark of MacroMind, Inc.

Microsoft Access is a trademark of Microsoft Corporation

Microsoft is a registered trademark of Microsoft Corporation

Microsoft is a registered trademark of Microsoft Corporation.

Mosiac is trademark of Mosaic Communications Corporation

Mosiac is trademark of Mosaic Communications Corporation

O2 from registered to Groupement D-interet Public Altair

Objectivity is a trademark of Objective systems SF AB

ObjectStore is a trademark of Object Design, Inc.

ObjectStore is a trademark of Object Design, Inc.

Ontos is a registered of Ontos, Inc.

Oracle is a registered trademark of Oracle Corporation

Postscript is a trademark of Adobe Systems

PowerBuilder registered trademark of Powersoft Corporation

PowerPoint is registered trademark of Microsoft Corporation

SMALLTALK is a trademark of Xerox Corporation

System 2000 is a registered trademark of SAS Institute Inc.

TeX is registered trademark of Personal Tex, Inc.

Toolbook is a registered trademark of Asymetric Corporation

Toolbook is a registered trademark of Asymetric Corporation

Versant is a registered trademark of Versant Object Technology

Visual Basic is a registered trademark of Microsoft Corporation

All other product names mentioned herein are the trademarks of their respective owners.

1

Basic Concepts and Terminology

This chapter discusses the following:

- The problems faced by users in locating, accessing, and integrating data from multiple databases.
- The requirements for a centralized database management system.
- The requirements for distributed data.
- The approaches used to manage multiple databases.
- How a database administrator selects the approach appropriate for his or her major application.
- How database administrators follow an integration path from several separate DBMSs to a distributed DBMS.
- How database administrators follow a distribution path from a centralized DBMS to a distributed DBMS.

Section 1.1 describes the problems users face in locating, accessing, and integrating data from multiple database management systems (DBMSs). These problems represent the motivating factors for distributed DBMSs.

Section 1.2 reviews the basic terminology and concepts for relational DBMSs. These terms and concepts will be used and extended to discuss distributed DBMSs.

1

Section 1.3 summarizes seven specific requirements for distributed DBMSs. Different types of distributed DBMSs satisfy these requirements to varying degrees.

Section 1.4 outlines six different techniques for meeting some or all of these requirements. While all six of these approaches involve some form of distribution, only two of them can really be called distributed DBMSs in the sense that they satisfy most of the requirements for distributed DBMSs. Database practitioners should carefully determine their data sharing requirements and then choose the data sharing technique that best meets those requirements. Section 1.5 presents examples of selecting data-sharing techniques.

Section 1.6 describes two migration paths for evolving centralized DBMSs into distributed DBMS. Several existing centralized DBMSs may be integrated into a distributed DBMS. A single existing centralized DBMS may be distributed into a distributed DBMS. Some distributed DBMSs result as a combination of these migration paths.

1.1   Users Cannot Locate, Access, and Integrate Data

The Situation. Information vital to running a modern enterprise is scattered across multiple, isolated information islands in a sea of computers and database systems. Users must locate, access, and integrate data from multiple databases and files from different computers located in different geographical locations. Many users cannot access these islands of information. We call them *islands of unreachability*, or *IOUs*, because they are out of reach of most users. Users don't want and don't need IOUs. Three factors contribute to the IOU problem: multiple computers, multiple data systems, and geographic distances separating computers.

1. *Multiple computers.* The number of computers within an organization is proliferating. Many enterprises own several mainframes containing data used by the enterprise as a whole. Most enterprises also own many workstations and personal computers. Users generate and store what are essentially private files and databases on these workstations and personal computers. Each computer contains several databases and files that users need to access; each computer is an IOU.

2. *Multiple data-management systems.* Two major types of systems have evolved for managing computerized data. Almost all computers have a file system for storing and retrieving data maintained on nonvolatile storage. Each *file system* typically contains files organized into a hierarchical directory structure. Many computers also support one or more database management systems. Each *database management system* (DBMS) contains several structured files containing interrelated data. Each file and database management system maintains separate information. Users of a database management system may not be able to access data in files, and users of the file

system may not be able to access data in the database management system. IOUs may exist within a single computer.

3. *Geographic distances between computers.* Computers may physically reside in different rooms, in different buildings, or in different cities around the world. This geographical distance makes it difficult for one user to access another user's data. The geographical dispersion of computers contributes to the IOU phenomenon.

How IOUs Arise. The way that an enterprise and its databases evolve and develop contributes to the increase of IOUs. Many companies encourage their enterprise units (divisions, departments, and subsidiaries) to be independent from each other. Independent enterprise units evolve differently with different data requirements. Applications are developed by various enterprise units at different times. Each enterprise unit designs its database to meet its particular needs. No one should be surprised to discover that the databases of different enterprise units contain different information used for different purposes. Unfortunately, independent enterprise units grow separate IOUs.

The decision to purchase several types of computers provides another factor resulting in IOUs. Mainframes from different vendors often support different operating systems, file systems, and database management systems. Users must access databases built under different systems using different commands and languages, leading to more information isolation.

The proliferation of PCs has greatly aggravated the IOU problem. The widespread use of PCs has resulted in many small information islands. Users frequently store data on floppy disks. Users must manually locate and place disks into the PC's disk drive before they access data. These off-line databases constitute multitudes of small, very isolated information islands.

The Problem. To be useful, data must be available when they are needed. Users often have difficulty in accessing and analyzing data scattered among several information islands. Users probably do not know what data are available in each database. Users might not know where to find data that they believe are available. This makes it difficult, if not impossible, for users to access needed data. Finally, users usually find it difficult to integrate data from scattered databases.

The Need. Users must perform three essential actions to obtain meaningful information from multiple IOUs.

1. *Locate.* Users must determine if relevant data are available somewhere among the IOUs. Users must then locate the appropriate IOUs containing the relevant data.

2. *Access.* Users must be able to formulate separate requests to each IOU to retrieve the data hidden within that island.

3. *Integrate.* Users must coordinate and integrate the results of their requests into an integrated format that they can review and use to make decisions.

Locating, accessing, and integrating information from IOUs require time, knowledge, and patience, three qualities that many users lack.

A Solution. Distributed data management provides facilities that enable users to locate, access, and integrate data from multiple IOUs, forming an information continent of sharing. Distributed data management enables users to perform the three essential actions of data:

1. *Locate.* Users examine a dictionary directory of available data to determine if relevant data are available, what the data mean, and where to locate them.
2. *Access.* User interfaces help users to formulate requests that extract the desired data from one or more IOUs. Communications services transfer requests and results among computers.
3. *Integrate.* Users invoke software for merging and integrating data from several IOUs. User interfaces format data for presentation to the user in a form that the user can quickly comprehend and use.

1.2   A Centralized DBMS Manages Interrelated Information

It is always wise to carefully define the meaning of terms to avoid confusion and misunderstandings. This section defines the basic concepts and terms used in relational database management systems. These terms will be used throughout this book.

We will use the term *user* to refer to either a human user or an application program that accesses a database. To access a database, the human user will use some type of *user interface*. The human user might use a query language, a form fill-in user interface, or a graphical user interface (GUI). To access a database, an application program uses an *application program interface (API)*. An application program interface consists of (1) data structures shared by the application program and the database management system, (2) database functions that the application program may invoke, and (3) messages and return codes from the database management system indicating the success or failure of those functions.

A *data type* is a set of values with an implied physical representation. Widely used data types in DBMSs include integers, floating-point numbers, and character strings. Additional data types are coming into use. These data types include graphics, images, audio, and video.

Figure 1.1 illustrates the relationship among the components of a typical database. In Figure 1.1, one-to-many relationships are represented by the inverted V at the end of the "many" side of the one-to-many relationship.

A *data item* is a data type and a value. Usually a database management system stores the type in a dictionary directory and the values in the database. For example, the data item (integer, 5) is represented by binary '00000101' in the database. Some database management systems store the data type with each value. These data items

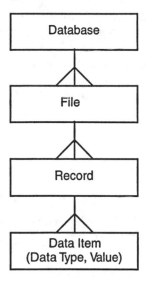

Figure 1.1   Components of a database

are said to be *tagged* in that the data type of each value is explicitly associated with the data value.

A *record* is a set of data values. For example, a record might contain the data values (5, 'John Doe', 1989), where each record contains an integer, character string, and another integer.

A *file* is an ordered set of homogeneous records. By homogeneous, we mean that each record contains values for the same data types in the same sequence. The following is logical view of three records:

(5, 'John Doe', 1989), (7, 'Jane Doe', 1991), (8, 'John Smith', 1992)

In relational databases, all records in the same file must contain values of exactly the same data types. The file is called a *relation* or *table*. Records are called *tuples* or *rows*.

A *database* is a collection of interrelated files. Two files are interrelated if they contain common data types that can be interpreted as being equivalent. For example, two files are interrelated if the integer data type that represents the identification number of a department record in a department file is also contained in a record in the employee file. The two files are said to be *logically linked*. Two files are also interrelated if the value of a data type of one file contains the physical address of a record in the other file. The two files are said to be *physically linked*. Users of relational database systems can see and manipulate logical links, but they can never see nor manipulate physical links. The use of logical links is one of the characteristics that makes relational databases different from other types of databases.

Enterprises typically use two types of systems to manage data: file systems and relational database management systems. These systems differ in the number of functions that they perform. A *file system* consists of hardware for storing files and software for accessing files by file name and location within a hierarchical directory. Popular file systems include the UNIX file system and MS-DOS file system.

A *database management system (DBMS)* is hardware for storing databases and software for accessing the database by content rather than location. The database management system software supports several features often missing from file systems:

- *Human interfaces*, such as query languages and form fill-in interfaces. Human users use these interfaces to save and retrieve records.

- *Security enforcement policies and mechanisms*. The DBMS authenticates users' rights to access data.

- *Business rules*. Business rules are enterprise-specific constraints about the values of data in the database. The DBMS verifies that values entered or modified by users conform to business rules. For example, a business rule might require that an employee's age must always be between 16 and 65 years. Business rules are important because they keep invalid data from entering into the database and thus enable users to avoid taking inappropriate actions based on erroneous data from the database.

- *Concurrency transparency*. Several users may try to modify the same data item at the same time. When this occurs, the changes entered by one user might be overwritten by a second user without taking into account the change entered by the first user. Multiple users need some type of concurrency control so that they don't inadvertently ignore changes made by other users. A DBMS supports concurrency transparency if multiple users can use the DBMS at the same time and not worry about updating the same data item at the same time. Each user of a DBMS that supports concurrency transparency is not aware that other users are using the DBMS. DBMSs on servers and mainframes usually support concurrency transparency. Because PCs are typically used by only one person at a time, PC-based DBMSs seldom support concurrency transparency.

- *Transaction processing*. A *transaction* is a sequence of database operations that must be executed as a unit. Transactions are desirable because they guarantee that the data satisfy business rules. If one of the operations of a transaction fails, then the entire transaction aborts and any changes made to the database by the transaction are automatically undone. This guarantees that data in the database always satisfy all business rules. The more expensive DBMSs support transaction processing.

- *Backup and recovery mechanisms*. These facilities enable users to make copies of their databases and to restore a database from a copy if the database is damaged. The DBMS may also make a log or journal of database changes. The DBMS uses logs and journals to restore the database to a previous point in time. While most mainframe and server DBMSs have copy and restore utilities, many PC DBMSs do not support journaling.

A *centralized database* is a database that is managed by a single DBMS. Note that a single DBMS may manage several centralized databases. This occurs when there are no interrelationships among the databases managed by the single DBMS. For example, a DBMS on a school district's mainframe may contain a database for each of several schools within the district. However, the databases are not interrelated in any way except that they have a common format so that the same software can be applied to each database.

Database administration is the role filled by individuals who design and manage databases. Individuals who fill this role are called *database administrators* (DBAs). DBAs also fine tune the DBMS so that users can access data in the database easily and efficiently.

1.3   A Distributed DBMS Meets Requirements

We will use the term *component DBMS* to refer to any of several DBMSs containing data that the user may wish to access. We will use the term *global DBMS* to refer to a collection of facilities enabling the user to access data in multiple component DBMSs. The global DBMS calls on the component DBMS to perform many tasks; however, there are some tasks that only the global DBMS can perform. The following enumerates the facilities and services of a global DBMS that enable users to access data in several component databases.

Global DBMS Enables Users to Access Data from Multiple Component DBMSs. Users may need to perform two tasks to access data from multiple component DBMSs:

1. Access descriptions of data so users can determine if the desired data are available in some component DBMS.

2. Formulate a request to access the desired data. The request itself may take either of two forms:

   a. *Multicomponent DBMS request.* A user writes a single request involving data from multiple component databases.

   b. *Single-component DBMS request.* A user writes several requests and each request is routed to a separate component DBMS for execution.

Users Obtain Up-to-date Results. The results of user requests reflect the most recent values available from the component DBMSs. In some situations, such as census and statistical databases, retrieving data that are a few hours or days old does not significantly affect the conclusions. In other situations, such as medical and security applications, up-to-date information may be critical.

Global DBMS Hides Data Location and Replication from Users. Automatic optimizers access dictionary directory information in order to determine where to find the desired data. *Data location and replication transparency* mean users are not aware of the location of data or whether the data have been replicated onto several component databases. Data location and replication transparency enable users to formulate requests without specifying to which component databases the request should be directed. Data location and replication transparency also enable DBAs to move data from one component database to another without forcing the user to change the specification of his or her requests. However, location and replication transparency require the use of automatic optimizers to partition the user's request into multiple subrequests and to determine which of the component DBMSs can process each subrequest.

Gateways Translate Queries. Gateways convert the queries to the format required by each component DBMS and convert the results into the format required by the user. Some distributed database management systems are heterogeneous in that different types of component DBMSs are used to manage different component databases. In this case, the user's request may need to be translated for processing by a different component DBMS. Automatic translating software called *gateways* perform these translations.

Global DBMS Merges Data. The data from multiple component databases are merged and integrated. If no data merging is performed, then the user sees results from multiple component databases and must manually merge and integrate the results. If the data from multiple component DBMSs are automatically merged and integrated, the user sees a single result that may be faster to comprehend and use.

Global DBMS Enforces Business Rules Involving Data in Multiple Component Databases. Business rules involving data in multiple databases are enforced. For example, if one database contains the value of "Engineering" for the department for which an employee works, then the separate Department database should also contain an entry for "Engineering." Business rules can be enforced using the following four approaches:

1. *Users enforce business rules.* The user verifies that no business rule is violated. If users enter or change data, causing the violation of one or more business rules, then users must correct the database values violating the business rules. Users don't always know what the business rules are, don't always take the time to verify that they are enforced, and may not correct data that violate a business rule.

2. *Each component database management system enforces business rules affecting data within its own component database.* The DBA of the component database specifies rules about data values that the component database management enforces. However, relational database management systems are limited in the types of business rules that they can enforce. Nor can these rules involve data in multiple component databases.

3. *Transaction processing automatically enforces business rules.* Programmers write transactions that update one or more of the component databases. If the programmers are careful, they write transactions in such a manner that, when executed to completion, each transaction enforces all business rule. If a transaction fails, then the transaction processing system removes all changes made to each of the component database by the failed transaction. This leaves each component database in the same state as when the transaction began processing and in a state in which all business rules are satisfied.

4. *A global DBMS facility enforces business rules that involve data in multiple component DBMSs.* Unfortunately, few distributed DBMSs support business rules that involve data in multiple component DBMSs.

Global DBMS Coordinates Recovery of Component DBMSs. The system maintains information useful in recovering from processing errors and destroyed media. Data in one or more component databases may become unusable because physical storage media are destroyed, the operating system fails, or transactions and application programs execute incorrectly, leaving invalid data in the database. Approaches for solving these problems include the following:

- Users must manually correct invalid data and reenter destroyed data in each affected component database. Users hate doing this and don't always correct invalid data.

- The DBAs of each component DBMS uses backup copies of component databases along with transaction logs to reconstruct component databases. To do this, each component DBA must (1) reload backup copies of component databases, (2) restore the effects of transactions that completed between the time the backup copies were created and the time the error occurred, and (3) restart transactions in progress when the error occurred. The DBAs of each component DBMS must coordinate with each other so that all component databases are consistent with each other.

- Global DBMS coordinates the automatic recovery of multiple component databases. However, not all distributed DBMSs support for the coordinated recovery of component databases.

As you can see, there are many requirements for a distributed DBMS. No existing commercial DBMS satisfies all these requirements. As we shall see in the next section, distributed DBMSs vary in their ability to satisfy each of the above requirements.

1.4   Users Access Multiple Databases

Figure 1.2 illustrates several configurations of component DBMSs, each differing in the degree to which they support each of the above requirements.

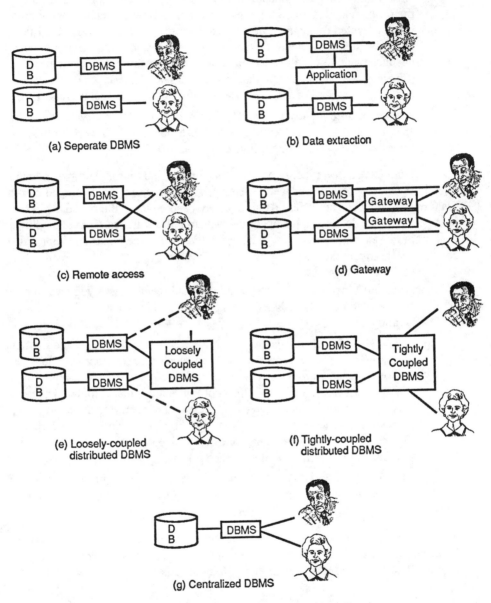

Figure 1.2   Approaches to distributed DBMS

Figure 1.2(a) illustrates the islands of information problem in which the user of one DBMS cannot access the data from another DBMS. This configuration supports none of the above requirements.

Each of the approaches illustrated in Figures 1.2(b) through (f) enables users to access data from multiple component databases. Each of these approaches differs in the degree to which they support the above requirements. Approaches 1.2(b) through (d) do not have a separate global DBMS. In these approaches, the component DBMSs have been extended to support some of the above requirements. Approaches 1.2(e) and (f) have a separate global DBMS. However, these two global DBMSs differ in which requirements they support.

Figure 1.2(g) illustrates multiple users accessing a centralized DBMS. This configuration supports none of the above requirements.

The following discusses how each approach satisfies each of the above requirements. Table 1.1 summarizes the characteristics of each approach.

1.4.1 Data Extraction

Figure 1.2(b) illustrates the data-extraction approach. Programmers must write special application programs to extract data from a component database, reformat the extracted data, and then merge the data into another component database. Users then

Table 1.1 Comparison of Approaches

	Data Extraction	Remote Access	Gateways	Loosely-Coupled Distributed DBMS	Tightly-Coupled Distributed DBMS
Users access data from multiple databases	Yes	Yes	Yes	Yes	Yes
Users obtain up-to-date results	No	Yes	Yes	Yes	Yes
System translates queries	No	No	Yes	Yes	Yes
System hides data location and replication from users	No	No	No	Yes	Yes
Transactions enforce semantic integrity constraints involving multiple databases	No	No	No	No	Yes
System merges data	No	No	No	Yes	Yes
System supports coordinated recovery	No	No	No	Yes	Yes

direct their data requests involving data from multiple component databases to the updated component database.

The advantage of the data-extraction approach is that users of the updated component database have immediate access to the extracted data without suffering from the communication costs and delays in accessing multiple component databases. However, data extraction satisfies only one of the distributed DBMS requirements outlined above. Users can access data from multiple databases, even though the extracted data becomes stale whenever the original component databases are updated. Data extraction does not guarantee that users will obtain up-to-date results when accessing the extracted data. There is no replication and location transparency. Developing the extraction, translation, and merging algorithms are time consuming for the programmer and add to the overall maintenance problem. A transaction applied to the extracted data is not reflected in other component databases. There is no coordinated data recovery.

1.4.2 Remote Access

Figure 1.2(c) illustrates the remote-access approach. Rather than periodically extracting and merging data, in this approach the user directly accesses data in each component database each time the user needs to access those data.

Remote access guarantees that results are always up to date. However, the user must be aware of the location of data. The user may also need to merge data returned from multiple component databases. A failed transaction that updates data in one component database but not other component databases may violate business rules that involve data in multiple component databases. There is no support for coordinated recovery.

1.4.3 Gateways

Figure 1.2(d) illustrates the use of gateways to access data. A gateway transforms a query into the format needed by the component DBMS and transforms results into the format needed by the user or application.

Gateways provide up-to-date results and automatically transform queries to the formats required by component DBMSs. However, users must be aware of the data that can be accessed using each gateway and must specify how data from multiple component databases should be merged. A failed transaction that updates data in one component database but not other component databases may violate business rules that involve data in multiple component databases. There is no support for coordinated recovery.

1.4.4 Loosely-coupled Distributed DBMS

Figure 1.2(e) illustrates a loosely-coupled distributed database management system in which users may access data in several component DBMSs. It performs all the necessary translations, optimizations, and data merging during the processing of a request. Some loosely-coupled distributed DBMSs support data location and replication transparency. However, a loosely-coupled DBMS does not enforce business rules that affect data in multiple databases. This is because, in a loosely-coupled DBMS, users may access component databases directly, bypassing the enforcement of any global business rule. Loosely-coupled distributed DBMSs do support coordinated recovery.

1.4.5 Tightly-coupled Distributed DBMS

Figure 1.2(f) illustrates a tightly-coupled distributed DBMS that is like a loosely-coupled DBMS except that it enforces business rules that span component databases. Users must submit all requests, even those that access a single database, to the tightly-coupled distributed DBMS. In this way, the tightly-coupled distributed DBMS can prohibit users from changing data in a way that violates a business rule that involves data in multiple component databases.

1.4.6 Centralized Approaches

In the centralized approach [Figure 1.2(g)], multiple databases are integrated into a centralized database that several users can access. It solves the islands of unreachability problem not by building bridges among the database islands, but by moving the islands together and building a single continent of data.

The client–server approach (Figure 1.3) is a variation of a centralized DBMS. To use the client–server model, data administrators extract data from multiple databases, merge the data, and place them onto a centralized computer called a server. Several users and applications working on clients (PCs and workstations) may access the server's data. Database requests from clients are automatically routed to the server, and results are automatically routed back to the requesting client. Unlike remote access, the server performs automatic backup and recovery. Unlike the gateway approach, command and data translation between the client and server is not necessary.

Servers provide up-to-date results to users. Programmers may write and apply transactions against data in the server. Because the data were merged onto the server, users do not need to worry about locating and replicating data, translating queries into the form required by databases, or merging data from multiple databases. A server makes a backup copy of its database and maintains logs of changes made to the database so that it can recovery from processing errors and data destruction.

There are several types of data servers. A *file server* manages files of data. When a client requests information, the server transfers a copy of the entire file to the client. A *database server* accepts queries and returns only the requested data from the database. File and database servers reside on general-purpose hardware. A *database computer* is a database server with specially designed hardware for database processing.

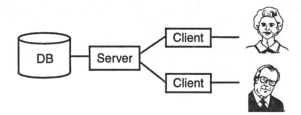

Figure 1.3   Client-server architecture

Problems with the client–server approach include reformatting data and integrating them into the database maintained by the server and modifying existing applications to access the server rather than a local database. Despite these problems, the client–server approach is frequently used to solve the IOU problem.

1.4.7 Other Approaches

Combinations of Approaches. An enterprise can combine the above approaches in various ways. For example, one enterprise may move some data to a server and leave the remaining data in a mainframe database. The distributed database management system may treat the mainframe database as one component database and the server database as another component database. As another example, some component databases are accessed through gateways, while other component databases are accessed using the remote-access approach. In practice, enterprises use many such combinations.

Distributed DBMS on a Single Computer. It is possible for two different DBMSs to both execute on the same computer. This usually occurs when an enterprise installs applications that use DBMSs from different vendors. Multiple DBMSs on the same computer can also be islands of unreachability. Approaches for bridging these islands of unreachability are the same as those illustrated in Figure 1.2 with one major exception: no intercomputer communication subsystem is necessary.

1.5   The Database Administrator Selects the Data-sharing Approach

To evaluate alternative solutions to managing multiple databases and select an approach appropriate for their enterprise, DBAs should first determine which of the above requirements apply to their enterprise. Then the DBAs choose the approach that best satisfies the enterprise's specific requirements. We illustrate this type of analysis with three examples.

1.5.1 Example 1: West Dakota Automobile Files

In the fictitious state of West Dakota, each of its 47 counties has its own driver's license system. Each driver in West Dakota obtains license plates from the Transportation Office within the county where he or she lives. The first two digits of the license plate number indicate which county issued the license plate. To manage license plate information, each county has developed separate files on different computers. Highway patrol officers can access each county's computer system via radio to check for outstanding warrants associated with license plate numbers. When a highway patrol officer queries about a license plate number to a county's computer system, it responds by listing any outstanding warrants associated with the license plate number. Each county uses its license plate file once a month to send notices to drivers whose license plates are about to expire. What approach for sharing data should the Transportation Office in West Dakota use to enable highway patrol officers to access license plate numbers quickly?

First, let's examine each of the proposed requirements listed in Section 1.3:

- *Users obtain up-to-date results.* Highway patrol officers follow different procedures when stopping cars depending on whether there is an outstanding warrant associated with the license plate. Highway patrol officers need up-to-date information about outstanding warrants associated with license plate numbers so that they can know which procedures to follow when stopping cars.

- *System hides data location and replication from users.* The first two digits of the license plate number identify the county issuing the license plate. Thus highway patrol officers already know the county issuing the license plate and direct their database queries directly to the appropriate county.

- *System translates queries.* No query needs to be translated because the query is very simple: the patrol officer only needs to enter the license plate number and be informed of any outstanding warrants.

- *System merges data.* Because all warrants associated with a license plate number are recorded on the file of the county issuing the license plate, patrol officers need information from only one county. The system does not require data merging.

- *Transactions enforce business rules involving data in multiple databases.* Patrol officers only retrieve information, not update it. Thus there is no need for business rules that span component databases.

- *System supports coordinated recovery.* If the data of one county are lost or become corrupted, the country can restore the lost data independently from the data of other counties. There is no requirement for coordinated recovery.

The only requirement for this system is that patrol officers obtain up-to-date results. Remote access, gateways, client–server, and distributed DBMS all support up-do-date results. However, each of these approaches, except for remote access, also supports other features that are not required. Thus remote access is the simplist approach for sharing data in this example.

1.5.2 Example 2: West Dakota Welfare Files

Each county in West Dakota also has its own welfare system. Each welfare system maintains its own files on its own computer with its own human interfaces. A client receives welfare payments only from a single county at a time. Information about a client should appear only in the files of the county from which the client is getting support. Social service counselors should access the computer systems of all counties to determine if a client is receiving welfare payments from any county in the state. What approach for sharing data should the Welfare Offices in West Dakota use?

- *Users access data from multiple databases.* Each social service counselor must submit requests to all 47 component DBMSs to determine if a client is receiving aid in any of the 47 counties.

- *Users obtain up-to-date results.* Each file should be up to date so that social service counselors can determine if a client is currently receiving aid.

- *System hides data location from users.* Social service counselors don't have the time (or the patience) to query each of 47 county welfare systems separately. The state-wide welfare system should automatically examine the component databases of all 47 counties and report to the social service counselor if the client is receiving aid from any county in West Dakota.

- *System translates queries.* To avoid forcing counselors to learn 47 different user interfaces, the welfare system should automatically translate queries about clients into the form required by each of the 47 county welfare systems.

- *System merges data.* Because no client should receive welfare from more than one county, there should not be data from multiple counties to merge.

- *Transactions enforce business rules involving data in multiple databases.* Each of the 47 county component DBMSs may have different qualification requirements and constraints on payments, and each county welfare system may enforce those business rules automatically when counselors attempt to modify the county welfare database. There is no constraint that spans counties.

- *System supports coordinated recovery.* If the data of one county are lost or become corrupted, the data can be restored independently from the data of other counties. There is no requirement for coordinated recovery.

The statewide welfare system requires counselors to have up-to-date results from a multiple component DBMS by submitting a single request that is automatically replicated, translated, and submitted to all 47 component databases. Either the tightly-coupled or loosely-coupled distributed DBMS approach supports these requirements.

Alternatively, we might extend the gateway approach, which satisfies all the requirements, except for hiding data location, by writing a special transaction that automatically queries all component databases with the single query, "Does this person get aid in your county?" While this special query does not provide general data location and transparency for all possible queries that users might submit, it docs provide location transparency for the single, most frequently submitted distributed query.

1.5.3 Example 3: West Dakota Fur Company

The West Dakota Fur company has small manufacturing facilities located in each of six cities in West Dakota. Each facility has a DB2® database containing the descriptions and amounts of fur pelts and other materials needed to make West Dakota Fur products. Because management is trying to keep overhead low, each facility keeps supplies at a minimum. Because supplies may run low on an almost daily basis, managers in each city must locate needed supplies frequently. Managers can cause supplies to be shipped from a neighboring town by executing a transfer transaction, which adjusts the inventory information in the component databases of the two facilities and notifies shipping to transfer the supplies.

- *Users obtain up-to-date results.* Managers need up-to-date inventory information from neighboring cities.

- *System hides data location from users.* Users will want to query neighboring facilities before facilities that are geographically more remote. Thus users will want to direct queries to specific databases. Data location should not be hidden from users.

- *System translates queries.* All queries are expressed in SQL, the DB2 database language. No query translation is needed.

- *System merges data.* Each query is directed to a single remote site. The system does not need to merge data from multiple sites.

- *Transactions enforce business rules that involve data in multiple component databases.* Because transactions involve changing the inventories at two sites, transactions must enforce the following business rule: During a transfer transaction, the total number of supplies neither increases nor decreases (i.e., supplies are neither lost nor gained when shipped between facilities).

- *System supports coordinated recovery.* Local recovery is needed to guarantee that each database reflects local inventories.

The West Dakota Fur Company requires up-to-date results and transactions that enforce business rules involving multiple component databases. A tightly-coupled distributed DBMS supports these requirements. As an alternative solution, consider integrating data from all the component databases into a single centralized server.

1.6   The Database Administrator Determines the Path to Distributed DBMSs

Figure 1.2 shows seven approaches for data sharing, beginning with no sharing [Figure 1.2(a)] and ending with maximal sharing [Figure 1.2(g)]. An enterprise is said to follow an *integration path* if it shifts approaches from separate DBMSs [Figure 1.2(a)] toward a distributed DBMS [Figure 1.2(f)]. The integration path solves the islands of information problem. Most loosely-coupled distributed DBMSs are the result of logical integration.

Enterprises should follow the integration path if there are several applications that access all or most of the data. This frequently occurs if the enterprise exercises centralized control on the use of data and there is a need for strong centralized planning. Data should be centralized if users in all areas frequently submit queries that access major portions of the database. Centralized data are especially desirable if users need current, up-to-the-minute information.

An enterprise is said to follow the *distribution path* as it shifts approaches from centralized [Figure 1.2(g)] to tightly-coupled [Figure 1.2(f)] or loosely-coupled [Figure 1.2(e)]. Beginning with a centralized DBMS, the DBA partitions the centralized database into multiple databases. Physical partitioning causes data to be distributed to the location where they can be quickly and easily accessed by users. The tightly-coupled distributed DBMS enables users to access data that are physically distributed across multiple component DBMSs. Most tightly-coupled DBMSs are the result of physical partitioning. The migration may continue to loosely-coupled distributed DBMS if there are no business rules that span databases.

Enterprises should follow the distribution path if data should be distributed to different locations. This should be done if the data usage is different at each location, data are generated and used at individual locations, and sharing of data between locations is infrequent. If end users at each location are responsible for manipulating and maintaining their own data, then the data should reside at the user's location. Data should be distributed if they are locally controlled, or excessive centralization may result in individuals losing their responsibility for maintaining accurate data. If this approach is followed to its extreme [Figure 1.2(a)], the islands of information problem may result.

What are the steps in each of these two paths?

1.6.1 Logically Integrate Distributed Databases

To build a loosely-coupled DBMS from several independent databases, the database administrator performs three steps:

1. Construct a single global description of all the data in the component databases. This description will act as a dictionary directory of available data and enable the distributed DBMS to locate and access any data in any local database

2. Provide a user interface for users to formulate queries involving any of the data.

3. Construct or purchase a mechanism to partition and route requests to the appropriate component DBMS and to coordinate and integrate the results returned from the component DBMSs. In effect, buy or build the distributed DBMS software. Users will invoke this software when they need to access data not located in their local component database, and they do not want to be concerned about the details of locating, formulating, coordinating requests to multiple component databases, and integrating the results. Distributed DBMSs differ in the degree to which they support these tasks.

1.6.2 Physically Partition a Centralized Database

There is another path to a loosely-coupled distributed DBMS. This path occurs when the enterprise has a centralized database but desires to distribute it to two or more component DBMSs. This may be desirable when the central computer becomes a bottleneck, when the centralized computer becomes saturated, or when the enterprise recognizes that it can benefit from distribution of data.

To build a distributed DBMS from a centralized database, the database administrator performs four steps:

1. Partition the centralized database into fragments that can be moved to other locations.

2. Allocate each fragment to one or more component DBMSs on different computers.

3. Provide a user interface for users to formulate queries involving several component DBMSs.

4. Construct or purchase a mechanism to partition and route requests to the appropriate component DBMSs and to coordinate and integrate the results returned from the component DBMSs.

Note that the last two steps of logical integration of distributed databases are the same as the last two steps of physical partitioning of centralized databases. Chapter 5 will describe approaches for performing step 4. These approaches are useful in distributed databases constructed by either partitioning a single centralized DBMS or by integrating multiple isolated DBMSs.

Chapter Summary

Users need to locate, access, and integrate data from multiple databases. A distributed DBMS performs these tasks on behalf of the user. Centralized DBMSs evolve to distributed DBMSs along either of two migration paths. Database administrators either integrate several existing centralized DBMSs into a distributed

DBMS, or they distribute a single existing centralized DBMS into a distributed DBMS.

Techniques for locating, accessing, and integrating data from multiple databases include data extraction, remote access, gateways, loosely-coupled distributed DBMS, and tightly-coupled distributed DBMS. Each of these techniques differs in the degree to which it supports the following requirements for distributed data:

- Access to data in multiple databases
- Up-to-date results
- Location and replication transparency
- Query translation
- Data merging
- Business rule enforcement across multiple databases
- Coordinated recovery

Database practitioners should carefully determine their data-sharing requirements and then choose the data-sharing technique that best meets their requirements.

Further Reading

This chapter defines the basic concepts and terminology for distributed DBMSs. Chapters 2 through 6 present more details about distributed relational databases. Chapters 7 through 10 describes other types of database systems and how they may be distributed.

The following books provide additional details and supplemental information about distributed databases. For detailed information about a specific distributed DBMS, see the user and technical manuals provided by the vendor.

Ceri, Stefano, and Giuseppe Pelagatti, *Distributed Databases Principles and Systems*, McGraw-Hill, New York, 1984. First book describing distributed database systems. Includes descriptions of early prototype and commercial systems.

Date, C. J., *An Introduction to Database Systems*, 4th Ed., Addison-Wesley, Reading, MA, 1986. Basic text for relational database management systems. Chapter 24 overviews distributed systems.

Date, C. J., *An Introduction to Database Systems, Vol. II*, Addison-Wesley, Reading, MA, 1986. Advanced topics in relational database management systems. Chapter 7 overviews distributed databases.

Elmasri, Ramez, and Shamkant B. Navathe, *Fundamentals of Database Systems,* Benjamin/ Cummings, San Francisco, 1989. Basic text for data modeling and database management systems. Chapter 21 overviews distributed databases.

Larson, J. A., and S. Rahimi, eds., *Distributed Database Management*, IEEE Computer Society Press, Silver Spring, MD, 1985. Contains reprints of key papers dealing with distributed databases.

Ozsu, M. Tamer, and Patrick Valduriez, *Principles of Distributed Database Systems*, Prentice Hall, Upper Saddle River, NJ, 1991. Theory, algorithms and methods that underlie distributed database management systems.

Ullman, Jeffrey D., *Principles of Database and Knowledge-base Systems, Volume I,* Computer
   Science Press, Potomac, MD, 1988. Theoretical description of database systems. Chapter
   10 describes distributed database management.

2

Software Architectures for Data Sharing

This chapter discusses the following:

- The five major dimensions of distributed DBMSs.
- The components and building blocks of distributed DBMSs.
- How a request proceeds through the distributed DBMS's building blocks.
- How to combine the building blocks to support the various sharing approaches.

A distributed DBMS requires several features in order to solve the problems of accessing data residing in multiple databases. Section 2.1 organizes these features into five *dimensions*, or classes of features. Distributed DBMSs differ in the features within each dimension that they support.

A distributed DBMS contains several software components to support features within each dimension. Distributed DBMSs differ in the software components they contain and the manner in which those components are organized. Section 2.2 presents an overview of the major software components for a centralized DBMS and how they may be reconfigured to form an architecture for a distributed DBMS. Section 2.3 describes a more detailed view of the software components needed in a distributed DBMS. This section also describes how each distributed DBMS software component relates to the five dimensions described in Section 2.1.

A software architecture for a distributed DBMS consists of several software components organized to provide specific features. Section 2.4 explains how to organize software components into software architectures supporting each of the approaches described in Chapter 1.

2.1   Distributed DBMSs Support Features Along Five Dimensions

This section describes five major dimensions of distributed DBMSs. We will see that the software architecture for each type of distributed DBMS is strongly related to the degree it supports features in each of these dimensions. Descriptions of these five dimensions follow:

Degree of Global Query Optimization. Distributed DBMSs provide different degrees of global query optimization. The following list describes three of the various degrees of query optimization.

1. *No query optimization.* The user must locate each file to be accessed, formulate a subrequest to access each file, and merge the results of the subrequests.

2. *Replication and location transparency.* Recall from Chapter 1 that a distributed DBMS supports location transparency if the user is not aware of the location or site of the data being accessed. A distributed DBMS supports replication transparency if the user is not aware that more than one copy of the data exists. When the distributed DBMS supports replication and location transparency, the user names the individual data elements to be accessed, and a software optimizer determines which copy to access and its current location.

3. *Fragmentation transparency.* Some distributed relational DBMSs support fragmentation transparency. In these systems, the DBA may partition or fragment a table into several pieces or fragments and store each fragment at a different location. A distributed DBMS supports fragmentation transparency if the user is not aware that a table has been fragmented by the DBA. When the distributed DBMS supports fragmentation transparency, a software optimizer determines how to reconstruct a table from its distributed fragments.

Data-Manipulation Language Transparency. The second software dimension involves data-manipulation language transparency. This type of data transparency is important if the distributed DBMS contains multiple types of component DBMSs. For example, a distributed DBMS interconnects an Ingres® DBMS located on one site, a CODASYL (DBTG network) DBMS on a second site, and an IMS® DBMS on a third site. When a distributed DBMS supports data-manipulation language transparency, the user formulates requests in using a single data-manipulation language such as SQL. Gateways translate each request to the appropriate languages understood by each component DBMS. Distributed DBMSs differ in the number of gateways that they support and the corresponding types of component DBMSs whose data-manipulation language can be hidden from the user.

Number of User Interfaces. A distributed DBMS can support a wide variety of user interfaces. Some user interfaces are tightly-coupled to the distributed DBMS. Others may be tools separate from the distributed DBMS. In addition to the *application program interface* (API) used by application programmers to construct applications that access the database directly, user interfaces may include the following:

- *Keyword-oriented commands.* The user formulates commands and specifies their parameters using a formal keyword-oriented syntax. SQL, DOS commands, and UNIX commands are examples of keyword-oriented commands.

- *Question and answer.* The user interface prompts the user to enter commands and parameters by asking questions to which the user enters simple responses.

- *Menu and fill-in form.* The user interface prompts the user with menus and fill-in forms rather than questions. The user responds by selecting options from menus and entering simple responses into the slots of the fill-in form.

- *Natural language.* The user types a request using English or some other natural language.

- *GUI (graphical user interface).* Information is presented to the user as graphical images that the user manipulates using a pointing device such as a mouse. This style of user interface, made popular by the Macintosh computer, is now widely available on many computers.

Degree of Component DBMS Control. This refers to the ability of a component database administrator to control how a distributed DBMS user may access data in his or her local DBMS that participates as a component within the distributed DBMS. Some distributed DBMSs give component database administrators the power to enable or disable distributed DBMS user to access component data. Other distributed DBMSs do not provide component database administrators with these options.

Number of Component Databases That Users of the Distributed DBMS Can Update in a Single Request. Some distributed DBMSs do not permit updates; users of these distributed DBMSs can only retrieve data. Some distributed DBMSs allow users to only update data in a single-component database; updates to data that involve data at two or more component databases are not allowed. Other distributed DBMSs allow users to update data in several component databases using a single request or transaction. Chapter 6 describes how these distributed DBMSs support sophisticated distributed concurrency control mechanisms that guarantee that two or more users don't attempt to update the same data at the same time. Chapter 6 also describes how these distributed DBMSs support distributed commit protocols that enable the distributed DBMSs to determine when updates to all component databases are completed. The distributed concurrency control and distributed commitment add to the complexity of the distributed DBMS as well as to the communication cost and response time of distributed requests.

2.2   Distributed DBMSs Contain Three Major Components

This section presents the major components of a distributed DBMS, and the next section describes subcomponents of these components. As illustrated in Figure 2.1(a), a centralized DBMS consists of three major components, a database, a database engine, and at least one user interface.

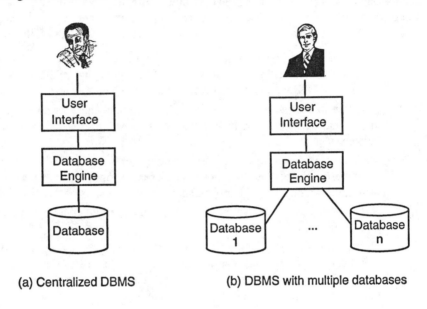

(a) Centralized DBMS   (b) DBMS with multiple databases

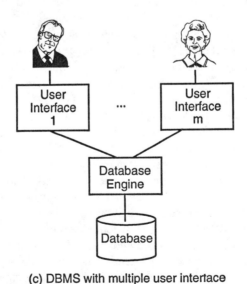

(c) DBMS with multiple user interface

Figure 2.1   Components of a centralized DBMS

The *database* contains the data managed by the database management system. The database consists of (1) one or more homogeneous sets of records and (2) a schema that describes each homogeneous set of records and the interrelationships among records. Some DBMSs manage multiple databases [Figure 2.1(b)]. These DBMSs are able to switch from one database to another, allowing a user to formulate and execute requests involving any one of the several databases. However, a user may not formulate a request that accesses data within more than a single database at a time.

The *database engine* is the workhorse of a DBMS. It performs requests to access the database. The database engine contains components that accept requests to access the database, determines if the user may perform the request, locates and accesses the desired data, records all changes made to the database, and prohibits multiple users from updating the same data at the same time.

The *user interface* is a front end to the database engine that (1) aids users in formulating requests to access the database and (2) formats and displays the results in a form useful to the user. Some DBMSs support only a single style of user interface, such as SQL commands or a graphical user interface. Other DBMSs [Figure 2.1(c)] support multiple types of user interface types.

Each of the above three components of a centralized DBMS also appears in a distributed DBMS, illustrated in Figure 2.2. A distributed DBMS has two additional components, global and local managers.

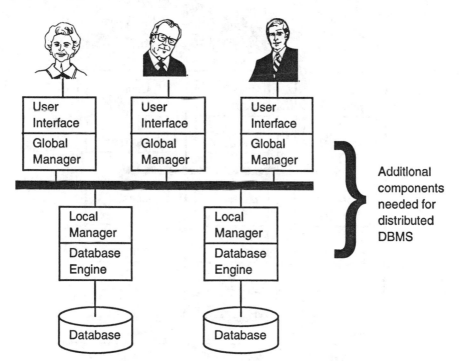

Figure 2.2   Components of a distributed DBMS

The *global manager* accepts a request from a user interface. It examines the request and routes it across a communication subsystem to one or more local managers. If necessary, the global manager coordinates several local managers in processing parts of the request and exchanging temporary data. Each *local manager* accepts requests from the communication subsystem and prepares them for execution by the component database engine. The local manager accepts results from the component database engine and routes results according to instructions from the global manager. The global manager causes results from multiple local managers to be merged and then transfers the merged results to the user interface for display to the user.

Figure 2.2 illustrates the global manager as residing on the same computer as the user interface. The global manager may instead reside on the same computer as one of the component DBMSs, or even on a separate computer. The global manager is often placed on the same site as one of the component databases in order to (1) minimize the copies of the data dictionary directory in the distributed DBMS, and (2) minimize the software on the computer supporting the user interface. For example, neither the data dictionary directory nor global manager is expected to reside on a mobile PC.

Figure 2.3   Logically and physically distributed

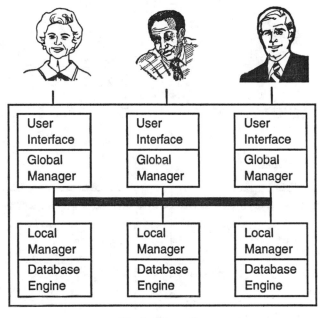

Single Computer

Figure 2.4   Logically distributed and physically centralized

Figures 2.3, 2.4, and 2.5 illustrate several types of distributed DBMSs. In Figure 2.3, a communication system connects three computers. Each computer has both a user interface and a database engine. Here the data are both *logically and physically distributed*. The data are logically distributed to three different databases. The three databases are physically distributed to three different computers connected by a communication subsystem, represented by the dark line in Figure 2.3.

Figure 2.4 illustrates a distributed system in which the data are logically distributed into three different databases, but the databases themselves are physically centralized and reside on the same computer. Here the data are *logically distributed but physically nondistributed*. In Figure 2.4, the dark line connecting the three DBMSs is not a communication system, but a mechanism supporting interprocess communication within a single computer.

Figure 2.5 illustrates a combination of the previous two types of distributed databases. Data are logically distributed to three separate databases. Two of the databases are physically centralized to a single computer, while the third database is physically distributed to a separate computer. Note also in this example that one computer has multiple user interfaces while the other doesn't. The dark line in Figure 2.5 represents both a communication system connecting DBMS in multiple computers and interprocess communication mechanisms for connecting DBMSs within the same computer.

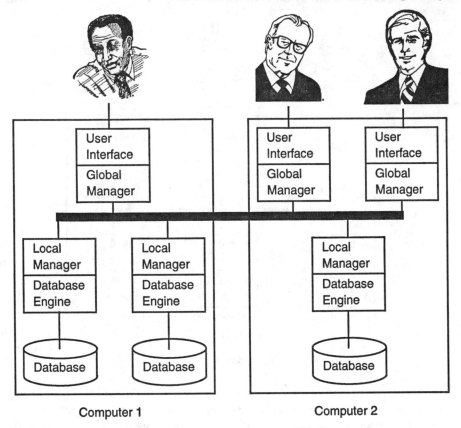

Figure 2.5 Logically distributed and partially physically centralized

2.3 DBMS Components Require Several Building Blocks

This section describes the basic building blocks that constitute each of the four major DBMS components of a distributed DBMS introduced in Section 2.2.

2.3.1 User interface component

As shown in Figure 2.6, the user interface component consists of two building blocks that we will call (1) the request constructor and (2) the user interface translator.

Request Constructor. A request constructor provides an interface used by human users. A request constructor helps a user to formulate requests by accepting and examining the commands and parameters entered by the user and validating them for syntactical correctness. Some request constructors assist users in formulating data-

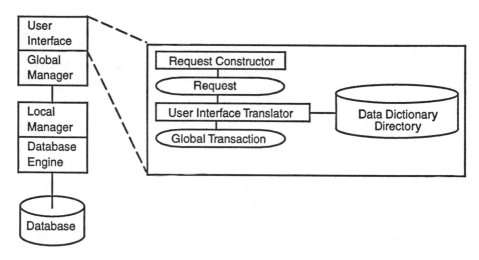

Figure 2.6 User interface

base transactions by displaying menus of currently valid options. Some request constructors display error messages describing syntactically incorrect portions of the request and enable users to easily enter corrections. Several request constructors are possible, one for each type of user interface supported by a distributed DBMS.

User Interface Translator. For each request constructor supported by the distributed DBMS, there is a user interface translator. The user interface translator converts the request constructed by its corresponding constructor into a global transaction for processing by the other components of the distributed DBMS. A *global transaction* specifies the data in one or more databases to be accessed. A global transaction may be a query in which data are retrieved from one or more databases, or it may update one or more databases. Each user interface translator hides the user interface from the other distributed DBMS components. The user interface translator performs two types of translations:

1. *Name translation.* The names of data objects used by the user may be different from the internal names used by component DBMSs. The translator performs this name translation by consulting a data dictionary directory.

2. *Syntax translation.* The user interface translator converts the command syntax and format generated by the request constructor component into commands expressed in a format used by the rest of the distributed DBMS components. Many distributed DBMSs use SQL as the format for representing global transactions.

Some database applications perform their own request construction by constructing global transactions using SQL. These applications provide their own user interface. Of course, some users formulate global transactions by entering and editing SQL directly.

2.3.2 Global Manager

As shown in Figure 2.7, the global manager consists of three building blocks:
(1) the transaction optimizer, (2) the distributed transaction manager, and (3) the
communication subsystem.

Transaction Optimizer. The transaction optimizer converts a user global transaction into a distributed transaction. The transaction optimizer isolates users from the
data structures used by the underlying component database management systems. To
illustrate, consider the following three relational database tables.

Employee1 at Site 1

Name	Salary	Department
Ackman	5000	Car
Baker	4500	Car

Employee2 at Site 1

Name	Salary	Department
Carson	4800	Toy
Davis	5100	Toy

Employee2 at Site 2

Name	Salary	Department
Carson	4800	Toy
Davis	5100	Toy

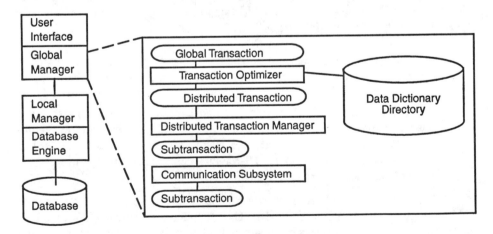

Figure 2.7   Global manager

In order for the user to retrieve salaries for employees named Davis, the user would need to retrieve information from the Employee1 table from Site1 (the user must look at site 1 to discover that it contains no information about Davis) and information from the Employee2 table from either Site1 or Site2 and then merge the results. The following illustrates a distributed transaction to accomplish this request:

```
Request 1 executed at Site 1:
    select Salary from Employee1 where Name = "Davis";
    send results to Site 2;

Request 2 executed at Site 2:
    select Salary from Employee2 at Site 2 where Name = "Davis";
    receive results from Site 1;
    union the results from Site 1 with the results from this
    site;
    send final results to the requesting global manager;
```

If the location and replication of the Employee table information are hidden, the user needs only to formulate the following global transaction:

```
    select Salary from Employee where Name = "Davis";
```

The transaction optimizer generates Request 1 and Request 2 from the above global transaction. The distributed transaction examines the data dictionary directory to determine where each table is located in the distributed DBMS. Using a transaction optimizer simplifies the job of the user or programmer in formulating requests.

A transaction optimizer has an additional benefit. Whenever a database administrator moves tables from one site to another and makes the appropriate changes to the data dictionary directory, the users and programmers do not need to modify their requests. Instead, the transaction optimizer reoptimizes the requests using updated information about the data in the dictionary directory

Distributed Transaction Manager. As its name implies, the distributed execution manager executes distributed transactions. The distributed transaction manager sends commands from the transaction optimizer to the appropriate local transaction managers via the communication subsystem. The distributed transaction manager also executes the synchronization aspects of the distributed transaction, causing temporary files to be transmitted between local managers. The distributed transaction manager is also responsible for the following:

- *Distributed concurrency control*, which guarantees that multiple local databases are updated in a well-behaved fashion (discussed in chapter 6).
- *Distributed commitment*, which guarantees that all local databases are updated consistently (also discussed in Chapter 6).

Communication Subsystem. The communication subsystem accepts messages from the distributed transaction manager and transmits them to the appropriate local managers. These messages, which we will call *subtransactions*, may contain (1) instructions for performing local database accesses and (2) data to be inserted into one of the component databases. The communication subsystem may also transmit data among local managers and from local managers to the distributed transaction manager. If distributed databases reside on the same computer, then the communication sub-system is just an interprocess communication mechanism that transmits messages among the DBMS processors executing on the same computer.

2.3.3 Local Manager

As shown in Figure 2.8, the local manager consists of two building blocks (1) the local transaction manager and (2) the gateway.

Local Transaction Manager. The local transaction manager accepts subtrans-actions from distributed transaction managers via the communication subsystem. It accepts results from the local database engine and places them on the communication subsystem for delivery to other local transaction managers or to a distributed trans-action manager. The local transaction manager also executes local synchronization aspects of the distributed transaction.

Gateway. Some distributed DBMSs support multiple types of database en-gines. When this occurs, each request or part of a request to be executed by one of the database engines must be translated to a format that the database engine can execute. A gateway coverts standard data-manipulation commands into the data-manipulation language appropriate for the database engine. The gateway uses information from the data dictionary directory to resolve any differences in data item names and formats. Sometimes this information is stored within the gateway itself. The gateway hides the heterogeneity of the local DBMSs from the remainder of the distributed DBMS.

2.3.4 Database Engine

As shown in Figure 2.9, the database engine consists of two building blocks: (1) the local optimizer and (2) the runtime support processor.

Local Optimizer. The local optimizer determines an optimal or near-optimal strategy for processing each request from the local manager. We will illustrate how

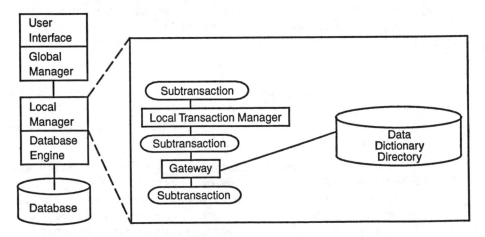

Figure 2.8   Local manager

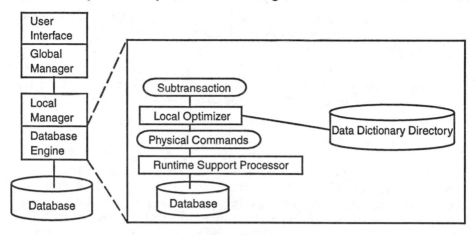

Figure 2.9   Database engine

the local optimizer works with two examples. Suppose that a component database contains two files, a Department file, containing DepartmentName and Budget, and an Employee file containing EmployeeName, Salary, and the name of the department for which the employee works.

The local optimizer converts the SQL request:

```
select * from Employee where DepartmentName = "Car";
```

into a program containing file I/O commands. Depending on the file structures used by the file system data manager, this program may do any one of the following:

- Search all records in the Employee file linearly for those records with value "Car" for the DepartmentName field.

- Binary search if the records in the Employee file are ordered by the Car field.

- Index look up if the records in the Employee file are indexed by the Car field.

The local optimizer converts the SQL request

```
select *
from Department, Employee
where Department.DepartmentName = Employee.DepartmentName;
```

into a program that accesses and concatenates records from both the Department and Employee files that have the same value for the DepartmentName field. Depending on the file structures used by the file system data manager, the this program may do any of the following:

- *Nested (inner–outer) loop.* For each record in Employee, retrieve each record in Department and test whether they match.

- *Use index.* For each record in Employee, use the index for DepartmentName to retrieve matching records in Department.

- *Sort–merge join.* If both Employee and Department are physically sorted by DepartmentName, then scan both files at the same time to locate matching records.
- *Hash join.* Transform the values of DepartmentName in both Employee and Department files into a set of empty slots. Examine each slot for Employee and Department records that have the same value for DepartmentName.

The Local optimizer uses information found in the data dictionary directory to perform these optimizations.

Runtime Support Processor. The runtime support processor is the workhorse of a component DBMS. It is responsible for accessing the database in response to the commands passed to it through the local transaction manager from one or more global managers. It schedules and performs these requests. The runtime support processor also enforces local concurrency control, ensuring that two concurrently executing requests do not try to update the same data at the same time. It also creates a journal log of changes made to the database. This log is used to restore the database to a previous state if the database becomes corrupted.

2.3.5 Putting All the Pieces Together

Figure 2.10 illustrates how all the subcomponents fit together to form the distributed DBMS of Figure 2.2. First we will describe what happens to a request as it travels down the path from the user to multiple databases. Then we will describe the return journey of data extracted from the multiple databases as they travel back up the path to be presented to the user.

The Request Path

1. The request constructor helps the user construct a request to display all the employees named Davis. Suppose that the request constructor is a fill-in form. Initially the request constructor displays a blank form such as the one illustrated in Figure 2.11. The user enters the value "Davis" into the Name fill-in to indicate that only employees named Davis are to be displayed. The user presses the OK button to signal that the request has been completely entered.

2. In this example we will assume that the internal request format is SQL. The translator constructs the following global transaction from the information in the fill-in form:

```
select Salary
from Employee
where Name = "Davis";
```

3. The transaction optimizer uses information from the data dictionary directory to determine how data are distributed across the multiple databases of the distributed DBMS. Let's suppose that the employee information has been partitioned. Part of it is stored in the table named Employee1 located in component DBMS 1, and the remainder of the employee information is

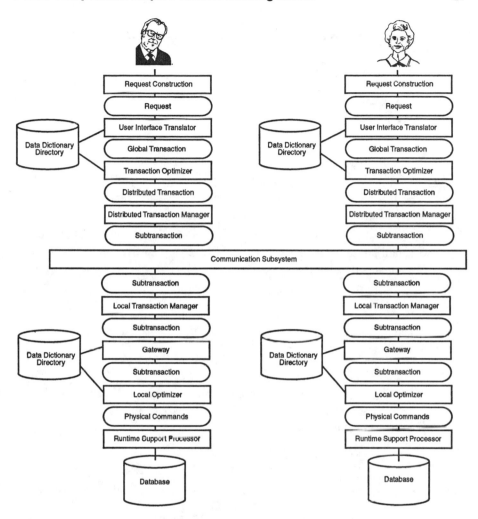

Figure 2.10 Detailed view of distributed DBMS of Figure 2.3

Figure 2.11 Fill-in form user interface

stored in the table named Employee2 located in component DBMS 2. The global request is translated to the following distributed transaction:

```
at Component DBMS 1:
select Salary from Employee1
where Name = "Davis";
send the results to Component DBMS 2;

at Component DBMS 2:
select Salary from Employee2
where Name = "Davis";
accept results from Component DBMS 1;UNION the results;
send the final results to the distributed transaction manager;
```

The distributed transaction manager routes the two subtransactions to the local transaction managers in component DBMSs 1 and 2.

4a. The local transaction manager at component DBMS 1 receives the subtransaction and delivers the following SQL request to the component database command translator:

```
select Salary from Employee1 where Name = "Davis";
```

4b. The local transaction manager at component DBMS 2 receives the subtransaction and delivers the following SQL request to the component database command translator:

```
select Salary from Employee2 where Name = "Davis";
```

5a. We will assume that the database engine at component DBMS 1 is a file system. A gateway translates the SQL request into the following algorithm to be executed against the file:

```
open Employee1 file;
  while not end of file do;
  read Employee1
  if EmployeeName = "Davis" then move Employee1 to TempFile;
  end do;
on end of file: close Employee1 file;
```

5b. We will assume that the database engine at component DBMS 2 is a SQL DBMS. No gateway is needed in this case, and the SQL request

```
select Salary from Employee2 at Site2 where Name = "Davis";
```

is passed directly to the local optimizer.

6a. There is no optimizer for the file system at DBMS 1, so the file program generated in step 5a is passed directly to the operating system, which acts as the runtime support processor.

6b. The SQL optimizer accepts the SQL request from step 5b and optimizes it. Suppose that there is an index on the field EmployeeName. Then the SQL optimizer converts the request to a table look-up on the EmployeeName index, followed by retrievals of each record identified in the index.

7a. The operating system in its role of runtime support processor executes the program generated in step 5a. It constructs a temporary file.

7b. The SQL processor in its role of runtime support processor executes the instructions generated by the SQL optimizer in step 6a. It constructs a temporary file to hold the results.

8a. The local transaction manager at component DBMS 1 executes the second part of its distributed execution plan. It transmits the temporary file created by the runtime support processor to the local transaction manager executing the other part of the distributed execution plan.

8b. The local transaction manager at component DBMS 2 receives the temporary file from the local transaction manager at component DBMS 1, which passes the temporary file to the runtime support processor.

9. The runtime support processor merges the temporary file from component DBMS 1 with the temporary file it created in step 7b, creating a new temporary file. The contents of the new temporary file are the results of the distributed request.

The Data Path

10. The local transaction manager at component DBMS 2 accepts the final results created by the runtime support processor in step 9. It transmits the results to the distributed transaction manager at the site where the request was formulated.

11. The distributed transaction manager accepts the results and gives it to the request constructor.

12. The request constructor converts the data into the format expected by the user. In this case the user expects several forms, one for each employee named Davis.

This example is very simple because no updates are involved. Transactions involving updates may be significantly more complicated because of two factors:

1. The distributed transaction manager must verify that each subtransaction does not interfere with the processing of other subtransactions from other users. This process is called distributed concurrency control and is discussed in Chapter 6.

2. The distributed transaction manager must verify that each subtransaction is actually completed. This process is called distributed commitment and is also discussed in Chapter 6.

The data dictionary directory plays an important role by storing information needed by the various components of a distributed DBMS. The data dictionary directory contains the following types of information:

- Relationships between user-oriented names and data descriptions and distributed DBMS-oriented names and data descriptions. This information is needed by the user interface translator.
- Location, replication, and fragmentation information needed by the transaction optimizer to generate a distributed transaction.
- Relationships between the distributed DBMS-oriented names and data descriptions and the component database names and data descriptions needed by the component gateway.
- Information about local access paths and data structures needed by the local optimizer.

Information in the data dictionary directory can be partitioned and replicated at several sites. Information needed by the user interface translator and transaction optimizer may be stored at each site where the user interface translator and transaction optimizer execute. Information needed by the gateway and local optimizer may be stored at sites containing the gateway and local optimizer. Whenever dictionary directory information is changed at one site, the corresponding information must also be changed at other sites.

2.4   Sharing Approaches Use Different Building Block Combinations

2.4.1 Data Extraction

Figure 2.12 illustrates the components needed for data extraction. Unused comments are grayed out. Database administrators extract data from remote databases and store them in the local database. Local users then access the extracted data using the components of the local DBMS.

2.4.2 Remote Access

Figure 2.13 illustrates the components needed for remote access. Because there is no transaction optimizer, users must formulate a request for each database to be accessed using the data-manipulation language supported by its DBMS. Individual requests are transmitted to the remote DBMS, where the local optimizer optimizes the request and the runtime support processor executes the request. Results from the remote DBMS are returned to the requesting site.

2.4.3 Gateway

Figure 2.14 illustrates the components needed for gateway access. This works similarly to remote access except that users may write requests using a single data-manipulation language. Each gateway converts the request to the data-manipulation language supported by the local DBMS.

2.4.4 Loosely-coupled and Tightly-coupled Distributed DBMSs

Figure 2.10 illustrates the architecture of both loosely-coupled and tightly-coupled distributed DBMSs. While both architectures contain the same components, the loosely-coupled distributed DBMS lacks the enforcement of business rules that involve data in multiple databases.

Chapter Summary

This chapter introduces the building blocks for a distributed DBMS:

- Request constructor helps users formulate requests.
- User interface translator converts the request into a standard format.

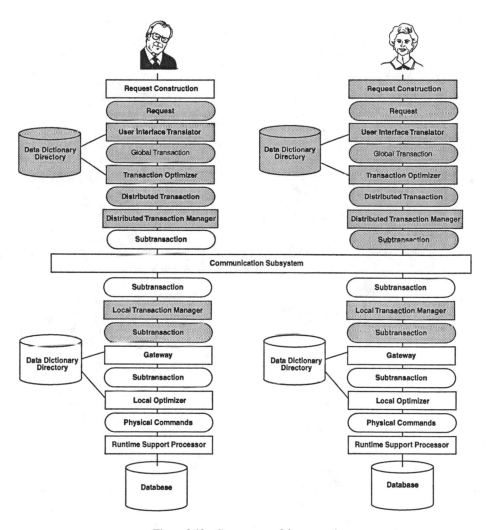

Figure 2.12   Components of data extraction

- Transaction optimizer supports location and replication transparency.

- Distributed transaction manager executes requests involving multiple sites.

- Communication subsystem transfers requests and data among sites.

- Local transaction manager executes subtransactions at each site of a request involving multiple sites.

- Gateway enables access to heterogeneous DBMS.

- Local optimizer supports data independence within the local DBMS.

- Runtime support processor performs accesses to data in the local database.

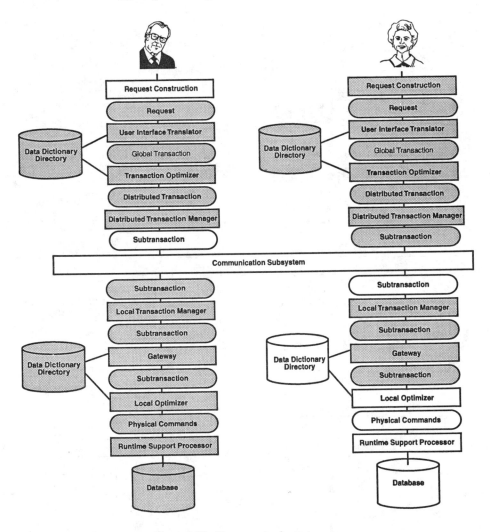

Figure 2.13   Components of remote access

These building blocks perform the major functions of a distributed DBMS. Not all distributed DBMSs contain all these building blocks and thus do not perform all the functions. These building blocks can be configured to form architectures for each of the approaches for sharing data discussed in Chapter 1. This list of building blocks can be used as a checklist of DBMS features (see Appendix B).

We will use this list of building blocks as an outline for exploring distributed DBMS issues. The remainder of this book is structured around this set of building blocks.

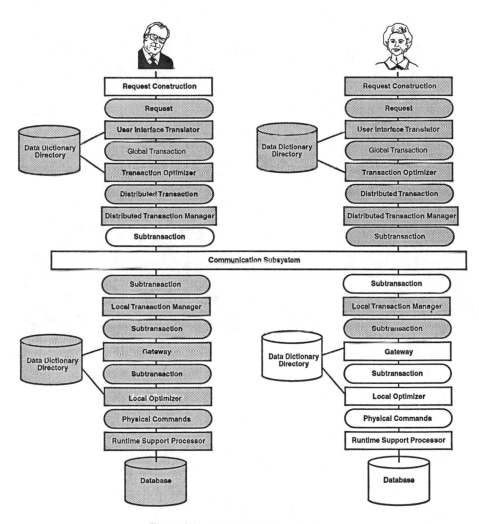

Figure 2.14 Components of a gateway

Further Reading

Larson, James A., "Four Reference Architectures for Distributed Database Management Systems," *Computers Standards and Interfaces,* Vol. 8, No. 1, 1988/89. Description of a reference model for distributed DBMS similar to the one presented in this chapter.

3

Federated Database Management Systems

This chapter discusses the following:

- Definition of a federated database.
- How federated databases offer an evolutionary path between several centralized databases and a tightly-coupled distributed database.
- How DBAs use gateways to construct a federated DBMS.
- How DBMSs negotiate the sharing of data within a federated database.
- Methodologies and tools for building federated databases.

A federated DBMS is a type of loosely-coupled distributed DBMS in which users of component DBMSs may continue to access the component databases without using any of the distributed DBMS facilities. Federated DBMSs provide an evolutionary approach to integrating multiple databases over time.

Section 3.1 explains how a federated DBMS works. Section 3.2 describes the lifecycle of a federated DBMS. Sections 3.3 through 3.5 describe how DBAs construct a federated database.

3.1   A Federation Assists Users in Accessing Distributed Data

When using a tightly-coupled distributed DBMS, the user is not allowed to directly access data of a component DBMS; all requests must be submitted to the distributed DBMS. This enables the distributed DBMS to enforce business rules that span component databases. No business rules spanning component databases are enforced by the loosely-coupled distributed DBMS, so users are allowed to directly access data in a component database by submitting requests directly to the component DBMS. A user can also access any data in a loosely-coupled distributed DBMS by using the distributed DBMS.

This chapter examines a type of loosely-coupled distributed DBMS in which the distributed DBMS user may not be allowed to access all the data of the component databases; some of the data in the component databases are hidden from the distributed DBMS user. Of course, users of the component DBMS are able to access all the component data. This type of loosely-coupled distributed DBMS is called a *federated DBMS*.

A federated DBMS is more flexible than a loosely-coupled distributed DBMS in that each component DBMS may participate in the federation in varying degrees:

- *Type of operations that federated users may perform.* Some component DBMSs may allow federated users to read but not modify data in the component database. Other component DBMSs may allow federated users to both read and modify data in their component database.

- *Amount of the component database federated users may access.* Some component DBMSs allow federated users to access all of their data, while other component DBMSs allow federated users to access only a portion of their data.

One significant aspect of a federated DBMS (and of all loosely-coupled distributed DBMSs) is that a component DBMS can continue its local operations and at the same time participate in a federation. Thus users may access the component DBMS directly, without using any of the federated DBMS facilities. Federated DBMSs are especially useful for the staged evolution of separate DBMSs into a distributed DBMS. In each stage, more data and functions are integrated into the distributed DBMS.

A component DBMS can participate in more than one federation. Figure 3.1 illustrates a federated DBMS that involves three component DBMSs and four federations. Site 1 is a mainframe containing a single component database that participates in two federations. Site 2 is a PC that contains a single component DBMS that participates in three federations. Site 3 is a PC that contains no component database, and site 4 is a database server that contains a single DBMS that participates in two federations. In this example, users of all but the leftmost federation may access data in more than one component database.

A component database administrator may use any of several mechanisms to specify rules for accessing component data by federated users. The component database administrator may build special views, formulate access control rules, or build a special schema called an *export schema*. To simplify the discussion, we will assume the use of an export schema for the remainder of this chapter.

The administrator of a component DBMS retains control over who may access data in his or her component DBMS by constructing export schemas. An export schema is a special type of schema that describes only the data in the component database that the component DBMS administrator will allow federation users to access. In effect, the export schema describes how federation users may access the component database. The component DBMS administrator constructs a different export schema for each federation in which the component database participates.

The administrator of each federation constructs a *federation schema* that describes all the data in the export schemas of participating component DBMSs. Federation users use data names and descriptions in a federation schema whenever they

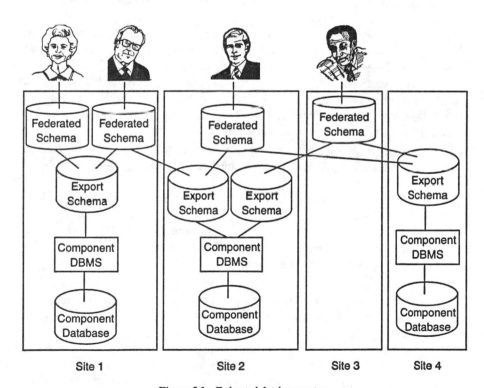

Figure 3.1 Federated database system

formulate requests to be processed by the federation. If the federation contains a transaction optimizer, then the federation hides the existence of the export schemas from the federation user, who perceives that he or she is accessing a centralized database.

3.2   Federated DBMSs Follow a Life Cycle

There are two general approaches to enable users to access multiple centralized DBMSs: installing a distributed DBMS or adding a layer of software above existing centralized DBMSs to create a federation. In the first approach, installing a distributed DBMS requires (1) changes and disruption of the existing applications if they are not able to adjust to the dispersion of data across component DBMSs, (2) a complete change of the organization structure for information management as the distributed DBMS administrator gains control over component databases from the component DBMS administrators, and (3) replacement of the existing centralized DBMSs by a distributed DBMS.

The federation approach offers a more evolutionary path. It allows continued operation of existing applications, preserves most of the enterprise's organization structure, supports controlled integration of existing databases, and facilitates incorporation of new applications and new databases. Programmers do not need to change existing applications as component databases are integrated into a federated DBMS.

Constructing a federated DBMS involves identifying, subsetting, and integrating the component DBMSs that are to participate in the federated DBMS. Federated database designers perform these tasks in three phases: (1) preintegration, (2) federated development, and (3) federated database system operation. These phases need not follow serially from one phase to the next; the designer may perform each phase several times and revisit previous phases and their results.

The preintegration phase deals with how federated users access files not managed by any DBMS. Two general approaches are possible:

1. *Migrate the files to a DBMS.* Federated database designers migrate files to a DBMS by performing three activities: (a) develop a component schema that describes the data in the files, (b) load a component DBMS with data from the files, and (c) modify existing application programs to access the DBMS, rather than access the files directly.

2. *Extend the file system to support DBMS-like features.* By extending the file system to support DBMS-like features, a file system can be treated as a component DBMS. In this approach, the federated database designer performs the following activities: (a) create or generate a component schema that describes data in the files, (b) create backup and recovery facilities in the file system if federation users will perform updates to data in the file system, and (c) create appropriate gateways to convert commands expressed using the data manipulation language of federated DBMS's to file-oriented com-

mands. Many developers of federated DBMS use gateways rather than migrate file data to a database and modify all the existing applications that access the file.

The second phase, developing a federated database system, involves defining the export and federated schemas, defining the mappings between various schemas, and implementing the associated processors. Methodologies for this phase are described in Section 3.3.

The third phase, the federated database system operation, involves managing and manipulating several component databases using the federated DBMS. The processors and the federated schemas developed or generated in the second phase allow the selective, shared, and consistent access to data stored on several component databases. Of course, component DBMS users may continue to access their component DBMSs without using any of the facilities of the federated DBMS.

3.3   Federated DBMS Developers Follow Methodologies

Developing a new federated DBMS primarily consists of logically integrating existing component databases. Federated database designers may follow either of two methodologies: bottom up or top town. The *bottom-up* methodology consists of phases for translating and integrating several component schemas to form a new federated schema. Section 3.3.1 describes the bottom-up methodology in detail.

When new applications are developed using an existing federated DBMS, it is necessary to determine if the data requirements of the application are already supported by a federated schema. If they are not, it may be necessary to extend a federated schema. We will call this a *top-down* methodology. Section 3.3.2 describes the top-down methodology in detail. In practice, federated database designers use elements of both the bottom-up and top-down methodologies to develop federated DBMSs.

3.3.1 Bottom-up Methodology

A bottom-up federated DBMS methodology is used to integrate several existing databases into a new federated schema. For this discussion we will assume the export and federated schemas will be specified using the relational data model. Figure 3.2 illustrates the following bottom-up methodology:

1. *Translate schemas.* If the component schema is not expressed using the relational data model, then translate the nonrelational component schema of a component database into an equivalent relational component schema. Generate the mappings between corresponding objects in the two schemas. Develop (or identify if one already exists) the gateway to transform SQL commands into the commands that can be executed by the component DBMS or file system.

2. *Define export schemas.* Define export schemas from relational component schemas. The database administrators of the respective component DBMSs perform this step to specify which parts of their databases are to be included in the federated DBMS based on the negotiations with the federation DBA. Develop (or identify if one already exists) the appropriate mechanism for representing the access control rules by either (a) encoding the rules using the existing security mechanisms of the component DBMS or (b) creating a separate export schema that describes the data to be exported to the federation.

3. *Integrate schemas.* Select the set of export schemas to be used by a group of federated DBMS users and integrate it to form a federated schema. Derive a federated schema for each group of federated DBMS users. Develop (or identify if one already exists) a transaction optimizer that transforms the commands expressed on federated schemas into commands expressed on the corresponding export schemas.

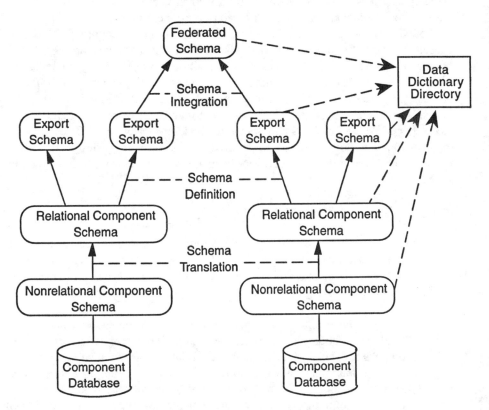

Figure 3.2   Bottom-up federated DBMS methodology

All the various schemas are all placed into the data dictionary directory. The federated schema and export schemas are used by the transaction optimizer to generate a distributed transaction. Then each pair of relational component and nonrelational component schemas is used by a gateway to translate SQL commands into commands that can be processed by the component DBMS

3.3.2 Top-down Development Process

A top-down federated DBMS development process is used when a federated DBMS already exists and additional user requirements (e.g., to support a new application) are placed on it. Figure 3.3 illustrates the following top-down process:

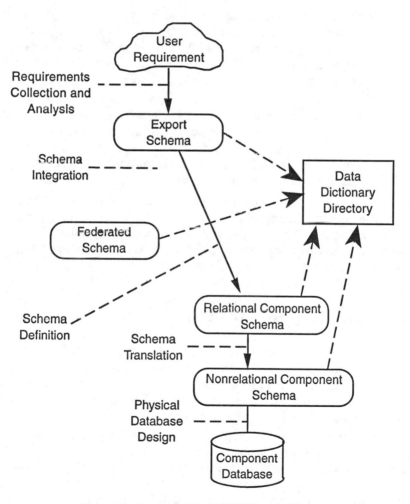

Figure 3.3 Top-down federated DBMS methodology

1. *Define the new export schema.* Collect federated user requirements and analyze them to define new export schemas.

2. *Integrate the export schemas into the appropriate federated schema*, so that federated users can access the required new information.

3. *Identify the relevant component databases.* One or more of the component databases will need to support the export data. Federated database administrators may accomplish this in one of three ways:

    a. The export schema is already contained by one or more component database(s). In this case, identify the component relational schemas containing the description of required data and negotiate with their administrators to grant appropriate access rights.

    b. The export schema is not contained in any component database, and a component database administrator is willing to place the required data in his or her component database. Modify the relational component schema. If the component DBMS is not relational, then modify the nonrelational component schema of the relevant databases.

    c. The export schema is not implemented in any component database, and no component database administrator is willing to place the required data in his or her component databases. In this case, the export schema is implemented as a separate database of an existing component DBMS. Define the relational component schema. If the component DBMS is not relational, then define the nonrelational component schema.

The various schemas are added to the data dictionary directory. The federated schema and export schemas are used by the transaction optimizer to generate a distributed transaction. Then each pair of relational component and nonrelational component schemas is used by a gateway to translate SQL commands into commands that can be processed by a component DBMS.

3.4   DBAs Negotiate the Sharing of Data

A federation DBA manages federated schemas. A component DBA manages the export schemas defined over the component DBMS he or she manages. A federation DBA and component DBAs must agree about the contents of the export schemas and operations allowed on the export schemas. This enables the federated DBA to define federated schemas over the export schemas.

Because the component databases are developed separately, there are usually no business rules that involve several component databases. In general, business rules that span component databases are not enforced by federated DBMSs. If business rules that involve data from several component databases must be enforced, then consider using a tightly-coupled distributed DBMS rather than a loosely-coupled federated DBMS.

Two additional aspects of federated DBMS operations may be problematic:

1. A component database administrator decides to withdraw access to a component schema object or change a component schema object. These changes should be reflected in the federated schemas.
2. A federation user decides that access to a schema object is not longer needed. The federated and underlying export schemas should reflect these changes.

Federated and component DBAs need to negotiate when these situations occur. Probably the simplest protocol is for the DBAs to telephone each other and verbally agree how to proceed in each situation. Heimbigner and McLeod [1985] present formal negotiation protocols for exchanging messages for this purpose.

Negotiation between the component and federated component database administrators may be necessary to agree on how to control data that some users are allowed to access and others are not. For example, suppose that component databases each contain information about commercial shipping and military shipping. One set of users may access only commercial shipping information, and another set of users may access only military shipping information. The following approaches are possible:

*   Each component database administrator includes schema objects describing both commercial and military shipping in their respective export schemas. This information is integrated into a single federated schema. The federation component database administrator creates two export schemas, one for accessing commercial shipping information and one for accessing military shipping. In this scenario, the local component database administrators trust the federation component database administrator to provide appropriate access controls on information described by each external schema.
*   Each component database administrator generates two export schemas, one describing commercial shipping information and the other describing military shipping information. The federation DBA creates two schemas, one containing commercial shipping and the other containing military shipping. In this scenario, the component database administrators control access to each export schema.

3.5   Middleware Enables Federated Databases

DBAs use several mechanisms to create federated databases. Many of these mechanisms are called *middleware* because they form a "middle" connection between applications and database systems. Examples of middleware include the following:

*   *Gateways*. If two databases are described using different data models, then a gateway may be used to translate the commands of one DBMS to a format suitable for the other DBMS. Most DBMS vendors provide a variety of

gateways so that users of their DBMS can access data maintained by other DBMSs and file systems. DBAs of the remote databases describe part of the remote data and provide mappings so that the gateway user can view the remote database as relational. In effect, construct an export schema for a federated database.

- *Command routers.* A command router is a simplified transaction optimizer that routes a transaction to the DBMS that can process the transaction and returns the response to the user. A command router examines a transaction to determine which data to access, examines a data dictionary-directory (or its own internal tables) to determine where the data reside, and routes the transaction to the appropriate DBMS. Command routers do not attempt to perform any optimizations.

- *Database links.* The Oracle® database server and Microsoft's Access™ software support *database links*, which act as database routers. If two databases are implemented using the same DBMS, then one database may be linked to another database. This linking establishes a path from the user's database to another database. When the user requests data, the user's request is redirected to the remote DBMS, which accesses the data and returns them to the user's DBMS. The location of the actual data is hidden from the user by this simple location transparency mechanism.

- *ODBC driver manager and drivers.* The Open Database Connectivity (ODBC) API is a call-level interface that can be used to access any ODBC-compliant database. Figure 3.4 illustrates the ODBC architecture. The ODBC-compliant application makes calls to the driver manager when it needs to access a database. The driver manager routes the transaction to the appropriate driver. The driver is a simplified gateway, which translates the request to a form that the component database can process, and returns the data to the driver manager, which returns the data to the ODBC-compliant application. There are two types of ODBC drivers. A single-tier driver manipulates the database directly. A multiple-tier driver generates SQL requests to be processed by a relational DBMS. ODBC drivers are available from vendors of most relational DBMSs and from vendors of ODBC-compliant applications. ODBC is Microsoft's version of a specification for accessing relational databases developed by the SQL Access Group (SAG), a consortium of DBMS vendors.

By using a combination of the above middleware, a DBMS can be extended to provide location-transparent access to multiple sources of data. This is a type of federated database system that both enables users to access selected data from any database, and yet enables users and existing applications to access data in their local databases.

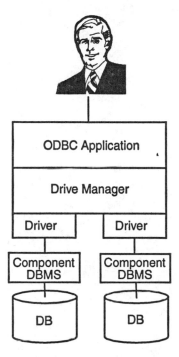

Figure 3.4   ODBC architecture

Chapter Summary

A federated DBMS is a type of loosely-coupled distributed DBMS in which users of component DBMSs continue to access the component databases without using any of the distributed DBMS facilities. Federated users can access selected pieces of component databases subject to security constraints imposed by component DBAs. Federated DBMSs provide an evolutionary approach to integrating multiple databases over time. Federated DBMSs seldom enforce business rules that span component databases. DBAs use gateways and other types of middleware to construct federated databases.

Further Reading

Heimbigner, D., and D. McLeod, "A Federated Architecture for Information Management," *ACM Trans. Off. Inf. Syst.,* Vol. 19, No. 3, Sept. 1985, 201–260. Describes protocols for negotiations between federated and local DBAs.

Sheth, Amit P., and James A. Larson, "Federated Database Systems for Managing Distributed, Heterogeneous and Autonomous Databases," *Computing Surveys*, Vol. 22, No. 3, Sept. 1990, 183–236. Overview of federated DBMS and examination of issues relevant to federated DBMSs. Overviews of architectures for four example federated systems.

Designing Distributed Databases

This chapter discusses the following:

- How data models are used to describe the contents, operation, and business rules of a database.
- Widely used data models and how do they differ from each other.
- Why most distributed DBMSs use the relational data model.
- How to convert data description and data manipulation to the relational data model.
- How DBAs integrate the descriptions of separate databases.
- How DBAs partition files and allocate the resulting fragments.
- Security mechanisms used to protect data.
- How business rules enforce data value constraints.

This chapter deals with three major issues in designing distributed databases:

1. *Multiple data models*. The first problem deals with differences in styles of describing data. These styles are called data models, and include relational, hierarchical, and CODASYL network styles of describing data. Section 4.1 reviews the four most widely used data models. Section 4.2 explains why

the relational data model is popular for distributed DBMSs. Section 4.3 discusses how to transform data descriptions using the popular nonrelational data models to the relational data model. Section 4.3 also discusses a widespread and difficult problem with distributed database management systems resulting from the large number of centralized applications written using single-record-per-command languages.

2. *Schema integration.* The second problem deals with one of the paths to distributed DBMS discussed in Section 1.3, the logical integration of data that already reside in several existing databases. Schema integration is necessary to provide an integrated view of multiple databases. Section 4.4 discusses schema integration.

3. *Data distribution.* The third problem deals with the other path to distributed databases, the physical partitioning of a centralized database and its allocation to multiple component databases. Data distribution and replication are needed when data are moved to one or more sites within a distributed DBMS. Section 4.5 discusses database partitioning and allocation.

Sections 4.6 and 4.7 discuss business rules and security constraints. Techniques for specifying and enforcing business rules and security constraints are described.

4.1 DBAs Use Data Models to Describe Data

Different component DBMSs of a distributed DBMS may use different data models. Figure 4.1 illustrates two component databases which use different data models. This section reviews four popular data models: relational, hierarchical, network, and file.

Some database experts use the term data model to refer to the description of the data in a specific database. We will use the term *schema* to refer to the description of data in a specific database and reserve the term *data model* to refer to a style of describing and manipulating data. A data model consists of three components to describe three important aspects of data:

1. Data description for describing the names, structure, and relationships of data in the database.

2. Data manipulation for describing the operations that users may apply to data in the database.

3. Business rules that describe the constraints users must obey when they manipulate data in the database.

Popular data models include the relational, hierarchical, and network data models. Although it is not generally recognized as a data model, we will include files as a database model because file systems provide the most widely used data-description and data-manipulation languages.

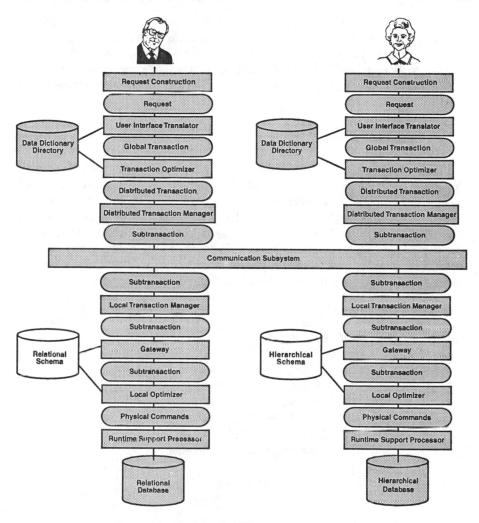

Figure 4.1   Resolving the differences between data models

Each data model has one or more execution engines. An execution engine is the software that processes data-manipulation commands and accesses data in the database. The relational database management systems Ingres, Oracle®, FoxBase®, and DB2 are examples of relational execution engines. The network database management system IDMS® is an example of network execution engines. System 2000® and IMS are examples of hierarchical execution engines. And, of course, every operating system has its own file I/O system. The file I/O system contains an execution engine that accepts commands from an application program to manipulate data in one or more files.

The remainder of this section describes each of these four major data models in greater detail. Readers already familiar with one data model may skip to the next data model. Recently, object-oriented is emerging as a new data model. Chapter 10 will describe this new data model along with its advantages and disadvantages. In Section 4.2 we will explain why the relational data model is frequently chosen to be the standard data model used in most distributed DBMSs. In Section 4.3 we will describe translators between the relational data model and the remaining three widely used data models.

4.1.1 File Data Model

The data description for a file data model is replicated within each of the application programs that accesses the file. The structure of each file is described in some type of file declaration section at the beginning of the program code for the application. In some programming languages, the file description is stored in a separate module called a *header file*. The file description names each data element in the file and declares its position and length within the file. Figure 4.2(a) illustrates a typical data description for a file containing two types of records. Figure 4.2(b) illustrates a sample file containing two department records and four employee records.

```
01  Department
     03 DepartmentFlag       Char (1)
     03 DepartmentName       Char (10)
     03 DepartmentEmployee   Integer
01  Employee
     03 EmployeeFlag         Char(1)
     03 EmployeeName         Char(10)
     03 EmployeeSalary       Integer
```

(a) File description

D	Car	45000000	Department record
E	Ackman	00005000	Employee record
E	Baker	00004500	Employee record
D	Toy	48000000	Department record
E	Carson	00004800	Employee record
E	Davis	00005100	Employee record

(b) File contents

Figure 4.2   Example file

The data-manipulation language for manipulating files consists of a set of *procedural commands*; each command accesses a single record. Generally, the commands fall into two classes, sequential and direct. Programmers use commands in the *sequential class* to access a file sequentially, usually beginning with the first record in the file and continuing until they reach the last record in the file. This class of commands includes open, read, write, and close. Programmers use these commands to access records in files stored on magnetic tapes. They use the *direct class* of file commands to access any record within a file directly using a record key, without having to read through the file sequentially. This class of commands includes open, read, insert, delete, modify, and close. Programmers use these commands to access records stored on magnetic disks. Report generators and fourth-generation languages support nonprocedural access to files, enabling users to formulate queries that access multiple records.

The file data model is weak in business rule enforcement. Most file execution engines are only able to verify that input data conform to a limited number of data types, such as integer, character, and decimal. This is the reason up to 50% of an application's program code deals with specifying and enforcing business rules.

4.1.2 Relational Data Model

Unlike the file data model, in which programmers replicate data description within each application accessing the file, data description for the relational data model is centralized to one place, the data dictionary. The term *schema* is frequently used to describe the data in a relational database. A schema describes several tables, called relations. Each table contains several rows. All the rows of a table contain the same item types called columns. Figure 4.3 illustrates an example of two tables and the relational schema describing these two tables. These two tables contain the same information as the file in Figure 4.2.

While the file data model enables programmers to access records in the file one at a time, the relational data model enables users to access entire tables with a single command. Relational database management systems support query languages. Queries expressed in these languages are called *nonprocedural* because the user specifies the data that should be accessed rather than how to access the data. The following are examples of the SQL query language, the standard query language used to access relational databases.

- *Select* some of the rows of a table:

```
select DepartmentName, DepartmentBudget
from Department
where DepartmentBudget > 5000000;
```

- *Project* some of the columns of a table:

```
select DepartmentName
from Department
order by DepartmentName;
```

- *Join* the rows of two tables if the rows have identical values in specific columns.

```
select EmployeeName, DepartmentBudget
from Department, Employee
where Employee.DepartmentName = Department.DepartmentName;
```

In addition, users may also execute commands to insert, delete and update rows within a table.

Table Department,
Column DepartmentName   Char(10) not null
Column DepartmentBudget Integer;

Table Employee,
Column EmployeeName   Char(10) not null
Column EmployeeSalary   Integer,
Column DepartmentName   Char(10);

(a) Database description

Department

Department Name	Department Budget
Car	450000000
Toy	480000000

Employee

Employee Name	Employee Salary	Department Name
Ackman	5000	Car
Baker	4500	Car
Carson	4800	Toy
Davis	5100	Toy

(b) Database contents

Figure 4.3   Example relational database

Relational database execution engines support three types of business rules:

1. *Type checking.* A user cannot enter a value into a specific column of a row unless its value conforms to the domain of that column. Type checking is used to prohibit obviously incorrect data from being placed into the database. For example, the character string "#$" (upper case "34") could not be accidentally entered into a column declared to be digits.

2. *Entity integrity.* Each row of a table must have one or more columns declared to be a primary key. No two rows of a table may have the same

value for their primary key. Each row of a table must have a value for its primary key. Entity integrity is used to enforce business rules that guarantee uniqueness; for example, no two employees may have the same employee number.

3. *Referential integrity.* A database administrator may declare a column of one table to be a *foreign key.* Each foreign key must either be null or contain a value that is the primary key of a row of another table. Commercial relational DBMSs are beginning to support the referential integrity constraint. Referential integrity is used to enforce business rules that relate two rows of different tables, for example, the value of the department name column of the employee table exists as a value in the department-name column of the department table.

4.1.3 Hierarchical Data Model

Data description for the hierarchical data model describes sets of records that form a hierarchy or treelike structure. Figure 4.4(b) illustrates the six records of Figure 4.2 structured as a hierarchy. Figure 4.4(a) illustrates pseudo syntax for describing a hierarchical schema. (The actual syntax used by IMS or System 2000 is more complicated than shown here.)

Data-manipulation for hierarchical databases is procedural and is designed for use within an application program. There are several versions of the *get* command for retrieving the first, next, or last record in a set of homogeneous records and for accessing the children records of a parent record. There are also commands for inser-

```
Record   Name=Department
     Type=Root of hierarchy
Data items=
   DepartmentName   Char(15)
   DepartmentBudget  Integer
   Key=DepartmentName
```

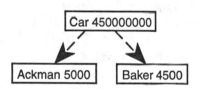

```
Record   Name=Employee
     Type=Child of Department
Data items=
   EmployeeName   Char(15)
   EmployeeSalary  Integer
```

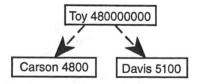

(a) Database description   (b) Database contents

Figure 4.4   Example hierarchical database

tion, deletion, and replacement of individual records. DBMS vendors have augmented most hierarchical DBMSs with SQL data-manipulation commands so that users can formulate nonprocedural queries.

Business rules include type checking, checking that a value falls into a prespecified range, and enforcing the creation and modification of parent-child relationships.

4.1.4 Network Data Model

Many organizations used the network data model (sometimes called CODA-SYL or DBTG after the names of the standard organization that specified the data model) in the late 1970 and early 1980s. Most of the major computer vendors of that period marketed versions of the data model. Several databases implemented using the network data model are still in use today.

Figure 4.5(b) illustrates the six records from Figure 4.2 organized as a network. Figure 4.5(a) illustrates a network schema, specified using a language known as DDL (Data Definition Language). In addition to the two record types, Department and Employee, Figure 4.5(b) illustrates two one-to-many relationships, called *sets* in DDL terminology. On set, named WorksIn, contains Employee records as members and a Department record as owner. For example, Ackman and Baker are members of the WorksIn set owned by the Car Department, and Carson and Davis are members of the WorksIn set owned by the Toy Department. In Figure 4.5(b), a thin arrow is drawn from each WorksIn owner to each of its members. Figure 4.5(b) also illustrates another set named ManagedBy. Thick arrows are drawn from each ReportsTo set owner to each member. Davis is ManagedBy Carson and Ackman is ManagedBy Baker.

```
Record Name is Department
Key is DepartmentName
03 DepartmentName   Char(15)
03 DepartmentBudget Integer


Record Name is Employee
Key is EmployeeName
03 EmployeeName     Char(15)
03 EmployeeSalary   Integer

SetName        is WorksIn
Owner          is Department
Member         is Employee
SetName        is ManagedBy
Owner          is Employee
Member         is Employee
```

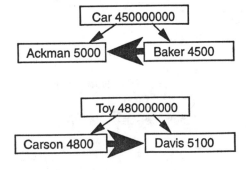

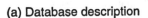

        (a) Database description   (b) Database contents

Figure 4.5   Example network database

The major procedural commands, known as DML (data-manipulation language), include the following:

find	Locate a specified record
get	Transfer a record from the database to the program work space
modify	Replace a record in the database with a record in the program work space
erase	Remove a record from the database
store	Insert a record into the database from the program work space
connect	Associate records in the database together
disconnect	Disassociate two records in the database
open	Make a collection of records available
finish	Terminate the availability of a collection of records
keep	Notify the DBMS that a record will be accessed again
free	Cancel keep
commit	Make all previous database updates permanent

DML is a procedural language for accessing records in the database. The language, with its various explicit and implicit parameters, is complex. When the relational data model began to become popular, most network DBMS vendors extended their products to support SQL so that users could formulate queries without having to write an application program using DML.

The network data model's strong point was its rich specification of business rules. In addition to type checking and range checking, it also supported a variety of insertion constraints that specify how records are to be automatically connected when they were inserted into the database and retention constraints that specified how these relationships are maintained.

Figure 4.6 summarizes the four data models with respect to the three aspects of data modeling: data structures, data manipulation, and business rules. We have categorized the file data model as a list in the sense that it can be thought of as a list of records that may be accessed sequentially or directly. All four data models are weak in their ability to enforce business rules. Newer data models, such as the object-oriented data model described in Chapter 10, are able to describe a greater variety of business rules.

4.2 Distributed DBMS Implementors Choose a Data Model to be Standard

A distributed DBMS must resolve the differences among heterogeneous data models and use a single data model in the data dictionary directory for describing data in all component databases. If multiple data managers containing different execution engines are to be supported in a distributed DBMS, then gateways are necessary to

	Data Structure	Data Manipulation	Constraints
File	List	Procedural	Very Few
Relational	Table	Nonprocedural	Few
Hierarchical	Tree	Procedural	Few
CODASYL/ Network	Network	Procedural	Some

Figure 4.6   Comparison of the four major data models

convert the commands and data formats among the data models used by these data managers. Each gateway must perform two functions:

1. Translate data-manipulation commands from the standard format used by the distributed DBMS to the data-manipulation language supported by each execution engine.
2. Translate data structures used by each execution engine to the standard format used elsewhere in the distributed DBMS.

Figure 4.7 illustrates two approaches for translators among the four most popular data models: network, relational, hierarchical, and file. Figure 4.7(a) illustrates six pairs of translators, two between each pair of data models. Figure 4.7(b) illustrates only three pairs of translators, two each between the relational data model and the remaining three data models. In Figure 4.7(b), the relational data model acts as a *standard data model* to and from which all remaining data models are translated.

Most distributed DBMSs have chosen the relational data model as the standard data model. The relational data model is the standard data model of choice for several reasons, including the following:

- *The relational data model minimizes communication costs.* The relational data model supports nonprocedural queries that access multiple database records. This means that there are fewer transmissions from a user to request data and a smaller number of (but larger sized) data transmissions to deliver the requested data back to the user.

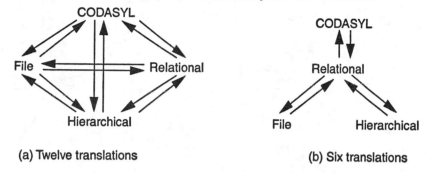

Figure 4.7   Translations among the four major data models

- *The relational data model avoids problems with pointers.* The relational data model is a flat file structure with no embedded pointers. This means that tables transported between computers have no dangling pointers that remain unresolved.

Figure 4.8 illustrates how the data dictionary contains two types of data description.

1. *Component relational schema,* which describes the data in the component database using the relational data model.
2. *Component nonrelational schema,* which describes the data in the component database using the hierarchical, network, file, or some other nonrelational data model.

A gateway converts relational commands into the commands that can be processed by the nonrelational database engine. The data structures of the component nonrelational engine must also be transformed into relational tables. To perform these transformations, the gateway uses data descriptions in both the relational and nonrelational schemas and the mappings between them. The remainder of this section describes the translations between the relational data model and the file, hierarchical, and network data models.

4.3 Software Translators Convert Both Data Description and Commands

4.3.1 The File Data Model

The file data model supports three major concepts: record types, fields, and unique identifiers. Each of these three concepts corresponds to similar concepts in the relational data model. A record type corresponds to a relational table. A field corresponds to a relational column. A unique identifier corresponds to a primary key.

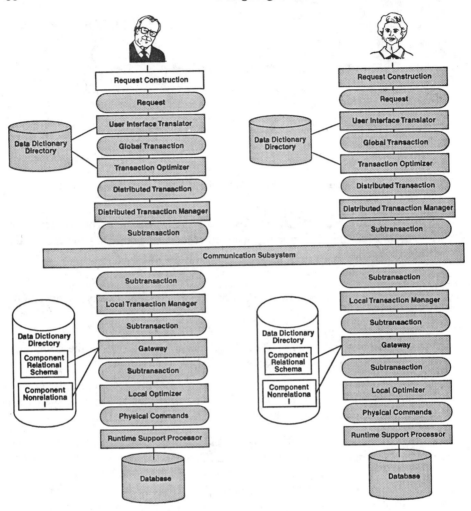

Figure 4.8   Use of a relational data model

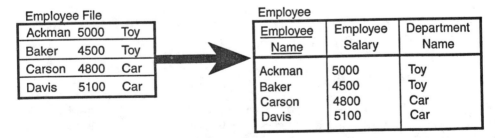

Figure 4.9   Mapping a file to a table

Figure 4.9 illustrates an example file and the corresponding relational table. The four records in the Employee file are translated to the four rows of the table with the same name. The three fields of the Employee file are mapped to the three columns of the Employee table. Finally, the unique identifier field of the file is mapped to the primary key, EmployeeName, in the relational table. (The names of primary keys are underlined.) While the file to relational data structure mapping is straightforward for this example, in general there are four problem areas:

1. *Some files do not have records with unique identifiers.* For example, Figure 4.10 illustrates a file with no unique identifier. One approach for solving this problem is to generate a new column that contains a unique identifier. In Figure 4.10, the Id column contains generated values that do not exist in the file.

2. *The order of records in a file implies information that is not represented in field values.* For example, the order of records in the file may imply a waiting list or ranking. One approach for solving this problem is to generate a new field that contains values from which the order can be generated. Figure 4.11 illustrates a file in which the order of the records implies a ranking among employees. In the corresponding relational table, this ranking is made explicit by the new column, Rank.

Employee

Ackman	44
Baker	50
Carson	33
Davis	20
Ackman	48
Davis	13

EmployeePoints

Id	Name	Points
1001	Ackman	44
1002	Baker	50
1003	Carson	33
1004	Davis	20
1005	Ackman	48
1006	Davis	13

Figure 4.10   Mapping a file with no unique identifier to a table

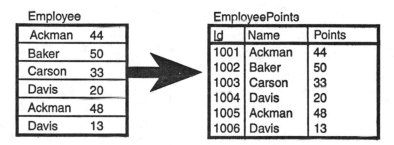

Employee File

Ackman	5000	Toy
Baker	4500	Toy
Carson	4800	Car
Davis	5100	Car

Employee

Rank	Employee Name	Employee Salary	Department Name
1	Ackman	5000	Toy
2	Baker	4500	Toy
3	Carson	4800	Car
4	Davis	5100	Car

Figure 4.11   Mapping a file with implied ranking

3. *A single record of a file may contain a repeating group.* A repeating group is
   a set of fields that may occur multiple times within a record. Figure 4.12
   illustrates an example of a file containing three records, with some of the
   records having a group of fields that repeats. One approach for solving this
   problem is to build a new table for the repeating group. In Figure 4.12, each
   row of the Child table contains values for fields of the repeating group. In
   order to relate values of each row of the Child table with the corresponding
   Employee, the new table also contains an Employee column whose values
   identify the Employee who is the parent or guardian of the child. (This
   Employee column in the Child table is sometimes called a foreign key and is
   an example of a referential integrity business rule.)

EmployeeFile

Jones	50000	3	Sally	80	Sam	82	Joe	84
Smith	51000	2	Fred	79	Phil	79		
Taylor	49000	1	George	88				

Employee

Employee	Salary
Jones	50000
Smith	51000
Taylor	49000

Child

Employee	Child	Birthdate
Jones	Sally	80
Jones	Sam	83
Jones	Joe	84
Smith	Fred	79
Smith	Phil	79
Taylor	George	88

Figure 4.12   Mapping a file with a repeating group to two tables

4. *Some files contain more than one type of record.* For example, Figure 4.13
   illustrates a file containing two types of records: Department records have a
   D in the first field, and Employee records have an E in the first field. Records
   of employees who work for a department follow the record of the department for which they work. The solution to this problem is to split the file
   into two tables, as shown in Figure 4.13. Note that the Employee Table contains a new column (Dept) that relates employees to departments.

It is necessary to translate relational data-manipulation commands to programs
containing file I/O commands that can be executed by the file system. To solve this
problem, an optimizer translates nonprocedural SQL commands to a program containing procedural data-manipulation commands that can be processed by the file

system. Sometimes this translation process is called optimization, because the result-ing program contains file I/O commands that depend on the data structures and access techniques of the file. Consider the following SQL request:

```
select DepartmentName, DepartmentBudget
from Department
where DepartmentBudget > 500000;
```

The translation of this request depends on the structure of the file containing the Department records. If the file is sequential but unordered, then the translator gen-erates a program that scans all the records in the file sequentially, checking each record to determine if its value for the DepartmentBudget field is greater than 500,000. If this check succeeds, then the program copies the DepartmentName and DepartmentBudget fields to another file. If the file is direct access and ordered by val-ues of the Department Budget, then the translator generates a program that does a bi-nary search to locate the first record whose value for the DepartmentBudget field is greater than 500,000. The program then copies the DepartmentName and Depart-mentBudget fields for all records following this record. If the file contains an implicit ordering, repeating groups, or multiple record types, then the program generated by the translator can be quite complex.

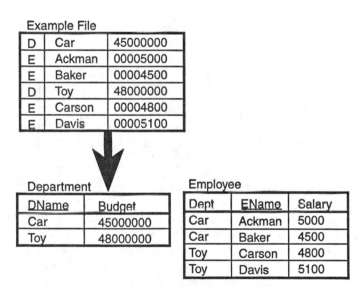

Figure 4.13   Mapping a file with multiple record types to two tables

4.3.2 The Hierarchical Data Model

Associated with the hierarchical data model are four major concepts: record types, fields, unique identifiers, and parent-child relationships. A record type corre-sponds to a relational table. A field corresponds to a relational column. A unique identifier corresponds to a primary key. The fourth concept, parent-child relationships, corresponds to a foreign key in the relational data model.

Figure 4.14 illustrates a hierarchical database consisting of two Department records and four Employee records. There are four parent-child relationships: Ackman and Baker work for the Toy department, and Carson and Davis work for the Car department. The two Department records are mapped to the two rows of the Department table. The four Employee records are mapped to the four rows of the Employee table. The WorksIn column of the Employee table is a foreign key. It contains the values of the DepartmentName primary key from the Department table. The WorksIn column of the Employee table contains the parent-child relationship information: Ackman and Baker work for the Toy department, and Carson and Davis work for the Car department.

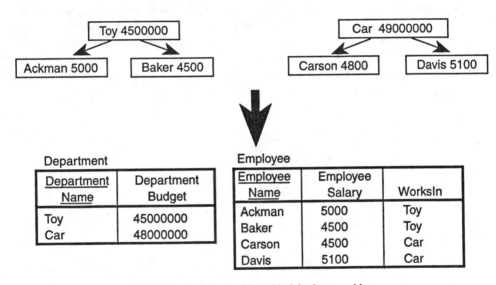

Figure 4.14   Mapping a hierarchical database to tables

The four problem areas of file-relational data-structure translation, no unique identifier, implicit ordering information, repeating groups, and multiple record types, may also occur in hierarchical-relational data-structure translation. These problems are solved in the same manner as in the file-relational data-structure translations. Figure 4.15 illustrates another problem that may occur in hierarchical-relational data-structure translation. The Baker record is duplicated so that it can be related to two different Departments. (One constraint of hierarchical systems is that a child cannot have two parents. Thus, if Baker works for two departments, the Baker record must be replicated so that Baker can be a child of two different Department records. The relationship between Department and Employee is really many-to-many rather than one-to-many. A department may have many employees working for it, and an employee may work for many departments. It is always difficult to represent many-to-many relationships using the hierarchical data model.)

One approach for solving this problem is to have two rows of the Employee table contain the same information about Baker. This approach is seldom used because it results in redundant information in multiple rows of the same table.

Figure 4.15 illustrates another approach in which a third table, WorksIn, is created. The third table contains the many-to-many relationship information in the form of two columns, both acting as foreign keys for each of the tables participating in the many-to-many relationship. Note in Figure 4.15 that Baker appears twice in the WorksIn table, indicating that Baker reports to both the Toy and Car departments.

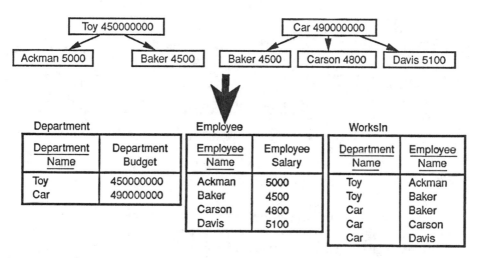

Figure 4.15   Mapping a hierarchical many-to-many parent-child relationship to three tables

4.3.3 The Network Data Model

The network data model supports four major concepts: record types, data items, record keys, and sets. Each record type corresponds to a table, data items correspond to columns, record keys correspond to primary keys, and each set (which is really a parent–child relationship) corresponds to a foreign key. Figure 4.16 illustrates an example network database containing two types of sets. The owners and their corresponding members of the WorksIn sets are represented by thin arrows from Department to Employee. The owners and members of the ReportsTo sets are represented by thick lines from the supervising Employee to the supervised Employee. No one supervises Baker and Carson, so the value for their ReportsTo column are null in the Employee table.

The four problem areas of file-relational data-structure translation, no unique identifier, implicit ordering information, repeating groups, and multiple record types, may also occur in network databases. These problems are solved in the same manner as in the file-relational data-structure translations.

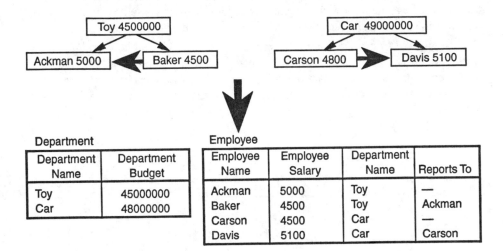

Figure 4.16   Mapping a network database to tables

4.3.4 A Big Problem for Distributed DBMS

Many existing applications are written using procedural data-manipulation commands. Most applications written using file, hierarchical, and network data-manipulation languages fall into this class. There are three approaches for enabling these applications to access data in a distributed DBMS. Unfortunately, all three approaches are costly.

1. Transmit many individual procedural requests and individual records between the application program and the distributed databases. This approach is very costly in terms of communication transmissions and may saturate the communication subsystem.

2. Rewrite the application to use nonprocedural data-manipulation commands in order to minimize the number of transmissions between the application program and the distributed databases. The programmer effort needed to rewrite these applications may be great.

3. Rewrite data-manipulation program fragments from application programs as triggers or stored procedures that execute in the local DBMSs. The programmer effort needed for this rewriting may be extensive.

There is no inexpensive solution to this problem. Applications written using procedural data-manipulation languages don't fit well into distributed DBMS. If you have lots of these types of applications, think carefully before implementing a distributed DBMS.

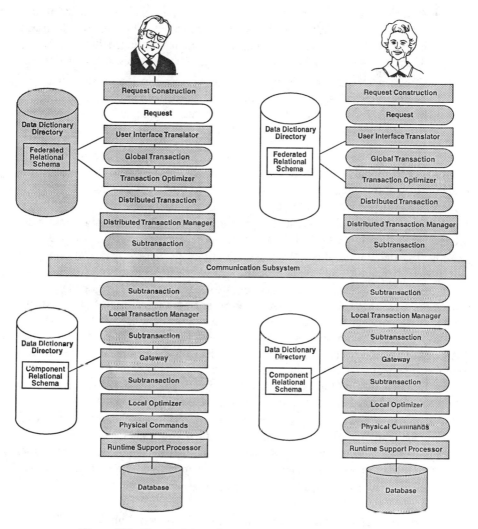

Figure 4.17 Use of a federated relational and component relational schema

4.4 DBAs Integrate Schemas

Chapter 2 presented five features of distributed DBMSs. One of these features is that the distributed DBMS hides the location and replication of data among component DBMSs from the user. In Figure 2.10, the transaction optimizer supports this feature by translating global transactions into distributed transactions. Chapter 5 will describe this translation process, which uses two types of information from the data dictionary directory:

- *Federated relational schema,* a schema expressed using the relational data model, which describes data in several component databases. As illustrated in Figure 4.17, the federated relational schema is in the data dictionary directory available to the user interface translator and transaction optimizer.

- *Component relational schemas,* schemas expressed using the relational data model, which describe data in one component database. As illustrated in Figure 4.17, the component relational schema is in the data dictionary directory available to the gateway.

This section describes how to construct the federated schema from several component relational schemas. The next section will describe how to construct several component relational schemas from a federated relational schema.

Chapter 1 presented two paths to distributed database management systems. One of those paths involved the logical integration of multiple, already existing databases into a distributed DBMS. This section addresses how to achieve logical integration by integrating descriptions of multiple databases and resolving the differences in data formats and data values.

The federated relational schema in Figure 4.17 provides an integrated view that a user can access via a distributed database management system. DBAs integrate the component relational schemas to form the federated relational schema. Typically, DBAs must solve two problems when designing a federated relational schema. Database administrators must (1) resolve differences in the data structures used by different component relational schemas and (2) determine how to resolve differences in data values that may exist in the different databases. We will first discuss the problem of detecting and resolving differences in component relational schemas.

In this section we will assume that component relational schemas are represented using the relational data model. This is the data model of choice for both the component relational schema and the federated schemas. Nonrelational database schemas can be converted to relational schemas using the mappings described in Section 4.3.

One strategy for schema integration follows:

1. *Identify pairs of tables that are candidates for integration.* One possibility is to consider each pair of tables in two component schemas as candidates for integration. If the two schemas have *m* and *n* tables, then there will be *m*n* candidate pairs to consider. Usually, DBAs are not interested in examining *m*n* candidate pairs, most of which will not be integrated. Instead, DBAs use heuristics to identify candidate pairs of tables. One heuristic is to consider only pairs of tables that have the same names, nearly the same names, or names that are synonyms. Another heuristic is to consider pairs of tables that have several columns with the same names, nearly the same names, or names that are synonyms.

2. *Determine the relationship of the rows of the table.* DBAs determines which of the following relationships holds among the rows of two tables, A and B. We will use the following tables as examples:

Engineer

Name	EmpId	Salary	NumberOfPatents
Able	13	13,000	2
Baker	14	14,000	3

Scientist

Name	EmpId	Salary	HighestDegree	School
Baker	14	14,000	MS	CMU
Carson	15	15,000	PhD	MIT

Secretary

Name	EmpId	Salary	WordsPerMin
Davis	16	12,000	80
Egbert	17	11,000	60

Equipment

Name	InventoryId	Location	
Gadget	97		Bin3
Widget	99		Bin4

Employee

Name	EmpId	Salary	HireDate
Able	13	13,000	1987
Baker	14	14,000	1988
Carson	15	15,000	1977
Davis	16	12,000	1990
Egbert	17	11,000	1991

NonExemptEmployee

Name	EmpId	Salary
Davis	17	12,000
Egbert	18	11,000

a. *Logical containment*. If each row in A always corresponds to a unique row in B, then we say that B logically contains A. For example, the DBAs may determine that each row of the Scientist table corresponds to a row in the Employee table. Thus Employee logically contains Scientist.

b. *Logical equivalence*. If each row in A always corresponds to a row of B, and each row in B always corresponds to a row in A, then we say that B is logically equivalent to A. For example, the DBAs may determine that every row in the Secretary table corresponds to a row in the NonExemptEmployee table and that every row in the NonExemptEmployee table corresponds to a row in the Secretary table. Thus Secretary is logically equivalent to NonExemptEmployee.

c. *Logical overlap*. If some of the rows in A correspond to some of the rows in B, and some of the rows in B correspond to some of the rows in A, then we say that A and B logically overlap. For example, the DBAs may determine that some of the Scientist rows correspond to rows in the Engineer table and that some rows in the engineer table correspond to the same rows of the Scientist table. Thus Scientist logically overlaps Engineer.

d. *Logically disjoint*. If none of the rows in A corresponds to any of the rows in B, and none of the rows in B corresponds to any of the rows in A, then we say that A and B are logically disjoint. For example, no row of Employee corresponds to any row of Equipment, and no row of Equipment corresponds to any row of Employee. Thus Equipment is logically disjoint from Employee.

3. *Determine which of the candidate pairs of tables to integrate*. Two tables may be integrated if they are logically equivalent, one logically contains the other, or they logically overlap. If two tables are disjoint, then they should only be integrated if the DBAs determine that they represent the same type of entity. For example, the Equipment and Employee tables should not be integrated, but the Secretary and Engineer tables may be integrated, resulting in an Employee table.

4. *For each pair of tables to be integrated, determine how many tables to create as a result of the integration*. There are two general approaches:

a. *Single-table approach*. Create a single table to replace the pair of tables to be integrated. The single table contains the UNION of the columns of the two tables, suitably renamed. Some rows of the integrated table may contain nulls in the columns that are not common to both original tables.

b. *Multiple-table approach*. Create multiple tables to replace the two tables to be integrated. One table contains the columns that are common to both original tables and contains rows in both tables being integrated. Two tables contain the key and the columns of one original table not present in the other original table. The extra tables in the multiple-table approach represent rows that are in one but not the other original table being integrated.

We will illustrate each of these approaches for each of the four types of equivalencies:

1. *Logical containment.* If Employee logically contains Scientists and we integrate using the single-table approach, the result is a single table with columns HighestDegree and School having values only if the employee is a scientist; otherwise, they are both null. The HighestDegree and School columns serve two purposes: (a) they contain the value, and (b) they indicate whether a row represents a Scientist or Employee.

Employee

Name	EmpId	Salary	HireDate	HighestDegree	School
Able	13	13,000	1987	2	null
Baker	14	14,000	1987	3	CMU
Carson	15	15,000	1977	null	MIT
Davis	16	12,000	1990	null	null
Egbert	17	11,000	1991	null	null

A disadvantage of the single-table approach is that it is possible that multiple attributes must either be null or all have values. In the example above, HighestDegree and School must both have values or both be null. If instead we integrate using the multiple-table approach, the result is two tables where Scientist.EmpId is a foreign key, containing the value from Employee.EmpId.

Employee

Name	EmpId	Salary	HireDate
Able	13	13,000	1987
Baker	14	14,000	1988
Carson	15	15,000	1977
Davis	16	12,000	1990
Egbert	18	11,000	1991

Scientist

EmpId	HighestDegree	School
14	MS	CMU
15	PhD	MIT

The disadvantage with the multiple-table approach is that data about one entity are in two places, which makes retrieval expensive and updates complex. In the previous example, Employee and Scientist must be joined to access all the Scientist's columns. Whenever a scientist resigns, a row must be deleted from both the Scientist and Employee tables.

2. *Local equivalence.* If Secretary is logically equivalent to NonExempt, then the resulting integrated table is...

Employee

Name	EmpId	Salary	WordsPerMin
Davis	16	12,000	80
Egbert	17	11,000	70

When two tables are logically equivalent, the single-table approach is almost always used. This avoids having two separate tables that represent exactly the same real-world entities.

3. *Logically overlap.* If Engineers logically overlaps with Scientists, then the resulting integrated table (using the single-table approach) is...

R&DStaff

Name	EmpId	Salary	HighestDegree	School	NumberOfPatents
Able	13	13,000	null	null	2
Baker	14	14,000	MS	CMU	3
Carson	15	15,000	PhD	MIT	null

where only engineers have values for NumberOfPatents, and only scientists have values for HighestDegree and School. If instead we used the multiple-table approach, then the resulting integrated tables are...

R&DStaff

Name	EmpId	Salary
Able	13	13,000
Baker	14	14,000
Carson	15	15,000

Scientist

EmpId	HighestDegree	School
14	MS	CMU
15	PhD	MIT

Engineer

EmpId	NumberOfPatents
13	2
14	3

where Scientist.EmpId and Scientist.EmpId are foreign keys.

4. *Logically disjoint.* If Scientist and Secretary are disjoint, but the DBAs determine that they both represent the same entity, then they may be integrated as follows (using the single-table approach):

Employee

Name	EmpId	Salary	HighestDegree	School	WordsPerMin
Baker	14	14,000	MS	CMU	null
Carson	15	15,000	PhD	MIT	null
Davis	16	12,000	null	null	80
Egbert	17	11,000	null	null	60

where HighestDegree and school have values only if the employee is a scientist and WordsPerMin has a value only if the employee is a secretary. The following is the result using the multiple-table approach:

Employee

Name	EmpId	Salary
Baker	14	14,000
Carson	15	15,000
Davis	16	12,000
Egbert	17	11,000

Scientist

EmpId	HighestDegree	School
14	MS	CMU
15	PhD	MIT

Secretary

EmpId	WordsPerMin
16	80
17	60

where Scientist.EmpId and Secretary.EmpId are both foreign keys.

5. *Merge columns that contain redundant information.*
   Consider the two tables

Employee1

EmployeeName	EmpId	Salary	BirthYear
Able	13	13,000	1945
Baker	14	14,000	1950

Employee2

EmployeeName	EmpId	Salary	BirthDate
Able	13	13,000	12/11/1945
Baker	14	14,000	3/15/1950

which integrate to the single table

Employee

EmployeeName	EmpId	Salary	BirthDate
Able	13	13,000	12/11/1945
Baker	14	14,000	3/15/1950

where BirthYear is the year in which the Employee was born and BirthDate is the month, day, and year when the Employee was born. BirthYear is redundant with BirthDate and can be eliminated without any loss of information.

6. *Resolve differences in the values from two columns that have been merged.* In the previous example, suppose that Baker's salary is 14,500 in table Employee 2 and 14,000 in table Employee 1. What value should the user see? It is tempting to automatically calculate the value using heuristics such as the following:

- Choose the minimum, maximum, or average of the two values for Baker's salary
- Choose the value from the table judged beforehand to be the most reliable.
- Replace the value by a symbol that the user interprets as conflicting values.
- Display both values to the user, and let the user resolve the problem.

We recommend that DBAs review the original source of the data to determine which value is valid. Great effort may need to be expended to determine the valid values of inconsistent data.

It is not an easy task to integrate two schemas. Knowledge about both databases and how they are used is essential to deriving an integrated schema. Rules must be specified for resolving conflicting values from different tables.

4.5 DBAs Partition Files and Allocate the Resulting Fragments

Section 4.4 describes schema integration and how it is used to achieve the logical integration of separate databases. This section deals with the other path to distributed databases described in Chapter 1. This path involves partitioning a centralized database into fragments and assigning each fragment to one or more component databases. Schema partitioning is necessary when the database administrator needs to physically distribute a centralized database. There are two steps in the process:

1. *Fragmentation*. Partition a table in a federated relational schema into multiple fragments for storage in different component databases. The DBA identifies fragments of a table such that all rows of the table fragment are accessed in the same way, and rows of different fragments are accessed differently.

2. *Allocation*. Determine in which component database to place each fragment. The DBA assigns each fragment to one or more component relational schemas for component databases where data are to be stored.

First we will describe three types of fragmentation: horizontal, vertical, and derived, and then discuss the issues associated with allocation.

4.5.1 Horizontal Fragmentation

Figure 4.18 illustrates an example table containing two sets of rows that two classes of employees access differently. Employees in Portland frequently access the rows of the table containing information about Portland employees, while the employees in Seattle seldom access these rows. Likewise, employees in Seattle frequently access the rows of the table containing information about Seattle employees, while the employees in Portland seldom access these rows. It is natural to partition this table "horizontally" into the two tables illustrated in Figure 4.19. Employees in Portland will frequently access the fragment named PortlandEmployee and seldom access the fragment named SeattleEmployee. Likewise, Seattle employees frequently access the fragment named SeattleEmployee and seldom access the fragment named PortlandEmployee. Each of these fragments are really tables that can be constructed by selecting rows from the Employee table as follows:

PortlandEmployee is defined by

```
select *
from Employee
where Location = 'Portland';
```

and SeattleEmployee is defined by

```
select *
from Employee
where Location = 'Seattle';
```

Employee

EmployeeName	EmpId	Location	Salary
Ackman	111-11-1111	Portland	4800
Baker	222-22-2222	Seattle	4900
Carson	333-33-3333	Portland	5100
Davis	444-44-4444	Seattle	5200

Figure 4.18   Table before partitioning

It should be possible to reconstruct the original table by forming the union of the fragments:

```
Employee = SeattleEmployee UNION PortlandEmployee;
```

In general, the DBA defines a horizontal fragment of a table by specifying a SQL statement for selecting rows of the fragment from the original table. The DBA constructs each fragment by executing this SQL statement and then deletes the original table because it is no longer needed.

PortlandEmployee

EmployeeName	EmpId	Location	Salary
Ackman	111-11-1111	Portland	4800
Carson	333-33-3333	Portland	5100

SeattleEmployee

EmployeeName	EmpId	Location	Salary
Baker	222-22-2222	Seattle	4900
Davis	444-44-4444	Seattle	5200

Figure 4.19   After horizontal partitioning of Figure 4.18

4.5.2 Vertical Fragmentation

Suppose that the Employee table of Figure 4.18 contains sets of columns that are accessed differently by different classes of users. The EmployeeName, EmpId, and Location columns are frequently accessed by employees in Seattle, frequently accessed by employees in Portland, and only occasionally accessed by employees in the accounting office in San Francisco. However, the EmpId and Salary tables are seldom accessed by Seattle and Portland employees, but are frequently accessed by employees in the accounting office in San Francisco.

It is natural to partition this table into fragments, as illustrated in Figure 4.20. Employees in Portland and Seattle frequently access the fragment named Employee-InfoForLocalUse and seldom access the fragment named EmployeeInfoForAccountingOffice. Employees in Portland and Seattle frequently access the fragment named EmployeeInfoForLocalUse and seldom access the fragment named EmployeeInfo-ForAccountingOffice. Each of these fragments is a table that can be constructed by selecting columns from the Employee table:

EmployeeInfoForLocalUse is defined to be

```
select EmployeeName, EmpId, Location
from Employee;
```

EmployeeInfoForAccountingOffice is defined to be

```
select EmpId, Salary
from Employee;
```

It is possible to reconstruct the Employee table from these two fragments as follows:

```
select *
from EmployeeInfoForLocalUse, EmployeeInfoForAccountingOffice
where EmployeeInfoForLocalUse.EmpId =
EmployeeInfoForAccountingOffice.EmpId;
```

In general, the DBA defines a vertical fragment of a table by specifying the SQL statements for projecting the columns of the original table. The DBA constructs the fragment by executing these SQL statements and then deletes the unneeded original table.

EmployeeInfoForLocalUse

EmployeeName	EmpId	Location
Ackman	111-11-1111	Portland
Baker	222-22-2222	Seattle
Carson	333-33-3333	Portland
Davis	444-44-4444	Seattle

EmployeeInfoForAccountingOffice

EmpId	Salary
111-11-1111	4800
222-22-2222	4900
333-33-3333	5100
444-44-4444	5200

Figure 4.20   After vertical partitioning of Figure 4.18

4.5.3 Derived Fragmentation

The goal of derived fragmentation is to horizontally partition one table in the same way that another table was previously partitioned so that the corresponding fragments can be stored at the same component database. Figure 4.21 illustrates two horizontal fragments, Division1 and Division2, that are to be stored in different component databases. It is desirable to horizontally partition the Employee table so that rows representing employees in Division1 can be stored in the same component database as Division1, and rows representing employees in Division2 can be stored in the same component database as Division2. Figure 4.22 illustrates the result of the derived fragmentation, which is defined as follows:

Employee1 is defined to be

```
select EmpId, Name, Employee.DeptNumber
from Employee, Division1
where Employee.DeptNumber = Division1.DeptNumber;
```

Employee2 is defined to be

```
select EmpId, Name, Employee.DeptNumber
from Employee, Division2
where Employee.DeptNumber = Division2.DeptNumber;
```

As expected, it is possible to reconstruct the original Employee table by forming the union of Employee1 and Employee2. Derived fragmentation is just a special case of horizontal fragmentation in which the selection criteria involve a join with horizontally partitioned fragments, instead of a simple selection criteria involving only attributes in the table to be fragmented.

Employee

EmpId	Name	DeptNumber
111-11-1111	Ackman	9
222-22-2222	Baker	13
333-33-3333	Carson	7
444-44-4444	Davis	5
555-55-5555	Egbert	5
666-66-6666	Fox	9

Division1

DeptNumber	DeptName	Budget
5	Toy	80K
7	Shoe	50K

Division2

DeptNumber	DeptName	Budget
9	Men's	50K
13	Women's	60K

Figure 4.21   Before derived fragmentation

Employee1

EmpId	Name	DeptNumber
333-33-3333	Carson	7
444-44-4444	Davis	5
555-55-5555	Egbert	5

Division1

DeptNumber	DeptName	Budget
5	Toy	80K
7	Shoe	50K

Employee2

EmpId	Name	DeptNumber
111-11-1111	Ackman	9
222-22-2222	Baker	13
666-66-6666	Fox	9

Division2

DeptNumber	DeptName	Budget
9	Men's	50K
13	Women's	60K

Figure 4.22   After derived fragmentation

4.5.4 Fragmentation Rules

Some DBAs perform successive fragmentations on a table, first partitioning it horizontally and then partitioning one or more of the resulting fragments vertically. Some data administrators first partition a table vertically and then partition it horizontally. The final result should be the same irrespective of the order in which horizontal and vertical partitioning is performed.

DBAs follow three rules when developing fragments:

1. *Vertical completeness.* Each column name in the original table is also in some fragment table. This rule is necessary to guarantee that the user can access all the data in each column of the original table.

2. *Reconstruction.* The original table can be reconstructed from the fragment tables. Note that the primary key of the original table must be present in each vertical fragment in order to be able to join the vertical fragments to reconstruct the original table.

3. *Horizontally disjoint.* A row in the original table appears in, at most, one horizontal fragment. This rule is needed to avoid updating multiple tables if just a single row of the original table needs to be changed.

4.5.5 Allocation

In this phase the DBA determines in which component database to store each fragment. The process of assigning a fragment to one or more component databases is called *fragment allocation*, or more simply *allocation*. Each fragment must be stored at least one component database in order for any user to be able to access data in that fragment. The DBA may determine that a fragment may be stored in multiple component databases if users at those sites frequently access the fragment. To perform the allocation step, the database administrator must solve the following problem: Determine the component database(s) at which to place each fragment given (1) how frequently applications and groups of users submit requests at sites where the component database resides, and (2) how frequently each of these requests accesses each fragment.

Optimization algorithms that calculate into which component databases each fragment should be stored are complex. See Section 5.4 of Ozsu and Valduriez for a descriptions of these algorithms.

4.5.6 Problems with Estimations

Often the DBA may not precisely know how often applications and users submit requests from each site and how frequently each of these requests accesses each fragment. Even if the database administrator can derive estimates for these parameters, there is no guarantee that users will continue to submit requests according to these estimates. For this reason, we recommend that the DBA do the following:

1. Find a reasonable allocation of fragments to sites.

2. Measure user access frequencies using that allocation.

3. Reallocate fragments to component databases only when the anticipated savings in access costs are greater than the cost of rearranging the fragments among component databases.

A distributed DBMS can itself measure the access frequencies using the current allocation. Database administrators use these measurements to determine if reallocation should occur. Future distributed DBMSs may automatically reallocate one or more fragments by moving fragments from component database to component database whenever it determines that reallocation is appropriate.

4.6 Security Mechanisms Protect Data

Data need to be protected from both accidental and malicious access by unauthorized users. Access to data may need to be restricted for reasons including the following:

- Information contained in a database may give competitors an advantage.
- For legal and moral reasons, access to the data should be restricted.
- Accidental or malicious modification may cause the data to become corrupted and unusable or, worse, may result in database users taking inappropriate actions.

DBAs employee several mechanisms to control access to the database. Data are encrypted so that they appear meaningless to individuals without access to the description algorithm. Database files, processors, and terminals are located in secure areas. Computers are shielded to avoid electronic eavesdropping. Users are required to pass security clearance procedures. To regulate which data each user may access, the database administrator uses both an identification and authentication component and an authorization component, as illustrated in Figure 4.23.

4.6.1 Identification and Authentication

The identification and authentication component is responsible for identifying users and verifying that users are who they claim to be. Because one or more pairs of users may have the same name, database administrators usually assign unique identifiers to users. Users enter their identifiers when they sign onto the DBMS. The database administrator places user identifiers and other user-oriented information into a special database called the *user profile*.

Many DBMSs use passwords to authenticate users. Users enter their passwords when they first log onto the DBMS. While passwords provide some degree of authentication, passwords can be easily compromised. A better approach is to ask the user questions that only the user is likely to be able to answer. Typical authentication questions ask to user to enter the maiden name of his or her mother, enter his or her birthdate, or supply other information known only to the user.

Alternatively, the user may perform an authentication procedure in which the user performs some simple function on a number or character string supplied by the DBMS. For example, the user might reverse the digits a three-digit number displayed by the DBMS and then add 12 to the result. Individuals observing the user are unlikely to determine this function, especially if the DBMS displays a different three-digit number each time the user signs on. The DBA places authentication questions and functions into the user profile. The DBA maintains control of access to the user profile so that its contents are not compromised.

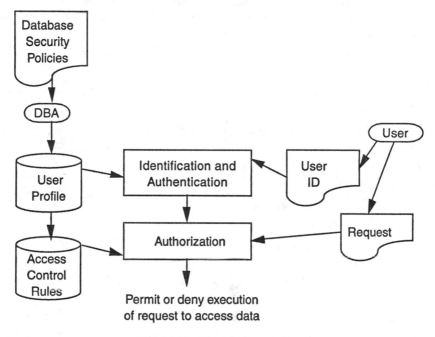

Figure 4.23 Data-access regulation

4.6.2 Authorization

Database security policies are high-level guidelines that characterize which users may access which data. Policies are dictated by legal constraints, enterprise regulations, user needs, and common sense. Generally, database security policies specify if control of access to data should be centralized to a single database administrator or distributed among several database users. Database security policies specify if users should access data only on a need to know bases or whether data sharing should be maximized. Some database systems are open in the sense that a user may access any data unless explicitly forbidden. Other databases are closed in that users may access data only if explicitly authorized to do so. Generally, the enterprise management defines database security policies.

The DBA implements database security policies through the use of access rules. Data-access rules specify the conditions under which classes of users may access data, and the nature of permitted accesses. Data-access rules may vary along the following dimensions:

- How the DBA groups users into user classes.
- How the DBA groups data into data classes for access-control security purposes. Rules regulating access to data may be specified at any of several levels of granularity, ranging from the database as a whole to individual data items within individual records. Generally, a finer level of granularity gives more control over how users may access data, but at an increased overhead in access-control specification and enforcement.
- What categories of operations should the DBA grant to users in a user class to apply to data objects in a data class.

The following illustrate some of the access operation categories allowed by various database systems.

1. Bell and LaPadula's access operations (frequently used in military applications).
   a. No access (neither observe nor alter)
   b. Read (observe only)
   c. Append (alter only)
   d. Write (observe and alter)
2. Lotus Notes® access operations
   a. No access
   b. Depositor access (may add new documents, but may not read documents deposited by others)
   c. Reader access (read documents)
   d. Author access (may add new documents to a database and may edit their own documents)
   e. Editor access (may delete or edit other users' documents)
   f. Designer access (may add, delete, or edit forms and views of a database)
   g. Manager access (may modify the access control matrix.)

The authorization component verifies that the user is permitted to perform each request or query. Whenever the user submits a request to the database management system, the authorization component selects and applies access-control rules to determine if the request should be executed. One simple mechanism for representing rules is illustrated in Figure 4.24. An access-control matrix is used to specify precisely which operations users in each class may perform against data objects in each data object class. Each row represents the data-access capabilities of users in a user class. Each column represents the control list of users and the operations they may perform on data objects in a data object class.

The manager access operations of Lotus Notes are an example of discretionary control. Users with *discretionary control* may grant other users the right to access data. In effect, users with discretionary control change the rules by modifying the access-control matrix. Users with discretionary control *grant* other user classes the right to perform an operation on a data class by adding the operation into a cell of the access control-matrix and *revoke* that right by removing the operation from a cell of the access-control matrix.

Some database management systems permit data-dependent access rules. For example, the CLERK user may READ the EMPLOYEE record only if the SALARY field of the EMPLOYEE record is greater than $20,000. The data-access rule includes a condition that must be satisfied if the DBMS is to perform the data-access. Some data-access rules include multiple data-dependent conditions, which must all be determined to be true before operation is performed.

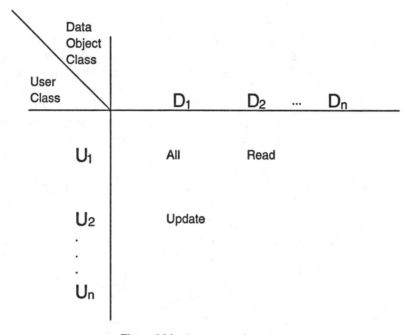

Figure 4.24   Access-control matrix

The data-dependent data-access rules can only be enforced after the DBMS has accessed the data and is able to test the data-dependent conditions. For this reason, data-dependent access rules are enforced by the runtime support processor. At least two approaches may be used to support data-dependent data-access rules:

1. Store the data-dependent rules in a database available to the runtime support processor. The runtime support processor retrieves data and determines if the user request should be completed by applying the appropriate data-dependent rules. In effect, the runtime support processor acts as a rule processor when it applies data-dependent rules to accessed data.

2. The data-dependent rules are incorporated into each user's request by the user interface translator or the component database command translator. For

example, to enforce the data-dependent condition of SALARY > 2000, the clerk's request

```
select * from EMPLOYEE;
```

is automatically modified to

```
select * from EMPLOYEE where salary > 20000;
```

When executed by the runtime support processor, only data that satisfy the data-dependent condition salary > 20000 are returned to the CLERK.

Nondata-dependent access rules may be enforced in several places:

1. The runtime support processor enforces nondata-dependent data-access rules by examining the control list associated with each data object. The control list is basically a column of the access-control matrix that indicates the operations that users in each class may perform on that data object.
2. The user interface translator or the component database command translator examines each request to determine if it satisfies access-control rules from the access-control matrix. If the request does not satisfies an access-control rule, the translator returns a message informing the user why the request cannot be processed.
3. The request constructor does not allow the user to formulate a request that violates a data-access rule. The user profile for each user contains the row of the access-control matrix. The request constructor uses this information to enable the user to specify only allowable operations on data objects that the user may access. If a data-access rule prohibits a user from accessing a data class, then that class is not represented in the menu of objects that the user may access; the user cannot include the name of the data class in any request that he or she formulates. If a user may not update data in a data class, then the update option is "grayed out" on the command menu whenever the user selects the data class.

4.7 Business Rules Enforce Data Value Constraints

Section 1.3 presented facilities of distributed DBMSs. One of these facilities is business rule enforcement. Examples of business rules include the following:

1. *Constraints on a single data item.* For example, the value of a person's age must fall into the range 0 to 119. (This example illustrates a *domain constraint* because it restricts values of a data item to take on one of the values within a domain of allowable values.)
2. *Constraints among records within a file.* For example, no two employee records may have the same value for employee identifier. (This example illustrates *entity integrity constraint* described in Section 4.1.3, which is supported by most relational database management systems.)

3. *Constraints between records in two different files.* For example, the department number of the department for which an employee works must exist as a value for the primary key of the department file. (This example illustrates the *referential integrity constraint* described in Section 4.1.3. Some relational database management systems support this constraint.)

Business rules can be categorized as validity constraints and data-dependent constraints. *Validity constraints* can be enforced without accessing data from the component databases. Domain constraints fall into this category. These constraints can be efficiently enforced by the request constructor or user interface translator. The request constructor prohibits the user from specifying a request that violates a validity constraint. For example,

- The user is not able to enter a value that violates a domain constraint.

- The user interface translator refuses to translate a request to change a field to a value disobeying a domain constraint and instead reports a business rule violation to the user.

Data-dependent business rules can only be enforced by accessing data in one or more of the component DBMSs. Examples include the entity and referential integrity constraints. If the data-dependent constraint involves data in a single component DBMS, then the runtime support processor of that component DBMS enforces the constraint. If data-dependent constraints involve data in two component databases, then a combination of the request optimizer and the runtime support processors for the component databases enforces the constraint. This is illustrated by two examples.

Example 1. *Enforcement of an entity integrity constraint that spans two component databases.* Suppose the Employee table of Figure 4.18 has the entity integrity constraint that no two employees may have the same value of EmpId. Also suppose that the Employee table is partitioned into two fragments, as illustrated in Figure 4.19. These two fragments are stored on two separate component DBMSs, one located in Portland and the other located in Seattle. When the user enters a request to insert a new employee into the distributed database, the distributed request optimizer may generate a distributed transaction consisting of the following steps:

1. The component DBMS in Portland must verify that the EmpId of the new employee does not exist in the Portland fragment.

2. The component DBMS in Seattle must verify that the EmpId of the new employee does not exist in the Seattle fragment.

3. If the EmpId of the new employee does not exist in either fragment, then insert a new row for the employee into the appropriate fragment.

The runtime support processor of the component DBMS in Seattle performs step 1 and possibly step 3. The runtime support processor of the component DBMS in Portland performs step 2 and possibly step 3.

Example 2. *Enforcement of a referential integrity constraint that spans two component databases.* Suppose that the Department table is stored in component DBMS at site 1 and that the Employee table is stored in the component database at site 2. Also assume that there is a referential integrity constraint requiring that the value of each employee's department number must exist in the Department table. After the user formulates a request to insert information about a new employee into the Employee table, the transaction optimizer might generate the following distributed transaction:

1. Examine the Department table in the component database at DBMS 1 to verify that it contains the department identifier of the department to which the new employee is assigned.
2. If the result of step 1 is affirmative, then insert the new row into the Employee table in DBMS 2; otherwise, report an error to the user.

In both examples the distributed transaction optimizer generated distributed transactions that involved data in two or more component databases. At least one local runtime support processor accessed its component database to obtain information necessary to determine if the business rule is violated. Intermediate results must be transmitted to a component DBMS where the decision is made to continue processing the distributed transaction.

Two observations can be made:

1. The transaction optimizer must be clever enough to generate a distributed transaction that, when executed by the runtime support processors of component DBMSs, enforces the business rule that spans component DBMS. If the transaction optimizer is not available or is unable to do this, then location and replication transparency is not possible and the user must formulate the distributed transaction himself.
2. There are several communications transmissions among sites to determine if the business rule is violated. These transmissions are both time consuming and expensive.

To minimize the communication overhead, some database administrators avoid business rules that span component DBMSs as follows:

1. By allocating fragments so that constraints do not span component DBMSs.
2. By electing not to automatically enforce the business rule during update processing. Instead, utilities periodically examine the database to detect and correct business rule violations.

Chapter Summary

The relational data model is the data model of choice for distributed DBMSs. If the distributed DBMS contains component DBMSs that are not relational, then the database administrator constructs a relational component schema for each nonrelational component schema. A gateway translates SQL requests to the data-manipulation language of the nonrelational component DBMS.

DBAs specify the federated schema and component relational schemas. If the component relational database already exists, then the DBAs integrate component relational schemas to form the one or more federated schemas. If an existing centralized database is to be distributed, then the DBA uses its schema as the federated schema and creates several component relational schemas.

DBAs specify security and business rules. If a business rule can be enforced without accessing any of the component databases, then the request constructor or user interface translator enforces the business rule or constraint. If a business rule involves data within a single component database, then that database's component DBMS enforces the business rule. If a business rule involves data within several component databases, then programmers write transactions that enforce the business rule whenever they are executed.

Further Reading

Ceri, Stefano, and Giuseppe Pelagatti, *Distributed Databases Principles and Systems,* McGraw-Hill, New York, 1984. Chapter 4 discusses fragmentation and allocation of fragments.

Elmasri, Ramez, and Shamkant B. Navathe, *Fundamentals of Database Systems,* Benjamin/Cummings, Menlo Park, CA, 1989. Chapter 12 describes how to map among the relational, network, and hierarchical data models via the entity relationship data model.

Larson, James A., "Bridging the Gap between Network and Relational Database Management Systems," *Computer,* Sept. 1983, pp. 82–92. Describes mappings between CODASYL and relational data models.

Navathe, Shamkant, Ramez Elmasri, and James Larson, "Integrating User Views in Database Design," *Computer,* Jan. 1986, pp. 50–62. Describes methodology for schema integration.

Ozsu, M. Tamer, and Patrick Valduriez, *Principles of Distributed Database Systems,* Prentice Hall, Englewood Cliffs, NJ, 1991. Chapter 5 discusses fragmentation and allocation of fragments. Chapter 6 discusses data security and business rule control.

Tsichritzis, D., and F. Lochovsky, *Data Models,* Prentice Hall, Upper Saddle River, NJ, 1982. Informally discusses data model equivalencies.

5

Designing Distributed Transactions

This chapter discusses the following:

- How distributed transactions guide a distributed DBMS to access data.
- How a distributed DBMS coordinates component DBMSs to access data.
- How an optimizer generates and optimizes distributed transactions.

We will use the term *global transaction* to refer to a request to access data in multiple databases without regard to where the data are located. A global transaction is written by a programmer or constructed from a user's request. A global transaction cannot be executed by itself. It must be modified to include information about how data are located among the several component databases before it can be executed. As illustrated in Figure 5.1, a transaction optimizer performs the task of converting a global transaction into a distributed transaction. When executed, a *distributed transaction* obtains and merges information from several component databases.

Section 5.1 discusses distributed transactions in general and enumerates the services needed to execute them. Every distributed DBMSs provides these services. Section 5.2 describes three models for executing distributed transactions. Each distributed DBMS supports one or more of these execution models. Query optimizers modify queries so that they execute efficiently. Section 5.3 presents typical strategies used by optimizers to convert queries to distributed transactions.

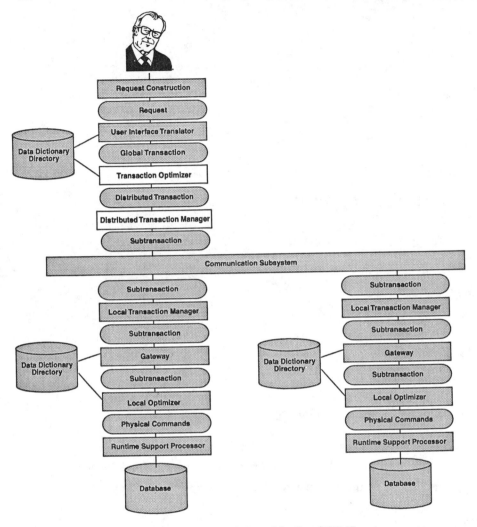

Figure 5.1   Detailed view of distributed DBMS

5.1 Distributed Transactions Guide a Distributed DBMS

Before it can be executed, a global transaction must be converted into a distributed transaction. A distributed transaction is a special type of distributed program in which component DBMSs (1) perform database requests and (2) transmit intermediate results between component database management systems. For example, consider the following global transaction:

Select X from Table1
Select Y from Table2
Select Z from Table3
Calculate the sum of X, Y, and Z
Display the result to the user

This global transaction may be converted to a distributed transaction such as the following:

1. At originating requester site:
   Send "Select X from Table 1" to component DBMS 1
   Send "Select Y from Table 2" to component DBMS 2
   Send "Select Z from Table 3" to component DBMS 3

2. At component DBMS 1:
   Receive instructions
   Perform instructions
   Send results to requester site

3. At component DBMS 2:
   Receive instructions
   Perform instructions
   Send results to requester site

4. At component DBMS 3:
   Receive instructions
   Perform instructions
   Send results to requester site

5. At requester site:
   Receive results from component DBMS 1
   Receive results from component DBMS 2
   Receive results from component DBMS 3
   Calculate sum of X, Y, and Z
   Display the result to the user

This distributed transaction describes how data are transmitted among the various component database management systems and how the results from each of the three component database management systems are synchronized and summarized at the requesting site. In general, four services are needed to manage the execution of a distributed transaction:

1. Remote process activation, which activates a database execution engine at a remote site.

2. Process synchronization, which coordinates processes at remote sites so that they perform pieces of the distributed transaction at the appropriate times.

3. Transmittal of intermediate data among processes executing at different sites.

4. Remote process deactivation, which deactivates a process at a remote site so that it no longer uses resources.

5.2 Distributed Execution Control Model Describes How to Coordinate Component DBMSs

Distributed transactions may conform to any of several control models. We use the term *control model* here to refer to any of several general approaches for coordinating the execution of the component database management systems of a distributed transaction. Control models for controlling the execution of a distributed transaction include master–slave, triangular, and hierarchical control.

Figure 5.2 illustrates a distributed transaction execution following the master–slave control model. A distributed transaction manager acts as the master and one or more local transaction managers act as slaves. In this model the distributed transaction manager controls all synchronization by sending and receiving messages to and from the local transaction managers. The distributed transaction manager activates each local transaction manager, tells it what to do, and may deactivate it when it has completed access to its component database and returned its results to the distributed transaction manager. However, intermediate results needed by another local transaction manager must first be transmitted to the global execution manager and then retransmitted to the appropriate local transaction manager.

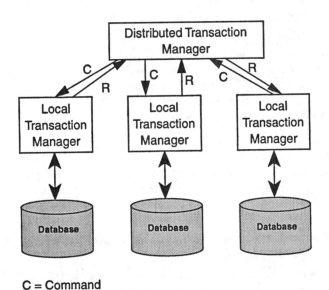

C = Command
R = Response

Figure 5.2   Master-slave approach to distributed execution

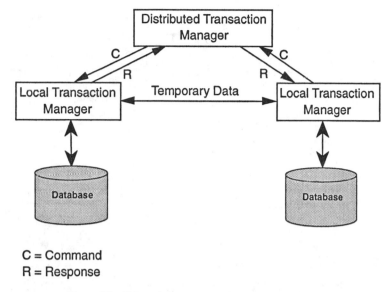

C = Command
R = Response

Figure 5.3 Triangular approach to distributed execution

Figure 5.3 illustrates the triangular control model. In this model the control is shared between the distributed transaction manager and the local transaction managers. Local transaction managers may send and receive data among themselves without the distributed transaction manager acting as an intermediary. This model avoids unnecessary data transmissions between the distributed transaction manager and local transaction managers. However, some synchronization is necessary among the local transaction managers so that they don't try to use intermediate data before they arrive.

Figure 5.4 illustrates the hierarchical control model. In this model each local transaction manager may itself act as a distributed transaction manager. This model permits incremental planning; when a local transaction manager receives a request from its global transaction manager and the local transaction manager is itself a global transaction manager, it may further optimize its transaction into another distributed transaction and distribute it for execution among other local transaction managers. This model is more complex than the previous two approaches.

The following table summarizes these three models of distributed execution:

Distributed Execution Control Model	Type of Control
Master–slave	Centralized
Triangular	Shared
Hierarchical	Distributed

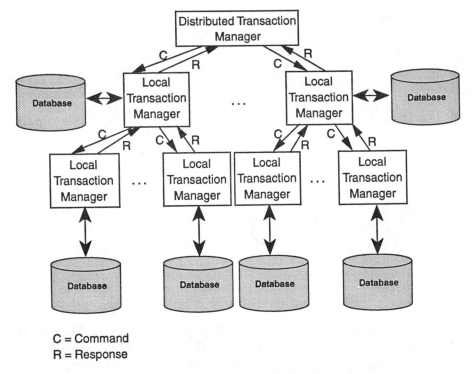

C = Command
R = Response

Figure 5.4   Hierarchical approach to distributed execution

A distributed transaction contains send and receive operations that conform to an execution control model. A query optimizer transforms global transactions into distributed transactions that conform to a distributed execution control model. Whenever programmers implement a distributed transaction, they embed a distributed execution control model into each transaction that they write.

5.3 Transaction Optimizer Generates Distributed Transactions

5.3.1 Motivation for Automatic Transaction Optimization

Database administrators have long strived to achieve data independence (more appropriately called program-data independence) in which they are able to make changes to the structure of data in the database without having to modify existing applications. One reason relational database management systems have become popular is that DBAs can add tables, add and remove indexes, and make other changes to the physical representation of the database without forcing users to modify their existing applications or queries. Data independence isolates users from the underlying data structures in a centralized database. Chapter 1 introduced three additional types of data independence in distributed databases:

1. *Fragmentation transparency*, in which the user is not aware of how tables have been fragmented.
2. *Location transparency*, in which users are not aware of the component database(s) to which fragments have been allocated.
3. *Replication transparency*, in which users are not aware if fragments have been allocated to more than a single component database.

To motivate the need for these types of data independence, consider the Employee table of Figure 5.5 and the two horizontal fragments, Employee1 and Employee2. Suppose that the DBA allocates the Employee1 to component DBMS 1 and the Employee2 fragment to both component DBMS 1 and DBMS 2. If there is no fragmentation, replication, or location transparency [Figure 5.6(a)], then the user must write the following SQL request to retrieve Davis's salary:

```
select Salary
from Employee1 at DBMS 1
where Name = "Davis"
UNION
select Salary
from Employee2 at component DBMS 2
where Name = "Davis";
```

Note that the user had to specify the location of each fragment.

Now suppose that the locations and replication of fragments are hidden from the user, but the user is still aware of the existence of fragments Employee1 and Employee2, as illustrated in Figure 5.6(b). To retrieve Davis's salary, the user must write the following SQL request:

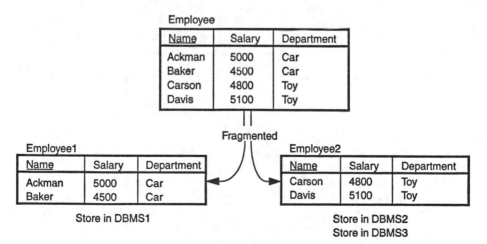

Figure 5.5 Employee table with its two horizontal fragments

Employee1   Site1   Employee2   Site2

Name	Salary	Department
Ackman	5000	Car
Baker	4500	Car

Name	Salary	Department
Carson	4800	Toy
Davis	5100	Toy

Employee2   Site 3

Name	Salary	Department
Carson	4800	Toy
Davis	5100	Toy

(a) Fragments and locations are visible to the user

Employee1   Employee2

Name	Salary	Department
Ackman	5000	Car
Baker	4500	Car

Name	Salary	Department
Carson	4800	Toy
Davis	5100	Toy

(b) Fragments are visible, but the locations of fragments are hidden from the user

Name	Salary	Department
Ackman	5000	Car
Baker	4500	Car
Carson	4800	Toy
Davis	5100	Toy

(c) Fragments and their locations are hidden from the user

Figure 5.6   Three versions of fragments

```
select Salary
from Employee1
where Name = "Davis"
UNION
select Salary
from Employee2
where Name = "Davis";
```

In this request, the user does not need to specify the actual component DBMS
containing each fragment.

Now suppose that the existence of fragments is hidden from the user, who sees a single table as illustrated in Figure 5.6(c). To retrieve Davis's salary, the user only needs to write the following SQL request:

```
select Salary
from Employee
where Name = "Davis";
```

By now the reader should be convinced that it is easier for users to write requests with fragmentation, replication, and location transparency than without. One more example should convince the most doubting reader that these types of transparencies really do save users time and frustration in formulating requests. Consider the Employee table illustrated in Figure 5.7(a) and the four fragments of this table illustrated in Figure 5.7(b). Suppose the user desires to change the value of Department from 3 to 15 for the employee with EmpID = 100. Using the table of Figure 5.7(a), the user writes the following simple SQL request:

```
select Employee
set Department = 15
where EmpId = 100;
```

However, using the fragments of Figure 5.7(b), the user must write the following complex SQL transaction:

Employee

EmpId	Name	Salary	Tax	ManagerNumber	Department
100	Smith	10000	1000	20	3
200	Jones	1333	122	40	14

(a) Fragments and their locations are hidden from the user

Employee1 (Department<10)

EmpId	Name	Salary	Tax
100	Smith	10000	1000

Employee2 (Department<10)

EmpId	ManagerNumber	Department
100	20	3

Employee3 (Department>=10)

EmpId	Name	Department
200	Jones	14

Employee4 (Department>=10)

EmpId	Salary	Tax	ManagerNumber
200	1333	122	40

(b) Fragments and their locations are visible to the user

Figure 5.7   Another example of fragmentation

```
select Name, Sal, Tax into $Name, $Sal, $Tax
from Employee1
where EmpId = 100;

select ManagerNumber into $ManagerNumber
from Employee2
where EmpId = 100;

insert into Employee3 (EmpId, Name, Department) (100, $Name,
15);
insert into Employee4 (EmpId, Sal, Tax, ManagerNumber) (100,
$Sal, $Tax, $ManagerNumber);

delete Employee1 where EmpID = 100;
delete Employee2 where EmpId = 100;
```

Fragmentation, replication, and location transparency make it much easier for users to formulate requests. They also isolate the user from changes in the structure of fragments and how fragments are allocated and replicated to sites. However, to support these types of transparencies, a distributed DBMS must support a transaction optimizer.

5.3.2 Transaction Optimization

The previous section demonstrated how much easier it is for users to formulate requests if they perceive the component databases to be a centralized database than a distributed database containing multiple, possibly replicated fragments. This section describes how to convert global transactions involving tables in a federated relational schema to equivalent distributed transactions involving fragments of a distributed database as described by several component relational schemas.

While we could continue to use SQL to describe transaction optimization, this and the following section will be easier to understand by switching notations. Instead of using SQL, we will use a notation involving directed graphs. The external nodes of the directed graph represent tables from a federated relational schema used by the user in formulating requests. Internal nodes of the directed graph represent relational algebra operations. Figure 5.8 illustrates the graphical notation for the relational operations of select, project, join, and union and their equivalent representations using SQL. It is possible to convert any SQL request to this style of notation.

The first step toward transaction optimization is to convert the global transaction involving tables in the federated relational schema to a global transaction involving fragments scattered throughout several multiple component relational schemas. Each external node of an operator tree represents a single table in the federated relational schema. Replace each external node by an operator tree that describes how to reconstruct the table from its constituent fragments. If a table was horizontally fragmented, then it can be reconstructed by forming the union of the horizontal fragments. If a table was vertically fragmented, then it can be reconstructed by forming the join of the vertical fragments. The result of this step is a distributed transaction involving fragments. Figure 5.9 illustrates a query tree and the global transaction that results by replacing each centralized table by its derivation from its fragments. Now we are ready to proceed with transaction optimization.

Select * from Product
where ProductName="widget"

select CustomerName
from Customer

select * from Customer, Order
where Customer.CustomerNumber
=Order.CustomerNumber

Scientist union Engineer

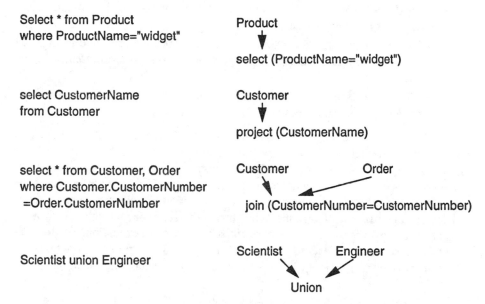

Figure 5.8   Graphical notation for relational algebra notation

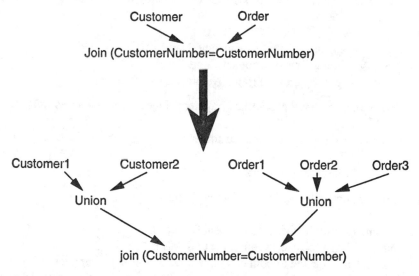

Figure 5.9   Replace leaf tables by operator trees defining leaf tables from their fragments

There are several possible goals for transaction optimization. Different optimization strategies attempt to optimize for one or a combination of the following objectives:

- *Maximize throughput.* Enable the distributed database management system to process as many requests as possible.
- *Minimize response time.* Minimize the response time, the time from when the user submits a transaction to the time the results are presented to the user.
- *Minimize transmission costs.* Minimize the number of data transmissions, and/or minimize the amount of data transmitted.

Some distributed database management systems perform no optimization. This may result in inefficiencies during the execution of the request. To overcome these inefficiencies, programmers may perform the optimization when they create distributed requests. While this may decrease the execution inefficiencies, it increases the personnel costs associated with transaction construction. An alternative approach is to develop optimization algorithms. While this optimization incurs some overhead, it may be offset by larger savings in more efficient transaction execution. The remainder of this section overviews some approaches to optimizing global transactions.

There are three major tasks to perform during transaction optimization:

1. Choose a query tree to represent the global transaction.
2. Choose component DBMSs containing data to be accessed.
3. Assign query tree operations to component DBMSs.

To illustrate these three tasks, consider the following three tables from a federated relational schema:

Customer [CustomerNumber, CustomerName, Address]
Product [ProductNumber, ProductName, Cost]
Order [CustomerNumber, ProductNumber, Date, Quantity]

Also suppose that the DBA has fragmented these three tables as follows:

Customer = Customer1 union Customer2
Product = Product1 union Product2
Order = Order1 union Order2

with the fragments allocated to the following sites:

Customer1 is allocated to component DBMS A
Customer2 is allocated to component DBMS B
Product1 is allocated to both component DBMS A and component DBMS B
Product2 is allocated to both component DBMS A and component DBMS B
Order1 is allocated to component DBMS A
Order2 is allocated to component DBMS B

Also suppose that a user submits the following SQL request involving the above tables:

select CustomerName
from Customer, Product, Order
where Customer.CustomerNumber = Order.CustomerNumber
and Order.ProductNumber = Product.ProductNumber
and ProductName = "Widget"
and Date = "June 1990";

Basically, this request asks the database management system to join the Customer, Product, and Order tables, select rows with "Widget" and "June 1990," and project the CustomerName column. How might the distributed transaction optimizer optimize this request?

1. *Choose query tree.* Figure 5.10 illustrates several possible query trees that derive results equivalent to this SQL request. Suppose that the optimizer chooses the query tree in the upper-left corner of Figure 5.10. Next, each leaf node is replaced by an operator tree that derives the original tables. The result is illustrated in Figure 5.11.

2. *Choose component DBMS.* In our example, the optimizer has two choices: Should it choose the copy of Product1 at component DBMS A or component DBMS B, and should it choose the copy of Order1 at component DBMS A or component DBMS B. Suppose the optimizer choose the fragments Customer1, Product1, Order1 at DBMS component A and Customer2, Product2, and Order2 at component DBMS B.

3. *Assign query tree operators to component DBMSs.* Figure 5.12 illustrates several possible ways to assign operations to component DBMSs. The star (*) by some of the arcs of the directed graph indicates that data must be transmitted from the component DBMS at the tail of the arc to the component DBMS at the pointer of the arc. Let's suppose that the optimizer might choose the operations as illustrated in the upper portion of Figure 5.12.

The transaction optimizer uses one of the control models described in Section 5.1 when assigning query tree operators to component DBMSs. If the master–slave control model is used, temporary results needed by a different component DBMS are first returned to the master, which forwards the results to the appropriate component DBMS. If the triangular approach is used, intermediate results are transmitted directly among component DBMSs. The distributed transaction generated by the distributed transaction optimizer must conform to the control model used in the distributed DBMS.

Transaction optimizers differ in major aspects. Different optimizers perform the above three tasks in different orders. For example, one optimizer may choose the query tree, then choose the component DBMS containing data to be accessed, and finally assign query-tree operations to the component DBMS. Another optimizer may first choose the component DBMS containing the data to be accessed, then choose the query tree, and finally assign query-tree operations to the component DBMS. A third optimizer may choose a component DBMS and query trees at the same time and finally assign query-tree operations to the component DBMS. Other approaches are also possible.

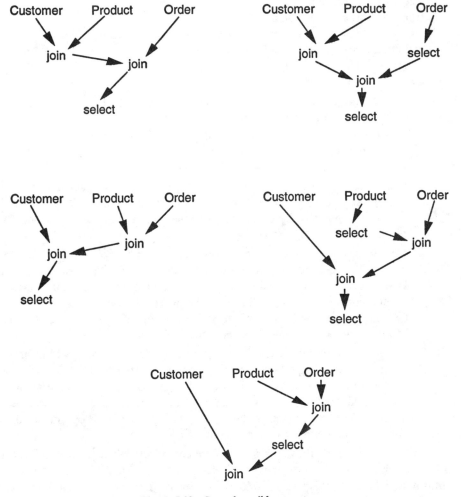

Figure 5.10   Several possible query trees

    Different optimizers may perform these tasks at various times. For example, one optimizer may perform all three tasks at compile time. Another optimizer may perform all three tasks at runtime. A third optimizer may perform one of these tasks at compile time and the remaining tasks at runtime. Some optimizers perform parts of each task at compile time and the remaining parts at runtime.

    Different optimizers may use different algorithms and heuristics for each of these tasks. For example, one optimizer may generate all possible query trees and then choose the best one, while another optimizer may generate one query tree and repeatedly transform it into a better one. The latter is called *heuristics-based optimization*. There are many possible heuristics that optimizers may perform. Figures 5.13 through 5.16 illustrate four examples of such heuristics.

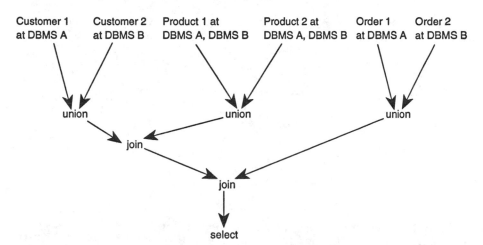

Figure 5.11 Replace leaf tables by operator trees defining leaf tables from their fragments

Figure 5.13 illustrates one optimization that is always useful. By migrating the select operation toward the external nodes of the operator tree, the size of fragments are reduced before they are combined by the join and union operators. This results in considerable savings because join and union are expensive operations, especially on large tables. In some cases the project operation may also be migrated toward the external nodes. Migrating selects and projects toward the external nodes is a useful optimization for both centralized and distributed transactions.

Figure 5.14 illustrates two branches of an operator tree that perform the same operation. These common branches can be combined so that the operations are only performed once rather than twice. This optimization is also useful for both centralized and distributed transactions.

Figure 5.15 illustrates an optimization that is only useful for distributed transactions. Suppose that the fragments Dept1 and Dept2 are defined as follows:

Dept1 is defined to be

```
select * from Department where DeptId <- 10
```

and Dept2 is defined to be

```
select * from Department where DeptId > 10.
```

Applying select (DeptId = 1) to the Dept2 fragment must result in null because the Dept2 fragment contains only rows with DeptId > 10. The optimizer is then able to determine that it is not necessary to perform this select operation. Because the select operation is not performed, no union operation needs to be performed. The query tree is modified to simply apply the select operation on the Dept1 fragment. This optimized query is much more efficient to perform than the original query.

Figure 5.16 illustrates another optimization that is only useful for distributed queries. This optimization applies to aggregate functions such as average, minimize, maximize, count, and sum that involve the values in the same column of several rows of a table. These aggregate operations can be distributed by applying aggregate operations locally and then combining the results.

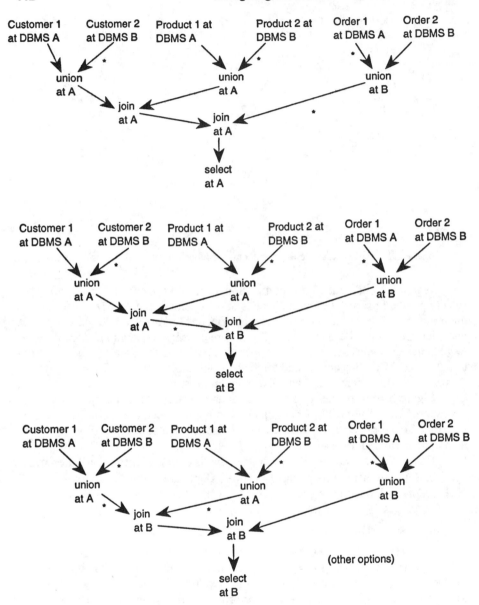

Figure 5.12   Assignment of operators to sites

Cost-based optimization uses statistics about the database to estimate the cost of different access strategies for processing a transaction. Statistics include such things as the number of rows in a table, the size of each table, and the number of distinct values in a primary key. Using a cost-based optimization approach, a join operation can be optimized to minimize the amount of data transferred between component databases by using information about the size of the tables to compute alternative ways to perform the join and then selecting the least expensive. The IBM OS/2 Extended Edition Database Manager, DEC Rdb/VMS, and the Microsoft SQL Server use cost-based optimization algorithms.

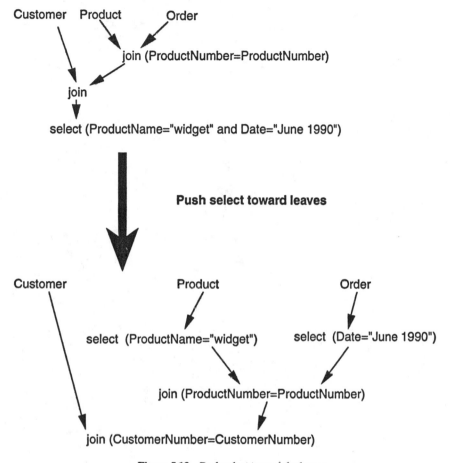

Figure 5.13 Push select toward the leaves

A join operation is both expensive and time consuming when the tables to be joined reside on two different component database management systems. One approach is to transmit one table to the component database management system of the other table. The following describes another approach in which the size of a table is reduced as much as possible before transmitting. We have already seen examples of reducing a table before it is transmitted to another component database management system by applying a select or project operation to a table which always makes it smaller. We will make the transmitted table smaller by transmitting only the rows of the table that will be joined. To select the rows to be transmitted, we will get the values used in the join from the other table. To join tables Department and Employee with the same value for Department Name:

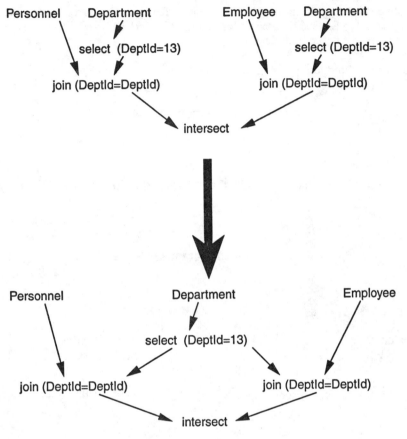

Figure 5.14   Merge common subexpressions

Department

DepartmentName	DepartmentBudget
Car	45,000,000
Toy	48,000,000
Hardware	36,000,000

Employee

EmployeeName	EmployeeSalary	DepartmentName
Ackman	5,000	Car
Baker	4,500	Car

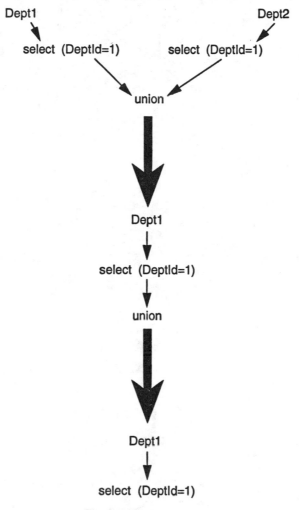

Figure 5.15   Trim branches

1. Construct Temp1 by projecting DepartmentName on Employee.

Temp1

DepartmentName
Car.

2. Transmit Temp1 to the component DBMS containing Department.
3. Construct Temp2 by joining Department with Temp1.

Temp2

DepartmentName	DepartmentBudget
Car	45,000,000

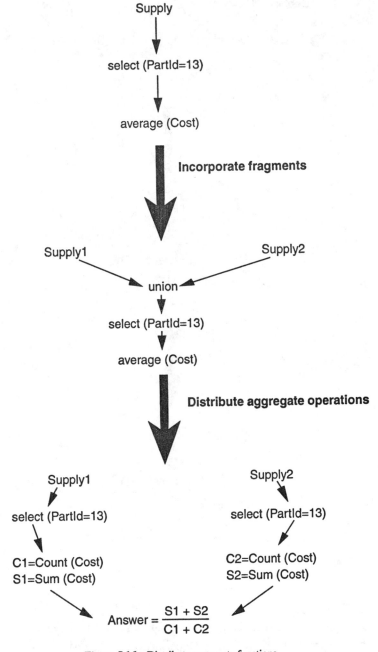

Figure 5.16   Distribute aggregate functions

4. Transmit Temp2 to the component DBMS containing Employee.
5. Construct Result by joining Temp2 and Employee.

Result

DepartmentName	DepartmentBudget	EmployeeName	DeptName
Car	45,000,000	Ackman	Car
Car	45,000,000	Baker	Car

If we assume that each field is 15 bytes long, the size of the transmission to send the complete Department table to the component DBMS containing Department is 30 × 3 = 90. The size of the transmission for sending the complete Employee table to the component DBMS containing Employee is 45 × 2 = 90. The transmission in the above scheme is 15 × 1 + 30 × 1 = 45, a definite savings in this case.

While this approach results in two transmissions rather than one, the amount of data transmitted may be significantly smaller. This same idea can be applied in many of the set operations, including the following:

- A intersect B
- A minus B
- A union B
- (A union B) - (A intersect B)

Additional complexities in transaction optimization may be introduced when the component database management systems are heterogeneous. The cost of performing an operation may differ from one component database management system to another. Some component database management systems may not even be able to perform some operations. For example, many database management systems do not support the union operation. This may influence which component database management system is chosen to perform certain operations. Some component database management systems do not support the creation and loading of temporary files. This may also influence the choice of system on which to perform operations.

Chapter Summary

In cases where performance is very critical, programmers may carefully design a distributed transaction that accesses data in multiple component DBMSs so that its execution is optimal or nearly optimal. However, usually it is more cost efficient to use automatic optimizers to hide fragments and their locations and replications from programmers and users, thus decreasing the time and effort necessary to formulate distributed transactions at a modest cost to perform the automatic optimization.

An execution control model describes how the execution of a distributed transaction is controlled. Three models of distributed execution control are master-slave, triangular, and hierarchical. Each distributed DBMS implements one or a combination of these control models.

A query optimizer performs three tasks: choose a query tree to represent the transaction, choose the appropriate component DBMSs containing the data to be accessed, and assign query-tree operations to component DBMSs. Distributed query optimizers of different distributed DBMSs use different heuristics to perform these tasks.

Further Reading

Ceri, Stefano, and Giuseppe Pelagatti, *Distributed Databases Principles and Systems*, McGraw-Hill, New York, 1984. Chapters 5 and 6 describe query optimization and query processing.

Khoshafian, Setrag, Arvola Chan, Anna Wong, and Harry K. T. Wong, *A Guide to Developing Client/Server SQL Applications*, Morgan Kaufman, San Francisco, 1992. Chapter 7 describes performance tuning and optimization.

Ozsu, M. Tamer, and Patrick Valduriez, *Principles of Distributed Database Systems*, Prentice Hall, Upper Saddle River, NJ, 1991. Chapters 7 through 9 describe query optimization and query processing.

6

Distributed Transaction Processing

This chapter discusses the following:

- The important properties of a transaction.
- How transactions enforce consistency.
- Why transaction histories should be serializable.
- How locking, time-stamp ordering, and optimistic protocols guarantee that transaction histories are serializable.
- Why replicated data must be kept consistent.
- How data replicators keep replicated data consistent.
- How commit protocols keep distributed data consistent.
- Why DBAs choose the two-phase commit protocol to keep distributed data consistent.
- How distributed DBMSs recover from failures.

Chapter 2 explained how a user's request is formulated into a global transaction by a user interface translator and how a transaction optimizer further transforms a global transaction into a distributed transaction. Chapter 5 explained how a distributed DBMS executes a distributed transaction. This chapter deals with the special problems of transactions that update data, that is, making sure that, when a transaction completes all its changes are recorded within the component databases.

Database operations are grouped into sequences called transactions. Each transaction involves one or more database operations. In this chapter, we will consider only transactions that involve one or more update operations. Transactions are written in such a manner that if the transaction completes then all business rules are satisfied by data modified by the transaction. If a transaction fails and the database might contain data that violate one or more business rules, the transaction processing system removes all changes made to each of the databases by the failed transaction. This leaves each database in the same state as when the transaction began processing.

There are several reasons why a transaction may not succeed. A user may cancel a transaction in progress. A transaction may detect that it cannot enforce a business rule, and cancel itself. The transaction processing system may determine that two or more transactions attempt to update a single data item and that the data item will not reflect the updates from these transactions. Also, operating systems occasionally fail while processing a transaction. When a transaction succeeds, we say that it *commits*. The results of a committed transaction are stored permanently in the database. When a transaction does not succeed, we say that it *rolls back*. Any changes made to the database are undone. The transaction can then be reprocessed, possibly at a later time.

This chapter describes transaction processing in distributed database systems. Section 6.1 overviews four important properties of transactions. The remaining sections discuss these properties in greater detail. Section 6.2 discusses consistency and how transactions persevere database consistency by enforcing business rules. Sections 6.3 through 6.5 discuss transaction isolation. To ensure isolation, distributed DBMSs use various approaches to concurrency control so that multiple users cannot update data at the same time. Section 6.6 describes the atomicity of transactions, which requires that all or none of a transaction's operations be executed. Section 6.7 addresses how to guarantee that the results of executing a transaction are always available.

6.1 Transaction Support Four Important Properties

A *transaction* is a distributed sequence of database operations that satisfies the following "ACID" properties:

- *Atomicity*: A transaction is atomic; either all or none of a transaction's operations are performed.
- *Consistency*: A transaction transforms the database from one consistent state to another consistent state. A database is said to be in a consistent state if all the data in the database satisfy a set of business rules.
- *Isolated*: If several transactions are performed concurrently, the results of one transaction are isolated or insulated from the other.
- *Durability*: A transaction is durable; committed, results are never lost.

This section explores each of these proprieties in detail.

6.2 Transactions Enforce Consistency

Section 4.7 discussed business rules. A database in which data-item values satisfy all business rules is said to be a *consistent database*; that is, the database values are consistent with respect to prespecified business rules. Programmers must write transactions, and transaction optimizers must generate transactions so that all business rules are enforced when each transaction is executed. The database administrator and database users should all precisely understand the business rules that the distributed DBMS must support. All transactions should enforce these business rules.

Figure 6.1 illustrates an example transaction. Bank customers use this transaction to withdraw cash from their account in a bank. Note that, if the customer attempts to withdraw more cash than there are funds in his or her account, the transaction will roll back any changes made to the database. This transaction enforces the following business rule:

- The funds in an account must always be equal to or greater than zero.

```
begin transaction withdraw (SourceAccountNumber, Amount);
   select Balance
   from Account
   where AccountNumber = SourceAccountNumber;

if <failure> then do
         display 'Source account not found';
         rollback;
         end do;

update Account
set Balance = Balance – Amount
where AccountNumber  = SourceAccountNumber;

if Balance < 0 then do
         display 'Insufficient funds in source account';
         rollback;
         end do;

display (Amount 'withdrawn');

commit;

end transaction withdraw;
```

Figure 6.1 The withdraw-funds transaction

```
begin transaction transfer (SourceAccountNumber, TargetAccountNumber, Amount);

select Balance
 from Account
 where AccountNumber = SourceAccountNumber;

if <failure> then do
            display 'Source account not found';
            rollback;
            end do;

update Account
set Balance = Balance – Amount
where AccountNumber = SourceAccountNumber;

if Balance < 0 then do
            display 'Insufficient funds in source account';
            rollback;
            end do;

select Balance
 from Account
 where AccountNumber = TargetAccountNumber;

if <failure> then do
            display 'Target account not found';
            rollback;
            end do;

update Account
set Balance = Balance + Amount
where AccountNumber = TargetAccountNumber;

display 'Transfer complete';

commit;

end transaction transfer;
```

Figure 6.2   The transfer-funds transaction

Figure 6.2 illustrates another transaction. Bank customers use this transaction
to transfer funds from one account, called the SourceAccount, to another account,
called the TargetAccount. Values for SourceAccount, TargetAccount, and Amount to

transfer are parameters that must be specified by the user. This transaction enforces two business rules:

- The funds in an account must always be equal to or greater than zero.
- The sum of the funds in both accounts at the end of the transaction must be the same as the sum of the funds in both accounts at the beginning of the transaction.

The last business rule guarantees that money is not created or destroyed during a transfer transaction.

Figure 6.3 illustrates a third transaction. Bank employees periodically use this transaction to credit each account with interest. When this transaction is executed, the value of each account balance is increased by 10%. This transaction enforces the following business rule:

- The sum of the funds in all accounts after the transaction is completed is 10% greater than the sum of the funds in all accounts at the beginning of the transaction.

All business rules must be enforced by each distributed transaction written by a user or generated by the transaction optimizer. To enforce business rules, the transaction optimizer must either (1) be programmed to include the enforcement of business rules in the distributed execution plans that it generates, or (2) obtain relevant business rules from the data dictionary directory and use them when generating distributed transactions.

The transaction optimizer of most commercial distributed DBMSs generates distributed queries that enforce only a few types of business rules. To compensate for this shortcoming:

- Programmers must write distributed transactions that enforce business rules.
- The DBA must periodically scan the database, detect nonconsistent data, and resolve them.
- Or the DBA elects not to enforce business rules that cannot enforced by the transaction optimizer.

```
begin transaction interest;

update Account
set Balance = Balance * 1.1;

end transaction interest;
```

Figure 6.3 The interest transaction

6.3 Transaction Histories are Serializable

One of the four properties of transactions is isolation. In a multiuser environment, users may execute several transactions concurrently. Isolation guarantees that two concurrent transactions do not interfere with each other. Several levels of isolation are possible. The strongest level of isolation is called *serializablity*. The concept of serializable is based on the idea that concurrently executing transactions produce results that are the same as if the transactions were executed serially. Before describing serializability, we first introduce the concept of history.

A *history* is a sequence of reads and writes of a set of transactions. We will use the notation

$$H = R_A[X] \ W_B[X] \ W_A[X] \ W_A[Y]$$

to mean that Transaction A reads X, Transaction B writes X, Transaction A writes X, and Transaction A writes Y.

A history of an execution of the transaction of Figure 6.1 might be

$R_{withdraw}$ [SourceAccountNumber.Balance]
$W_{withdraw}$ [SourceAccountNumber.Balance]

A history of an execution of the transaction of Figure 6.2 might be

$R_{transfer}$ [SourceAccount.Balance]
$W_{transfer}$ [SourceAccount.Balance]
$R_{transfer}$ [TargetAccount.Balance]
$W_{transfer}$ [TargetAccount.Balance]

Two transaction histories can be related in three ways:

1. *Serial*: One transaction completes before the other transaction begins to execute. The execution of the two transactions do not overlap in time.

2. *Concurrent*: One transaction starts before the other transaction completes. The executions of the two transactions overlap in time but don't modify the same data items.

3. *Conflicting*: Concurrent transactions in which one transaction needs to modify a data item that another transaction needs to reference.

Serial and concurrent transactions are isolated; they don't interfere with each other. Conflicting transactions are not isolated and may result in database errors.

Figure 6.4 illustrates three possible histories of the withdraw transaction from Figure 6.1 and the interest transaction from Figure 6.3. Histories 1 and 2 are both serial histories. Both of these transactions are consistent in the sense that each transaction enforces all relevant business rules. Note that these two histories do not produce the same result in the database. Both results are valid. Because there is no business rule that specifies the order in which these two transactions should be processed, the transaction management system does not enforce the order in which transactions should be executed; that is the users' responsibility.

A history of concurrent transactions is serializable if an equivalent serial history exists for it. History X and history Y are equivalent if transactions that access the same data item satisfy the following synchronization criteria:

- Read–write synchronization. If transaction A reads a data item before transaction B writes the same data item in history X, then in history Y transaction A must read the data item before transaction B writes it.

- Write–write synchronization. If transaction A writes a data item before transaction B writes the same data item in history X, then in history Y transaction A must write the data item before transaction B writes it.

History 3 in Figure 6.4 is a concurrent history. The withdraw transaction began before the interest transaction finished. History 3 is not serializable with History 1 because of the write–write conflict between the withdraw and interest transactions. History 3 is not serializable with history 2 because of the read–write conflict between withdrawal (read) and interest (write). Thus history 3 is not serializable to any serial history of the two transactions withdraw and interest. History 3 is undesirable because the result of the interest transaction (33) is overwritten by the result of the withdrawal transaction (20). History 3 has a final value of 20, which is not the same as either of the two valid histories with final values of 22 and 23. We want to avoid nonserializable histories because their results are not isolated and cannot be obtained under any serial processing of the involved transactions.

Figure 6.5 illustrates four more histories. Histories 4 and 5 are both serial. History 6 is a concurrent history that is serializable. However, history 7 is a concurrent history that is not serializable. In this history we have Rwithdraw[Source.Balance] proceeding Wtransfer[Source.Balance], which implies that the withdraw transaction must proceed the transfer transaction, and yet Wtransfer[Source.Balance] proceeds Wwithdraw[Source.Balance], which implies that the transfer transaction must proceed the withdraw transaction. This history is not serializable to either of the two possible serial histories.

History 1		History 2		History 3	
Initial value of x	30	Initial value of x	30	Initial value of x	30
RWithdraw[x]	30	RInterest[x]	30	RInterest[x]	30
WWithdraw[x]	20	WInterest[x]	33	RWithdraw[x]	30
RInterest[x]	20	RWithdraw[x]	33	WInterest[x]	33
WInterest[x]	22	WWithdraw[x]	23	WWithdraw[x]	20

Figure 6.4 Three histories for the withdraw and interest transactions

Initially Source.Balance = 360
Target.Balance = 220
WithdrawalAmount = 30
TransferAmount = 50

History 4 (Serial)	Source	Target
Rwithdraw[Source.Balance]	360	220
Wwithdraw[Source.Balance]	330	220
Rtransfer[Source.Balance]	330	220
Wtransfer[Source.Balance]	280	220
Rtransfer[Target.Balance]	280	220
Wtransfer[Target.Balance]	280	270

History 5 (Serial)	Source	Target
Rtransfer[Source.Balance]	360	220
Wtransfer[Source.Balance]	310	220
Rtransfer[Target.Balance]	310	220
Wtransfer[Target.Balance]	310	270
Rwithdraw[Source.Balance]	310	270
Wwithdraw[Source.Balance]	280	270

History 6 (Serializable)	Source	Target
Rtransfer[Source.Balance]	360	220
Wtransfer[Source.Balance	310	220
Rwithdraw[Source.Balance]	310	220
Wwithdraw[Source.Balance]	280	220
Rtransfer[Target.Balance]	280	220
Wtransfer[Target.Balance]	280	270

History 7 (Nonserializable)	Source	Target
Rtransfer[Source.Balance]	360	220
RwithdrawSource.Balance]	360	220
Wtransfer[Source.Balance]	310	220
Rtransfer[Target.Balance]	310	220
Wtransfer[Target.Balance]	310	270
Wwithdraw[Source.Balance]	330	270

Figure 6.5   Four histories for the withdraw and transfer transactions

Because many of the business rules are not known to the database management system, it cannot directly enforce them. It can, however, guarantee that transactions (which are written by programmers to enforce business rules) are executed in isolation from each other, either in serial order or in an order that is serializable and thus can indirectly enforce the business rules.

In general we want histories to be isolated: either serial or serializable. Serializable histories allow more concurrency than serial histories, but not so much concurrency that values of data are lost causing at least one business rule to be violated. We want to avoid nonserializable histories because they may leave the database in an inconsistent state that violates one or more business rules.

6.4 Transaction Serializability Is Guaranteed by Concurrency Control Protocols

There are three major protocols that guarantee that transaction histories are serializable. These protocols are (1) locking, (2) time stamp ordering, and (3) optimistic protocols. Of these three approaches, locking is the most widely used.

6.4.1 Locking

In the locking protocol, the transaction manager uses locks on data items to isolate the transaction execution. A lock controls access to a data item. It prohibits several transactions from simultaneously accessing the locked data item. If a transaction tries to access a locked data item, it must wait. Locks force transactions to execute in serializable order.

Figure 6.6 illustrates two transaction and how transaction B is forced to wait until transaction A is finished with data item X. Transaction A sets a lock on data item X, and reads the value 50 from the database into its work space. Transaction B tries to read data item X, discovers that it is locked, and is forced to wait. Transaction A performs its calculations involving X, in this case adding 20 to X, yielding a value of 70 in its work space. Transaction A writes X to the database, changing the value of X in the database from 50 to 70. Transaction A releases its lock on data item X. Transaction B is now able to read X, so it sets it lock on X and reads the value of 70 from the database into its work space. Transaction B subtracts 10 from its work space value of 70, yielding 60. Transaction B writes the value of 60 back into the database and releases the lock on data item X.

There are four locking principles that all transactions should obey:

1. A transaction should lock a data item before using it.
2. A transaction should release the lock after using the data item.
3. All locks must be eventually released.
4. A transaction should make all requests for locking before it releases any locked data items.

A:	Read[X]	B:	Read[X]
	X:=X+20		X:=X−10
	write[X]		write[X]

Operation	A Workspace	B Workspace	Database
A sets lock, reads X	50		50
B tries to read X, waits	50		50
A calculates X:=X+20	70		50
A writes X, releases lock	70		70
B sets lock, reads X		70	70
B calculates X:=X-10		60	70
B writes X, releases locks		60	60

Figure 6.6 Example locking

This last principle results in what is sometimes called two-phase locking protocol. (Note that two-phase locking has nothing in common with two-phase commitment, to be discussed later in this chapter.) Transactions have two phases. First there is a growing phase in which they acquire locks. Then they have a shrinking phase in which they release locks. Computer scientists have proven [Yannakakis, 1982] that, if all transactions obey these four locking principles, then all transaction histories will be serializable.

Unfortunately, there is a major problem with the locking protocol. Consider the following example: transaction A has locked data item X and needs to lock data item Y before it releases data item X. Transaction B has locked data item Y and needs to lock data item X before it releases data item Y. Transaction A waits for transaction B, which in turn waits for transaction A. This phenomenon is called a deadlock. A *deadlock* is a situation in which two or more transactions wait forever on each other.

Database systems use two protocols to handle deadlocks: deadlock prevention (avoidance) and detection. First we will discuss deadlock prevention.

Deadlock Prevention

An obvious approach to deadlock prevention is to start transactions only after they can acquire all locks that they will need during their processing. This is undesirable for at least two reasons. First, transactions may lock data items that they need for a small portion of the total transaction time. This prohibits other transactions from accessing these data items and decreases the potential concurrency. The second problem is that some transactions are not able to predict which data items they will need to lock at the beginning of the transaction.

Two viable alternatives to lock preacquisition are the wait die and the wound wait deadlock prevention protocols. With both of these protocols, each transaction is given a unique time stamp when it starts execution. This time stamp represents the time when the transaction begins execution. In a distributed system, the site number is appended to the end of the time stamp to guarantee that two transactions starting at the same time at different sites don't get the same time-stamp value.

Wait Die Protocol

Suppose that transaction A needs to lock a data item that is locked by transaction B. If transaction A is older than transaction B, then A is forced to wait. Otherwise, A dies (A is rolled back and restarted at a later time). Because a younger transaction never waits for an older transaction, a cycle of waiting transactions can never occur, and thus no deadlock can occur.

Wound Wait Protocol

Suppose that transaction A needs to lock a data item that is locked by transaction B. If transaction A is older than transaction B, then A wounds B (B is rolled back and restarted). Otherwise, A is forced to wait. Because an older transaction never waits for an younger transaction, a cycle of waiting transactions can never occur, and thus no deadlock can occur.

Deadlock Detection

The other major protocol to handling deadlocks is deadlock detection. In this protocol, locks are granted as they are requested. If a lock is not available, then the requesting transaction must wait for the lock. If a deadlock occurs, then it must be (1) detected and (2) resolved by selecting one of the deadlocked transactions, which is rolled back and later restarted. Distributed database management systems detect deadlocks by several mechanisms, including time-outs and wait-for graphs.

Deadlock Detection by Time-out

If a transaction makes no progress after T amount of time, the distributed DBMS assumes that the transaction is deadlocked and rolls back the transaction by undoing any changes it made to the database. If T is too short, then transactions that are not deadlocked are rolled back. If T is too large, then deadlocks tie up resources for long periods of time and limit the number of transactions that can process concurrently. The value of T is determined experimentally.

Wait-for Graphs

Figure 6.7 illustrates a wait-for graph in which subtransactions of transactions A and B are executing in two component databases. A cycle in the wait-for graph represents a deadlock. In Figure 6.7, transactions A and B are deadlocked. Each transaction is waiting for the other to release a lock.

One approach for detecting deadlocks is for the distributed transaction manager to construct a wait-for graph at a central site. The local transaction manager updates the wait-for graph each time a lock is granted or released. The distributed transaction manager periodically examines the wait-for graph to determine if any cycles (and hence deadlocks) exist. When it detects a deadlock, the distributed transaction man-

A   B   Denotes that A waits for B (data item lock)

A— — ► B   Denotes that A at one site is waiting for A at another
            site (information delay)

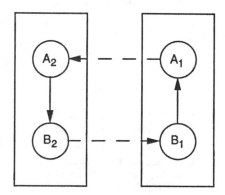

Figure 6.7   Waits-for graph

ager chooses a transaction involved in the deadlock to be rolled back. When the transaction is rolled back, the deadlock is broken, and the remaining transaction may continue processing. The rolled-back transaction is restarted at a later time.

There is a major disadvantage with the centralized detection of deadlocks. The distributed transaction manager may become a communication bottleneck. There may be a large communication cost associated with transmitting information about the locking and releasing of locks.

An alternative approach to overcome the disadvantage with centralized deadlock detection is to organize component DBMSs into a hierarchy, as illustrated in Figure 6.8. Each component DBMS performs local deadlock detection as follows:

1. Build a wait-for graph for data within the component DBMS.

2. A local deadlock detector selects any cycles in the wait-for graph within the component DBMS. Here a cycle represents a local deadlock.

3. An interdatabase deadlock detector detects chains of transactions that might be part of a deadlock involving several component DBMSs and passes those chains to its parent interdatabase deadlock detector.

In the local wait-for graph of Figure 6.9(a), CGH is a local deadlock. The chains S and ABCD may be part of an interdatabase deadlock and are thus passed to the interdatabase deadlock detector.

Each interdatabase deadlock detector performs the following tasks:

1. Builds a wait-for graph from the chains transmitted from its children.

2. Detects cycles that represent interdatabase deadlocks.

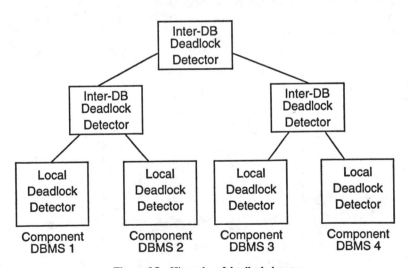

Figure 6.8   Hierarchy of deadlock detectors

3. Detects chains of transactions that might be part of a deadlock involving other databases and passes those chains to its parent interdatabase deadlock detector.

In the wait-for graph of Figure 6.9(b), $A_1A_2BCD_1D_2PQ$ is a regional deadlock, and S2S1 is a chain that may be part of a deadlock in a larger region.

Another approach to detecting distributed deadlocks is called the boomerang approach. It consists of sending messages from component DBMS to component DBMS along wait-for chains. If the message returns to the component DBMS from which it originated, then a potential deadlock exists. For example, in Figure 6.10, component DBMS 1 detects a wait-for condition from B_1 to A_1 and sends a boomerang message to component DBMS 2, which would detect the wait-for from A_2 to B_2, which in turn sends the boomerang message back to component DBMS 1. Because

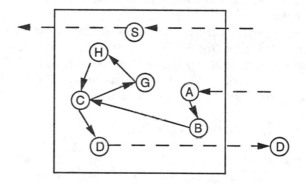

(a) Waits-for graph in local deadlock detection

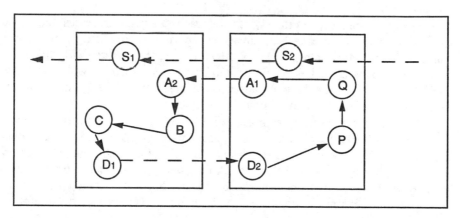

(b) Waits-for graph in an Inter-DB deadlock detection

Figure 6.9 Example deadlocks

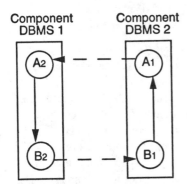

Figure 6.10 Distributed deadlock

messages can be delayed in a distributed system, a message may return even though a deadlock does not exist. A potential deadlock can be validated by sending another boomerang message.

Distributed deadlock detection is expensive. Messages must be transmitted among several component DBMSs. There is an overhead in building and analyzing wait-for graphs. And there is the expense of modifying existing DBMSs to perform distributed deadlock detection. For these reasons, many distributed DBMS developers have elected to use the simpler time-out approach, rather than wait-for graphs.

6.4.2 Other Approaches to Serializability

The major problem with locking is the potential for deadlocks. Another approach used in distributed DBMS is called time-stamp ordering. Deadlocks cannot occur when using this approach. When a transaction first enters the system, it is assigned a unique time stamp. Time stamps indicate a serial execution order. If a transaction attempts to execute in some other order, it is rolled back. Here is how this approach works.

A transaction leaves its time stamp with each data item it accesses. Each time a transaction needs to access a data item, it compares its own time stamp with the time stamp of that data item. If the transaction attempts to write a data item already written by a younger transaction, then the time-stamp serial execution order will be violated, so the transaction is rolled back. A transaction proceeds only if the resulting transaction histories are equivalent to the time-stamp order.

Locking and time-stamp approaches are said to pessimistic because they assume that deadlocks may occur and take appropriate precautions, such as setting locks and leaving time stamps. There is another class of protocols that takes a very different approach. Computer scientists call these protocols *optimistic* because they assume that deadlocks will not occur frequently and don't take detailed precautions, such as setting locks and leaving time stamps. Optimistic approaches consist of three phases:

Phase 1: Transaction read phase. In this phase, a transaction reads data items, performs calculations, and writes results to a temporary file.

Phase 2: Transaction validation phase. The transaction histories are checked for serializability.

Phase 3: Transaction Write phase. This phase is carried out only if the history is serializable. The results in the temporary file are moved to the database.

Optimistic approaches perform no checking while the transaction is executing. Violations of serializability are detected during the validation phase. If serializability is achieved, there is minimum overhead. However, if serializability is not achieved frequently, there may be lots of overhead in the form of rolling back and restarting transactions.

Table 6.1 summarizes the major features of each of the three approaches for enforcing serializability. Most distributed database management systems use two-phase locking and deadlock detection by time-out.

Table 6.1

	Two-phase Locking	Time Stamps	Optimistic
Avoid nonserializable histories	Waiting	Roll back and restart	Roll back and restart
Conflicts between two transactions determined	Each time transaction attempts to access a data item	Each time transaction attempts to access a data item	After all accesses have been performed
Serialization order determined by	Order of access to data items	Time stamp of transaction	—

Some DBMSs provide multiple levels of isolation among concurrently executing transactions. Rather than enforce serializability of all transactions, the serializability constraint is relaxed in one of the following ways:

- *Dirty reads.* A transaction may read a data item updated by a second transaction before the second transaction rolls back the change to the modified data item. A dirty read may be permitted in situations where the result is not significantly affected if the value of an item is modified, for example, in decision-making situations where a modified value does not change a trend sufficiently to alter the decision made by the database users.

- *Nonrepeatable reads.* A transaction may read a data item that may be changed by another transactions, so if the first transaction reads it again, the modified value will be retrieved. This form of isolation can be permitted if each transaction never reads a data item twice.

- *Phantom.* A record is created by a second transaction that satisfies the criterion of retrieval by the first transaction after the first transaction accessed the database. Phantom records can be permitted if transactions do not access values derived from multiple records.

For many transactions, the isolation provided by serializability is not required. In its place, the DBMS enforces a lesser level of isolation, which is easier and less expensive to enforce. For many applications, these lesser levels of isolation are sufficient.

6.5 Replicated Data Must Be Kept Consistent

Database administrators allocate table fragments to multiple component DBMSs for
two principal reasons:

1. *Availability.* If for some reason users cannot access the fragment in one component DBMS, users may access the fragment at an alternative component
   DBMS.

2. *Reduce communication costs.* If a fragment is stored at the component
   DBMS where users submit requests involving the fragment, then the costs
   of transmitting the request and returning the result are avoided. However, if
   the request involves updating the fragment, then all copies must be updated,
   which might increase the communication costs rather than reducing them.

   Consider these transactions:

Interest: Read X
              $X := X*1.1$;
              Write X;

Withdrawal: Read X;
              $X := X - 20$;
              Write X;

   Suppose that copies of the fragment containing X reside in both the Los Angles
component database and the San Francisco component database. Suppose also that
one request is issued at Los Angeles and the other is issued at San Francisco. It is possible that the two requests will be executed in different orders in the two component
DBMSs. Assuming that X initially contained the value of 50, the result of executing
the two requests in different orders at the two component DBMSs is shown in Figure
6.11. The values of X at the two component databases have diverged. Database administrators either (1) allow replicated component databases to diverge and then
force them to converge at a later time or (2) prevent replicated databases from diverg-
ing guaranteeing that the transactions are executed in the same sequence within the
replicated databases.

Los Angeles DB		San Francisco DB	
Initially	50	Initially	50
Withdrawal transaction subtracts 20	30	Interest transaction increases 10%	55
Interest transaction increases 10%	33	Withdrawal transaction subtracts 20	35

Figure 6.11   Updating replicated fragments at two sides

6.5.1 Dealing with Divergent Databases

Trying to synchronize divergent databases may be impossible. For example, suppose that Fred changes his address to Elm Street in one component database while his wife, Sally, changes her address to Helm Street in another component database. Which street, Elm or Helm, is the correct value to be placed in both component databases? There may be no way of choosing the correct street name short of asking Fred and Sally.

Lotus Notes is an example of a distributed application that supports multiple "notes" databases. A user of one database may check a copy of another notes database. Users of both databases may delete existing notes and insert new notes into their respective copies of the database. When a user modifies a note, the Notes system deletes the old note and creates a new note in the user's database. No attempt is made to keep the replicated databases consistent. The replicated copies diverge as users modify their respective copies of the replicated database.

The Lotus Notes system supports an operation that compares the two databases and copies all new notes from each database to the other. Changes made by users on the copies of the same note result in two separate notes that replace the original note in both databases. In this way, the replicated copies are made consistent.

6.5.2 Locking

If a transaction needs to read a data item, then any copy of the data item can be read. However, if a transaction needs to update a data item, then all copies of the data item must be updated. An interesting question is how many copies of the data item must be locked before the transaction can proceed?

- *Lock all copies of the data item to be updated.* This approach is called *mutual agreement.* In this approach, a transaction must obtain locks on all copies before the transaction can perform the update. However, if a component database containing a copy of the data item is down (temporarily off line), then the transaction cannot proceed, nor can the transaction release locks on other data items. This situation is called *blocking.* Clearly, blocking is undesirable.

- *Lock more than half of the copies of the data item to be updated.* This approach is called *majority consensus.* This approach may avoid some of the blocking problems associated with the mutual agreement approach. Updated values are propagated to the remaining copies when they become available.

- *Lock a single, primary copy.* This approach is called the *primary copy* approach. All modifications are first made to the primary copy. Other copies are updated later during a batch update mode. Variations of this approach include migrating the primary copy or leaving the primary copy fixed.

With locking, mutual agreement is the simplest to implement. Migrating the primary copy appears attractive, but is more complex to implement.

6.5.3 Time-stamp Ordering

The second approach to controlling replicated fragments is based on time-stamp ordering. This approach is similar to using time stamps to guarantee serialization, except that multiple component DBMSs collectively decide if an update should be applied to all copies of a data item in multiple component DMBSs. Each component DBMS votes on accepting or rejecting the update by comparing its time stamp with the transaction's time stamp. The distributed transaction manager forces all component DBMSs to update the data item only if the transaction has acquired a majority of favorable votes. Otherwise, the distributed transaction manager declares the update rejected and instructs the local transaction managers to roll back any changes made to their component databases.

With locking, mutual agreement is the simplest to implement. Migrating the primary copy appears attractive, but is slightly more complex.

6.5.4 Asynchronous Replicators

Several new database products have recently been released for managing replicated databases. These products, called *data replicators*, use a cascading strategy to synchronize the values in a replicated fragment or table. Replicators force users to update a primary copy of data and then migrate the changes to the remaining copies. Users may retrieve data from the secondary copies, but users are prohibited from updating the secondary copies.

Replicators are useful for managing replicated databases in several situations, including the following:

- Distribute read-only reference data to branch offices.
- Copy data from branch offices to a central site for overnight processing at the end of the day.
- Copy data and construct a decision support system that does not require up-to-the-minute information.
- Make a backup copy of critical data.

Replicating data allows companies to divide up a database and ship information closer to the users that work with it the most. Response time improves because the information is stored locally rather than at a central site. And users avoid the communication costs of accessing data from a central site.

Various data-replication products differ in two aspects: (1) when data are captured at the primary copy and (2) when the captured data are applied to the secondary copies.

Data to be copied are captured at the primary copy into a capture file or queue before being transmitted to the secondary copies in different component DBMSs. Several approaches are used for capturing data:

- *Data driven.* As update transactions modify the primary copy, information about the data changes is captured and copied into a capture file or queue. Some replicators use database triggers to capture data as they are updated. Other replicators use the recovery log, created by the component DBMS.

- Timer driven. Data are captured automatically by the system at user-defined intervals. Oracle 7 Complex Snapshot uses this approach.

- *Application driven.* An application event will cause the system to copy data from the primary copy to the captured file or queue. Prism Warehouse Manager uses this approach.

Data can be applied to a secondary copy in three ways:

- *Data driven.* Changes made by an update transaction at the primary copy are copied, transmitted, and immediately applied to the secondary copies. Hewlett-Packard's AllBase/Replicate, Open Ingres Replicator, and Sybase Replication Server fall into this category.

- *Timer driven.* Changes made by an update transaction at the primary copy are applied at user-defined intervals. IBM's Data Propagator/Relational, Open Ingres Replicator, and Oracle 7 Simple Snapshot fall into this category.

- *Application driven.* An application event will cause the system to update the secondary copy from the captured file or queue. Prism Warehouse Manager uses this approach.

Data replicators are useful for keeping replicated databases synchronized. However, if transactions involve nonreplicated data that have been distributed to multiple sites, then a two-phase commit protocol is required.

6.6 Transactions Are Atomic

6.6.1 Motivation for Commit Protocols

Commit protocols are distributed algorithms that guarantee the atomic property of transactions. If a transaction commits, then the commit protocols guarantee that all the operations of a transaction are executed and the results stored permanently in the component databases involved in the transaction. If a transaction fails, then the commit protocols roll back, guaranteeing that any changes made to any of the component databases are removed from those databases.

We need commit protocols because an executing transaction may fail. A transaction may fail itself if it receives incorrect inputs or if it detects that it will violate some business rule associated with the database. A transaction may also be canceled by the operating system because of system overload. A transaction may be canceled to avoid consistency problems such as nonserializable histories or deadlocks. Various types of system crashes may also result in transaction cancellation.

When a transaction has been committed, all modifications it has made to each involved database are made permanent. The modified database values are then made available to other transactions.

There are several alternative commit protocols, including one phase, two phase, three phase, and commitment under network partitioning. These protocols differ in the way that the commit-rollback decision is reached and in the manner in which the decision is enforced. However, all these alternative commit protocols have the following in common:

- Each has a mechanism to determine whether the distributed transaction should be committed or rolled back.
- If the decision is commit, then changes are permanently made to each component database.
- If the decision is rollback, then changes to each component database are undone.

The distributed transaction manager acts as the *coordinator*. It interacts with local transaction managers to guide the component database systems in performing their part of the distributed execution strategy. The distributed transaction manager also interacts with the local transaction managers to determine if the transaction should commit or roll back.

A *time-out* is the time period after which the distributed transaction manager assumes that a local transaction manager has failed. Time-outs are needed because it is possible for a local transaction manager to fail during the processing of commitment protocols. It is also conceivable that the distributed transaction manager may fail during the processing of commitment protocols. If a distributed transaction manager fails, usually the local transaction manager located at the same site as the distributed transaction manager also fails.

Figure 6.12 illustrate two subtransactions for the bank account transfer transaction illustrated in Figure 6.2. As illustrated in Figure 6.13(a), the successful execution of this transaction proceeds as follows:

1. The distributed transaction manager will send each subtransaction to the appropriate local transaction manager as part of an "Execute" messages.
2. Each local transaction manager executes the subtransaction it received from the distributed transaction manager and responds by sending the distributed transaction manager the results in a "Done" message.

However, occasionally one of the local transaction managers may not be able to successfully complete the subtransaction it receives from the distributed transaction manager. This is illustrated in Figure 6.13(b). This results in an unfortunate situation: Local transaction manager 2 has changed its component database, but local transaction manager 1 was not able to change its database. The two component databases are now inconsistent.

```
begin transaction debit (SourceAccountNumber, Amount);
select Balance from Account where AccountNumber=SourceAccountNumber;
if <failure> then do
          display 'Source account not found';
          rollback;
          end do;
update Account
 set Balance=Balance–Amount
 where AccountNumber=SourceAccountNumber;
if Balance < 0 then do
          display 'Insufficient funds in source account';
          rollback;
          end do;
send 'debit done';
end transaction debit;
```

(a) Participant 1

```
begin transaction credit (TargetAccountNumber, Amount);
select Balance from Account where AccountNumber=TargetAccountNumber;
if <failure> then do
          display 'Target account not found';
          rollback;
          end do;
update Account
 set Balance=Balance+Amount
 where AccountNumber=TargetAccountNumber;
send 'credit done';
end transaction credit;
```

(b) Participant 2

Figure 6.12   Two subtransactions for the debit transaction shown in Figure 6.2

This problem can be resolved by the distributed transaction manager if it examines all the messages it receives form the local transaction managers and determines if any parts of the transaction have failed. Figure 6.14(a) illustrates the case in which all local transaction managers report "Done"; the distributed transaction manager instructs all local transaction managers to commit their subtransactions. Figure 6.14(b) illustrates the case in which one of the local transaction managers reports "Rollback"; the distributed transaction manager instructs all local transaction managers to rollback their subtransactions.

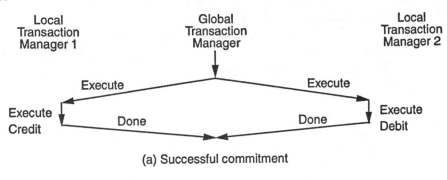

(a) Successful commitment

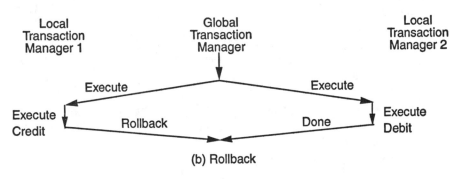

(b) Rollback

Figure 6.13 No-commit protocol

6.6.2 One-phase Commit Protocol

Figure 6.14 illustrates the *one-phase commit protocol*. After the execution phase in which each local transaction manager receives and executes subtransactions, the distributed transaction manager examines the messages returned by each local transaction manager (or assumes that a local transaction manager is down if the time-out period has expired) and determines if the total transaction should be committed or rolled back. In the commit phase, the distributed transaction manager transmits it decision to each local transaction manager, who carries out instructions to either commit or roll back local changes to the database.

A major problem with the one-phase commit protocol is illustrated in Figure 6.15. Here local transaction manager 1 executes its subtransaction quickly and returns its "Done" message to the distributed transaction manager, while local transaction manager 2 takes longer to complete its subtransaction and return its "Done" message. While local transaction manager 2 is executing its subtransaction and after local transaction manager 1 has completed, local transaction manager 1 aborts. The distributed transaction manager has already received the "Done" message from local

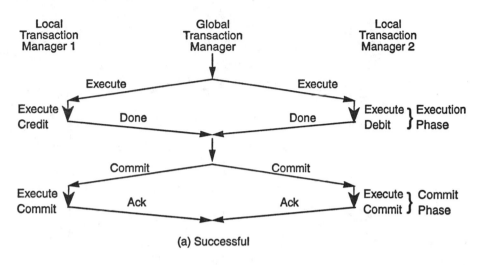

(a) Successful

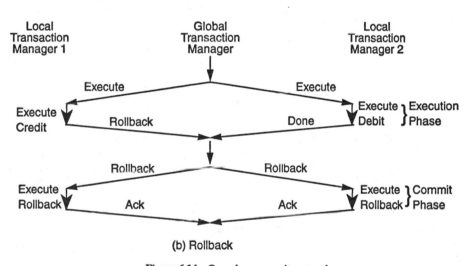

(b) Rollback

Figure 6.14 One-phase commit protocol

transaction manager 1. The global transaction manager is not aware that local transaction manager 1 has aborted, so it sends commit messages to both local transaction
managers. Local transaction manager 2 makes its changes to its database permanent,
but local transaction manager 1 doesn't because it is currently down. When local
transaction manager comes back to life, the component databases will be inconsistent.

One-phase commit protocol suffers from long in-doubt periods, the time between when a local transaction manager signals that it is "Done" and the time it receives a "Commit" message. We can shorten the in-doubt period by transmitting

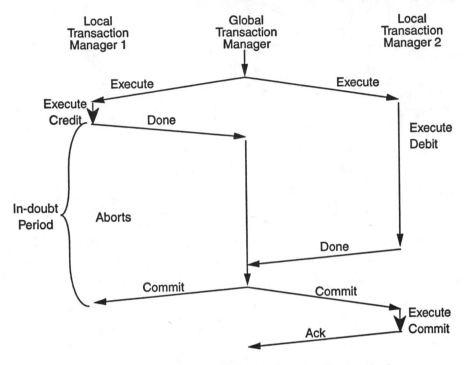

Figure 6.15   Long in-doubt period in the one-phase commitment protocol

extra messages between the distributed transaction manager and local transaction managers. These extra messages turn the one-phase commit protocol into the two-phase commit protocol. (Note that the only thing in common between the two-phase commit protocol and the two-phase locking protocol is that they both have two phases. Otherwise, they are entirely different protocols for achieving entirely different goals.)

6.6.3 Two-phase Commit Protocol

Figure 6.16(a) illustrates how the two-phase commit protocol has a much smaller in-doubt period. This is because local transaction managers can quickly respond to the "Prepare to commit" protocols, leaving very short the time between the "Ready to commit" messages and the "Commit" messages, with little chance of the local transaction manager failing within this time period. Figure 6.16(b) illustrates what happens when local transaction manager 2 rolls back under the two-phase commit protocol; all local transaction managers are told to roll back in the first phase of the two-phase commitment protocol. The second phase of the two-phase commit protocol is not needed in this case.

6.6.4 Three-phase Commit Protocol

While the two-phase commit protocol is generally used to implement distributed commitment in distributed database management systems, it is not a perfect so-

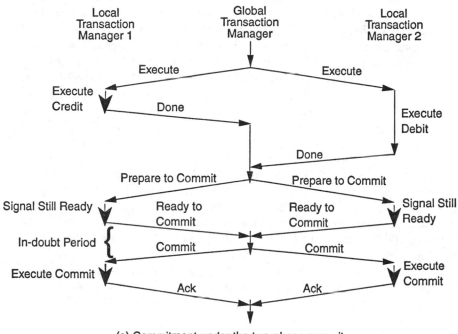

(a) Commitment under the two-phase commit

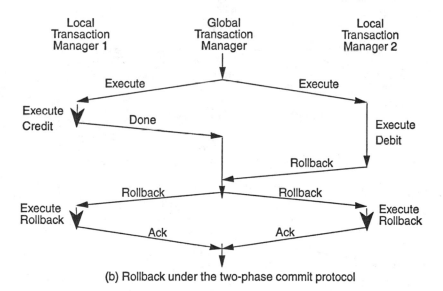

(b) Rollback under the two-phase commit protocol

Figure 6.16   Two-phase commit protocol

lution. It is still conceivable (although unlikely) that a local transaction manager can abort, leaving the distributed database in an inconsistent state. Two-phase commit protocols also suffer from the high overhead of four messages between the distributed transaction manager and each of the local transaction managers. The two-phase commit protocol may result in blocked transactions, as illustrated in Figure 6.17.

A local transaction manager is *blocked* when it is unable to determine whether it should commit or roll back. In Figure 6.17, local transaction manager 2 does not know whether the distributed transaction manager decided to commit or roll back. Suppose that local transaction manager 2 unilaterally decides to roll back. Then the databases would be inconsistent if local transaction manager 1 was able to commit before it died. On the other hand, suppose that local transaction manager 2 unilaterally decides to commit. Then the databases would be inconsistent if local transaction manager 1 was able to roll back before it died. The only safe thing for local transaction manager 2 to do is to wait until either the global transaction manager or local transaction manager 1 comes back to life so that it can find out whether to commit or roll back. While local transaction manager 2 is blocked, it cannot release its locks, causing other transactions to wait.

A three-phase commit solves the blocking problem in some situations, but not for network partitioning. Because it adds another set of messages to be transmitted between the distributed transaction manager and each local transaction manager, it is not widely used.

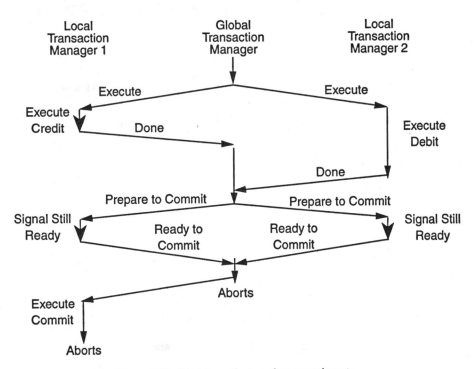

Figure 6.17   Blocking under two-phase commitment

6.6.5 Commitment under Network Partitioning

A communication network is *partitioned* when a communication link goes down, leaving two sets of component DBMSs, with component DBMSs in one set able to communicate with each other but not with component DBMSs in the other set. Figure 6.18 illustrates a typical network consisting of five component DBMSs. The partitioned network consists of one partition containing two component DBMSs and the other partition containing three component DBMSs. The following approaches may be used to enable users to do useful work within a partition of a partitioned network.

- *Token approach.* Each data item has a token associated with it. The partition containing the token can modify the data item, but other partitions cannot modify their copy of the data item.

- *Primary-component DBMS approach.* Each data item has a primary-component DBMS. The partition containing the primary component DBMS can modify the data item, but other partitions cannot modify their copy of the data item.

- *Quorum-based commit approach.* In this approach, local transaction managers send "commit" or "not commit" messages. The global transaction manager counts the messages and determines if it received messages from a quorum (more than half of the local transaction managers). The distributed transaction manager decides whether to commit or roll back. At most one partition can contain a quorum.

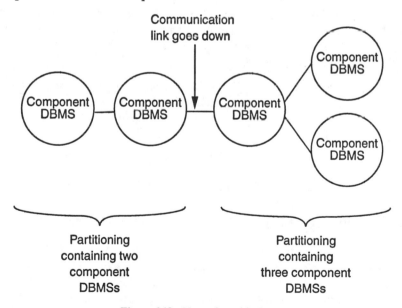

Figure 6.18 Network partitioning

In any event, component DBMSs in separate partitions cannot update the same data items. When the partition is repaired, the updates of one partition are cascaded to the other partitions so that all copies converge to the updated values.

6.6.6 Implementing Distributed Updates

There are two major problems with distributed DBMSs that support distributed updates:

1. The messages among component DBMSs may be excessive, due to the distributed concurrency control and distributed commit protocols.
2. Many existing DBMSs do not support distributed concurrency control and distributed commit protocols.

There are three approaches for avoiding these problems:

1. The distributed DBMS supports only transactions that read data several component DBMSs, but updates no data. Clearly, this type of distributed DBMS needs no distributed concurrency control and distributed commit protocols.
2. The distributed DBMS supports global transactions that access nonreplicated data in several component DBMSs, but update data at only one component DBMS. No distributed concurrency control and distributed commit protocols are needed for this type of distributed DBMS. All necessary concurrency control and commit protocols are already available within each component DBMS.
3. The distributed DBMS supports global transactions that update data replicated at multiple sites. A data replicator that restricts users to updating a primary copy and then migrating the updated information to the secondary copies avoids distributed commit protocols.

These restricted types of distributed database management systems are useful in many situations. For example, many ad hoc queries require no updates. Nor do generating organization-wide reports and summaries. If updating multiple databases within a single transaction is not an absolute requirement, then the above types of distributed database management systems appear very attractive.

6.7 Distributed DBMSs Recover from Failures

6.7.1 Preparing for Distributed Database Recovery

Every computer user needs recovery mechanisms because data are sometimes lost. When the operating system fails, users need to recover their data. When a transaction fails and rolls back, changes made to the database by the failed transaction need to be removed. Sometimes the media on which the database is itself stored are lost. Experienced users realize the need to recover from these types of problems. It is wise to store recovery information to help recover lost data. One big advantage of some DBMSs is that they automatically store the necessary recovery information.

Figure 6.19 illustrates the steps for executing a subtransaction and capturing of information that can be used for database recovery.

1. The subtransaction enters the local transaction manager of the component database.

2. The subtransaction is copied to the log. If the component database is restored to an earlier point in time, subtransactions on this log can be reexecuted to bring the component database up to date.

3. Data from the component database are retrieved for use during subtransaction processing.

4. The "before" images (values of data before updating) are copied to the log.

5. The subtransaction is executed, possibly modifying the data values retrieved from the component database in step 3.

6. The "after" images (values of data after updating) are copied to the log.

7. If the distributed transaction manager indicates that the transaction should be committed, the local DBMS enters a commit transaction entry in the log.

8. Any revised values not already written to the component database are written in the database.

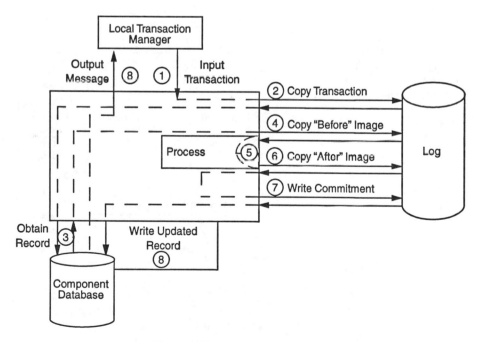

Figure 6.19 Transaction execution steps

6.7.2 Recovering from Failed Transactions

The two approaches used to recover from failed transactions are illustrated in Figure 6.20. Figure 6.20(a) illustrates the use of an incremental log with deferred updates. With this approach, the component database is not changed until the transaction commits. Instead, the changes to the component database are recorded in the log

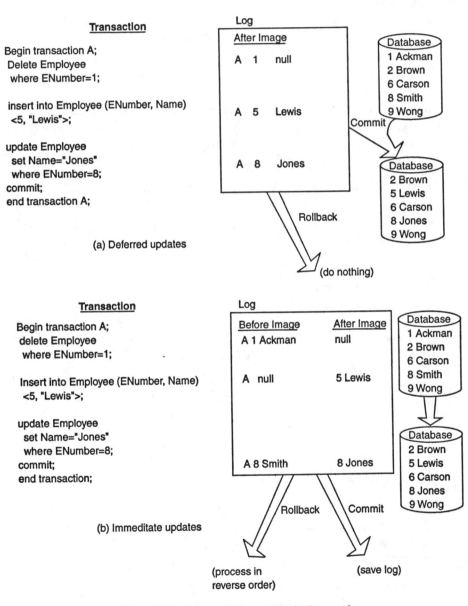

Figure 6.20   Recovery from an aborted subtransaction

as after images. If the transaction commits, then the after images are removed from the log and merged into the component database. If the transaction fails, then rolling back consists of removing the after images from the log.

Figure 6.20(b) illustrates the use of an incremental log with immediate updates. With this approach, the component database is updated as the transaction executes. The before and after values of each updated item are also written to the incremental log. If the transaction commits, there is nothing to do because the component database has already been updated. If the transaction rolls back, the updates in the component database must be undone. This is accomplished by processing the incremental log entries in reverse order, by replacing the after image in the component database by the before image from the log.

6.7.3 Recovery from System Failures

When a computer system fails, the contents of the main storage and I/O buffers are lost. While the component database is safe, transactions in progress must be canceled and rolled back because they cannot continue without the contents of main storage. Three approaches for recovery from a system failure follow:

1. *Search the entire transaction log.* Figure 6.21(a) illustrates the algorithm for this approach. However, if the component database has been in operation for any reasonable length of time, the process of searching the transaction log from the beginning may be impractical. To avoid searching the entire transaction log, the component database management system may use a quiet point. During a *quiet point*, the component database management system accepts no new transactions until all the currently execution transactions have committed. A quiet point entry is written to the log, and a pointer to this entry is recorded in a restart file.

2. *Search the transaction log from the most recent quiet point.* Figure 6.21(b) illustrates the algorithm for this approach. Unfortunately, this approaches requires the database management system to stop accepting transactions during the quiet point. This problem is overcome by using a checkpoint. During a *checkpoint*, the database management system creates a checkpoint entry on the log that contains the identifiers of all active transactions. A pointer to the checkpoint entry is recorded in the restart file.

3. *Search the transaction log from the most recent checkpoint.* Figure 6.21(c) illustrates the algorithm for this approach. Due to system delays, it is possible that some updated values of committed transactions might not be written to the component database before the system crashes. This is why we need the REDO list. All transactions on the REDO list have been committed, but might not have been written to the component database. The results of these transactions are forced into the database during recovery. Figure 6.22 illustrates the use of recovery strategy of Figure 6.22(c). As illustrated in Figure 6.22, transactions T3 and T5 are canceled and rolled back because they did not commit before the system crash. The log information for transactions T2

UNDO := empty
Search entire log from beginning
  For each BEGIN TRANSACTION, place transaction identifier from UNDO list
  For each COMMIT TRANSACTION, remove transaction identifier from UNDO list
Rollback transactions on UNDO list and restart them

              (a) Recovery by searching the entire log

UNDO := empty
Search log beginning with most recent quiet point
  For each BEGIN TRANSACTION, place a transaction identifier on UNDO list
  For each COMMIT TRANSACTION, remove transaction identifier from UNDO list
Roll back transactions on UNDO list and restart them

        (b) Recovery by searching from the most recent quiet point

UNDO :=transaction identifiers in the most recent checkpoint entry
REDO := empty
Search log beginning with most recent checkpoint record
  For each BEGIN TRANSACTION, place transaction identifier on UNDO list
  For each COMMIT, move transaction identifier from UNDO list to REDO list
For each transaction on the UNDO list, roll back
For each transaction on the REDO list, force log info to database

        (c) Recovery by searching from the most recent checkpoint

Figure 6.21   Recovery strategies

and T4 is copied into the component database in the event that these values were not placed into the component database after these transactions committed, but before the system crash occurred.

In a distributed database, it is necessary to use a global checkpoint that causes each local DBMS to perform a local checkpoint. During recovery, the distributed database management system selects the most recent local checkpoint at the failed site and forces all sites to recover from the same checkpoint.

6.7.4 Recovery from Media Failures

The component database may be totally or partially lost. If this occurs, the database administrator restores the component database from an archive. The database

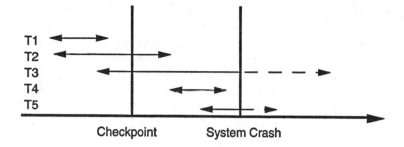

Checkpoint   System Crash

Log

<T1, Start>
<T2, Start>
<T1, Commit>
<T3, Start>
<Checkpoint:T2,T3>
<T2, Commit>
<T4, Start>
<T5, Start>
<T4, Commit>
System Crash

Recovery

Redo T2 and T4
Undo T3 and T5

Figure 6.22 Example recovery

administrator then reprocesses all transactions on the transaction log since the archive was recorded.

In the event that both the component database and the log are lost or damaged, restore the database to the most recent archive. Apply that portion of the log that is undamaged. (To avoid this problem, many database administrators create duplicate copies of the log on different storage devices.)

6.7.5 Practical Advice

Some transactions cannot be rolled back and restarted. For example, if the withdrawal transaction of a banking application has already distributed cash to a bank customer, the withdrawal transaction cannot be rolled back. It has already changed the real world, and their is little that the database management system can do to get the cash back. Once any transaction has displayed information to a user and the user acts on that information, it may be too late to effectively roll back a transaction.

Occasionally, a transaction performs an unexpected action. These actions are often called bugs, and the transactions that contain them are called *deviant transactions*. An appealing approach for fixing a component database when a deviant transaction has been discovered is to undo the transactions back to the time that the deviant transaction was executed, undo the deviant transaction, and then force all the log information after the deviant transaction back into the database. This approach will not always work, because a transaction executed after the deviant transaction may have used data written by the deviant transaction. Instead, carefully examine the database, correct errors caused by the deviant transactions, and correct errors propagated by other transactions that read the contaminated data. It is wise to correct these errors as soon as possible to avoid further database contamination.

Chapter Summary

A distributed transaction that updates one or more component databases should support atomicity, consistency, isolation, and durability. The transaction optimizer generates distributed transactions that guarantee consistency. Distributed concurrency control mechanisms guarantee isolation in the form of transaction history serializability. Two-phase commit protocols guarantee transaction atomicity. And distributed recovery mechanisms guarantee transaction durability. Much of the code of a distributed DBMS and much of the communication among component DBMSs are devoted to supporting, these properties.

Further Reading

Barghouti, N. S., and G. E. Kaiser, "Concurrency Control in Advanced Database Applications," *Computing Surveys*, Vol. 23, No. 3, Sept. 1991, 269–318. Survey of advanced concurrency control mechanisms for special situations. While these mechanisms are not generally available in commercial systems, they may be programmed for use in home-grown distributed database management systems.

Garcia-Molina, H., and K. Salem, "Sagas." In *Proceedings of the ACM SIGMOD 1987 Annual Conference*, May, 1987, ACM Press, New York, pp. 249–259. Sagas and compensation functions. A compensation function undoes the actions performed by a transaction. However, a compensation function does not affect changes to the database made by other transactions. A saga is a long transaction in which users may view intermediate results and in which compensation functions may undo intermediate results.

Khoshafian, Setrag, Arvola Chan, Anna Wong, and Harry K. T. Wong, "A Guide to Developing Client/Server SQL Applications," Morgan Kaufman, San Francisco, CA, 1992. Chapter 5 describes transaction processing.

Moss, J. E. B., *Nested Transactions: An Approach to Reliable Distributed Computing*, MIT Press, Cambridge, MA, 1985. Nested transactions in which a transaction may contain multiple subtransactions. A subtransaction may fail and can be restarted or replaced by another subtransaction without causing the whole nested transaction to fail or restart.

Pradel, U., G. Schlageter, and R. Unland, "Redesign of Optimistic Methods: Improving Performance and Availability, I, *Proceedings of the 2nd International Conference on Data Engineering*, Feb. 1986, IEEE Computer Society Press, New York, pp. 466–473. Snapshot validation, that distinguishes between serious conflicts which require restarting, and non-serious conflicts, which do not.

Salem, K., H. Garcia-Molina, and R. Alonso "Altruistic Locking: A Strategy for Coping with Long-lived Transactions." In *Proceedings of the 2nd International Workshop on High Performance Transaction Systems*, Sept. 1987. Long transactions, ranging from hours to weeks. Altruistic locking makes use of information about the access patterns of a transaction to decide which resources it can release.

Silberschatz, A., and Z. Kedem, "Consistency in Hierarchical Database Systems," *J. ACM*, Vol. 27, No. 1, Jan. 1987, 72–80. Tree protocols in which the two-phase locking protocol is relaxed if there is a partial ordering on the set of data items accessed by concurrent transactions.

Yannakakis, M., "Issues of Correctness in Database Concurrency Control by Locking," *J. ACM*, Vol. 29, No. 3, July 1982, 718–740. Demonstration that two-phase locking is both necessary and sufficient to ensure serializability by locking.

Ceri, Stefano, and Giuseppe Pelagatti, *Distributed Databases Principles and Systems*, McGraw-Hill, New York, 1984. Chapter 7 discusses distributed transactions. Chapter 8 discusses concurrency control, and Chapter 9 discusses commitment protocols.

Ozsu, M. Tamer, and Patrick Valduriez, *Principles of Distributed Database Systems*, Prentice Hall, Upper Saddle River, NJ, 1991. Chapter 10 discusses transaction management, Chapter 11 discusses distributed concurrency control, and Chapter 12 discusses DBMS reliability.

Papadimitriou, Christos, *The Theory of Database Concurrency Control*, Computer Science Press, Potomac, MD, 1986. Chapter 7 deals with distributed concurrency control.

7

Client-Server Architecture

This chapter presents an introduction to client-server architectures, including the following:

- The benefits of client-server computing.
- The types of services servers provide.
- How clients support user interfaces.
- IIow multiple servers implement distributed DBMSs.

Military generals have long used the strategy of divide and conquer. Generals attempt to divide the enemy and conquer the divided groups independently. The strategy of dividing and conquering is also useful for system designers. Designers strive to identify independent modules that can be designed and implemented separately. A recent trend in computing is the modularization of systems into two classes of modules called clients and servers. In general, a server provides services to one or more clients.

Previous chapters of this book have examined various ways to distribute data among multiple computers. In the client-server architecture, data are centralized on one computer (the server), with each user's computer (the client) connected to the server via a local-area network. While the client-server architecture distributes users, it centralizes data. A discussion about the client-server architecture is included in this book because it presents one way to solve the islands or unreachability problem: In the client-server architecture, the islands of data are integrated onto a centralized server.

7.1   Functions Are Distributed between Client and Server

A *server* is a process running on a computer that provides services to one or more client processes. For example, several users may share a single print server. Whenever a user using a spread-sheet application issues a print command, the spread sheet to be printed is transmitted to the print server. The print server contains a print queue that buffers the spread sheet until the printer is available. The print server eventually prints the spread sheet on behalf of the spread-sheet application.

A *client* is a process running on a computer that uses the services of a server. In the example above, we say that the spread sheet is an application that executes on a client of the print server.

The basic *client-server architecture* consists of one or more clients that interact with one or more servers.

7.1.1 Motivation for Client-Server Computing

Figure 7.1 illustrates a centralized computing environment typically found in business enterprises. It consists of an expensive mainframe computer with a centralized database with several terminals supporting command-line user interfaces. The enterprise also owns many PCs sitting on employee desktops, but not able to access data in the mainframe. There are three motivations for migrating from this environment to client-server computing:

1. Leverage the investment in PCs. Enable users to use the PCs sitting on their desktop to access and manipulate data from the mainframe database. Users should be able to use their PC applications to analyze and modify mainframe data.

2. Improve the user interface supported by the command-line user interface provided by "dumb" terminals by replacing the terminals with PCs that support graphical user interfaces. Many users, especially novice users, can be more productive using graphical user interfaces available on PCs than the cryptic, keyboard-oriented user interfaces supported by computer terminals.

3. Save dollars by replacing expensive mainframe hardware by less expensive hardware. The following table illustrates the cost of processing power (expressed in MIPS, millions of instructions per second) for various types of hardware:

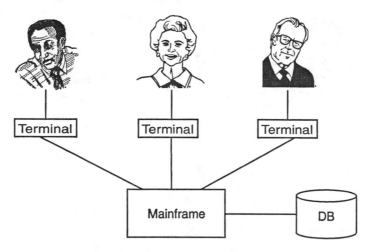

Figure 7.1   Centralized computing environment

Mainframe MIPS	$75,000 to $150,000
Midrange MIPS	$50,000
Desktop Micro MIPS	$300
LAN Server MIPS	$1,000 to $3,000

A large cost savings can be realized if mainframe computers can be phased out and replaced by servers and desktop computers.

7.1.2 Approaches to Client-Server Computing

Two popular client-server architectures are mainframe centric and network centric. Figure 7.2 illustrates the mainframe-centric client-server architecture. In this architecture, PC clients have replaced dumb terminals. Cost savings are realized by using PCs and eliminating older terminals. However, applications that existed on the mainframe are unchanged, except for enhancing their user interface to take advantage of the graphical user interfaces available on PCs.

Figure 7.3 illustrate the network-centric client-server architecture. In this architecture, print, fax, file, and database services are migrated to servers. Applications are segmented and distributed among clients and servers. Distributed applications communicate via messages. In this environment, the communication network connects the various clients and servers. Processors appropriate for each function are installed, leading to a variety of hardware adjustments, including the following:

- *Downsizing*. Reduce cost by replacing expensive mainframe hardware with cheaper, smaller systems. Often system administrators will reorganize office work flows and roles when downsizing occurs.

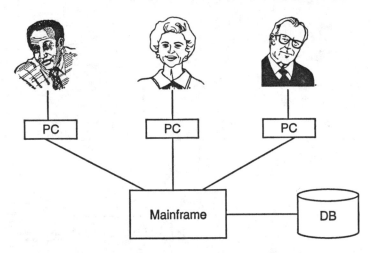

Figure 7.2   Mainframe-centric client-server computing

- *Rightsizing*. Use a processor that fits the task at hand. Often system administrators will improve the user interface and revise office work flows and roles when rightsizing.
- *Upsizing*. Evolve to bigger hardware to support increased processing needs. When upsizing, system administrators will sometimes add new functions to take advantage of the new hardware.
- *Smartsizing*. Reengineer the business processes by streamlining the internal work flow tasks and reimplementing existing automated systems onto smaller LAN-based platforms.

7.1.3 Other Benefits of Client-Server Computing

The clients and servers may execute on the same or different hardware. For example:

- All the clients and servers may reside on the same machine. Because this approach supports only a single user, the clients are usually migrated to other computers, as in the following two approaches:
- Each of the clients and servers may reside on different computers connected by a local-area network.
- Some clients and servers may reside on one machine, and other clients and servers may reside on another machine.

One advantage of the client-server architecture is that system administrators can assign clients and servers to hardware in various ways. This gives system administrators the flexibility to upgrade existing clients and servers or add additional clients and servers to the system by reassigning the servers to different hardware processors.

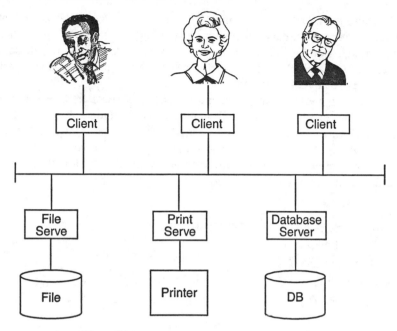

Figure 7.3 Network-centric client-server computing

System administrators may add hardware upgrades and/or additional hardware to support the new clients and servers. In some systems, servers may automatically migrate among computers, depending on workload characteristics.

Another reason why the client-server architecture is popular is that it enables multiple users to share hardware such as printers. Other types of hardware can also be shared. Several users can share the same scanner, the same fax hardware, and the same set of disk drives. Sharing expensive hardware is certainly less expensive that buying the same hardware for each user.

The client-server architecture also enables multiple users to share data. Each user uses a client to access data on a data server. Data servers can provide all the advantages of centralized databases. Users share up-to-date information managed by the server.

While most of the other approaches for solving the IOU problem are basically bridge-building strategies that tie multiple databases together, the client-server architecture uses a different strategy. Database administrators solve the IOU problem by merging data from several files and databases into the centralized database server. Thus the client-server is, in essence, a centralized architecture in that the data are centralized, much in the same way that a centralized DBMS manages a single database used by several users. While in the client-server architecture the data are centralized to the data server, applications that use the data are distributed as clients, often on different workstations connected to the data server by a local-area network.

Because the client-server architecture uses a centralized database, clients do not need to worry about data replication or merging data from multiple databases. The data-merging problem is solved by data administrators when the data server is populated with data. Replicated copies of the same data cannot become inconsistent because there are no replicated data.

Some enterprises use more than one server to store data. In this case, many of the benefits of a centralized database disappear without some mechanism to help users determine which server contains the desired data and to perform distributed locking and commit protocols to ensure data consistency across servers.

Several types of data servers are possible. Each of the following data servers will be described in greater detail in the remainder of this chapter.

- File server
- Database server (and database machine)
- Transaction server
- Document server
- Bulletin board server
- News server

7.2 Server Provides Access to Files

A file server manages files of data. As illustrated in Figure 7.4, the client contains a GUI (graphical user interface) and application code. The user manipulates the GUI to interact with the application. The application sends requests for files to the server. The server copies the requested file and returns it to the client, where it is processed by the application. Some file servers transfer the complete copy of the file to the client. Other file servers repeatedly transfer a portion of the file to the client, which processes that portion before the next portion is transferred.

One disadvantage of file servers is that the entire file is copied and transferred from the server and client. Even if the application needs only a single record from the file, the entire file is copied and transferred. While the file server is conceptually very simple, it can be expensive to transmit entire files between the file server and a client. The database server decreases the communication costs by sending only the needed records to the client.

File servers enable users to share files without having to explicitly replicate them. Instead, the user creating the file places it on the server, where other users can access it as needed. Many users find file servers a convenient way to share files that are coauthored by taking turns making corrections and enhancements.

7.3 Server Provides Access to a Database

Figure 7.5 illustrates the interaction between a client and a database server. The client consists of a GUI and application code that formulate database queries and trans-

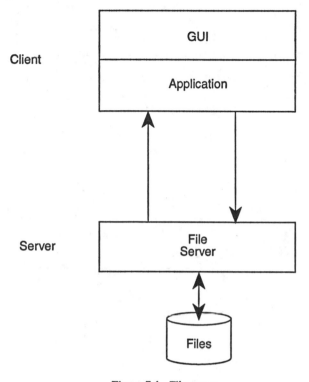

Figure 7.4 File server

fers them to the server. Generally, the query is formulated using SQL. The database server receives and executes SQL queries from several clients. When the database server executes a SQL request, it selects only the data that satisfy the SQL request. The selected data are then transmitted back to the requesting client, where the application processes the data.

Database servers decrease the amount of data that is transmitted from the server to a client. Database servers often provide additional functions, such as user identification and authentication, security constraint enforcement, business rule enforcement, journalizing, and automatic database backup.

7.4   Server Supports Transactions

A transaction server is a database server that is able to execute application-specific code. Figure 7.6 illustrates a transaction server that consists of application-oriented transactions and a database server. Programmers specify transactions that contain application-specific code. The client contains a GUI and part of the application that constructs transaction invocations that are transmitted to the server. The transactions

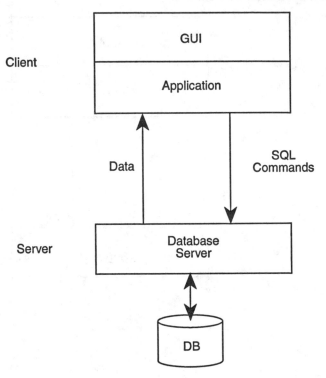

Figure 7.5   Database server

are executed on the transaction server, which guarantees the four ACID properties of transactions described in Chapter 6: atomicity, consistency, isolation, and durability.

By carefully designing transactions and the client applications that invoke them, programmers can minimize communication costs between the client and server. In general, designing transactions and client applications requires the talents of a skilled programmer.

7.5   Database Computers Use Special Hardware

File, database, and transaction servers use traditional hardware. Specially designed hardware can increase the throughput and decrease the processing time of individual transactions and database queries. A *database computer* is a database server that uses specially designed hardware to accelerate query processing. Most database computers process transactions from several clients. Some database computers are designed to process hundreds or even thousands of transactions per minute. For example, airline reservation systems use specially designed mainframes that act as transaction-oriented database computers. Database computers tend to be expensive

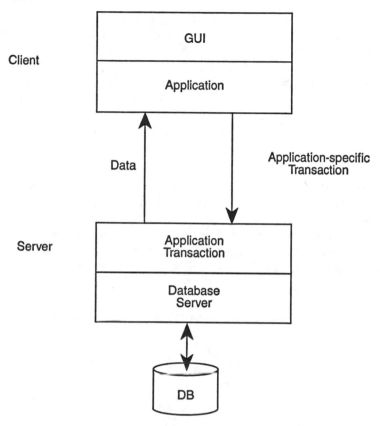

Figure 7.6 Transaction server

and are not widely used except in cases of very large transaction loads and/or critical processing speeds.

7.6 Servers Support Access to Documents

Many applications generate output called *documents*. Documents are often printed and distributed to interested users. However, with the advent of PCs and worksta-tions on employee desks, many documents are stored in electronic form. Users may access documents, display them on monitors, or print them. Using electronic mail and file transfer techniques, users may send documents to other users. Examples of documents include word-processing documents, spread sheets, electronic drawings and charts, presentations and "electronic slide shows," results of a database query, and reports generated by special applications.

A *document server* manages the documents on behalf of multiple users. In effect, the document server is an electronic file cabinet containing electronic documents. Users may delete existing documents from the document server, insert new documents into the document server, and retrieve documents from the document server. The document server also enables users to organize documents into "files" or "buckets" for easy retrieval. Document servers may also maintain attributes about a document, such as who created it, the date the document was created, the document size, and the application used to create or edit the document.

Examples of commercial products that support document servers include Key-File® and Imara®. Both of these products also support clients for accessing documents and presenting documents to users. Clients enable users to access documents by specifying values of document attributes. When a user accesses a document, the client automatically invokes the application that created the document so that the user can view and edit the document. Some document clients also enable the user to access documents whose text contains user-specified words. Most document servers support a keyword search capability to locate documents containing the user-specified words.

7.7 Servers Support Access to Bulletin Boards

A *bulletin board* is a database that contains messages about general announcements and news. Users view the database as a bulletin board where they can browse, examine posted notes, and post their own notes.

Examples of bulletin boards include NewsNet and Lotus Notes. Users may post messages to any of several categories in NewsNet and may review existing messages within any category. The messages themselves are maintained on NewsNet servers, which users access using a wide-area network.

The Lotus Notes client provides a user interface using an electronic filing cabinet metaphor consisting of three levels: (1) the cabinet consisting of six folders, (2) folders, each containing an arbitrary number of databases, and (3) databases, each containing an arbitrary number of notes. Users may insert, delete, and modify notes within a database and create, copy, and delete databases within a folder. The notes are maintained on a Notes server connected to the clients by a local-area network.

7.8 Servers Support Access to News

Streams of electronic news are broadcast over wide area networks by several news agencies, including the Associated Press, United Press International, and Reuters news services. Dow Jones also broadcasts stock market information. A *news server* captures broadcast information and stores it so that users can retrieve the information when it is needed. Users access information on the news server from clients on their desktop. In addition to capturing news, a news server may *filter* the news items, selecting specific items for each user conforming to a prespecified user profile and placing the selected news items into the user's "in box."

7.9 Servers Provide More Than Data Access

Data servers generally provide more than access to data. Most servers support the following properties:

- *Multitasking.* A data server can service multiple clients at the same time. It is able to accept a request from a client while processing requests from other clients and sending responses to other clients.

- *Security.* A data server can enforce security constraints on all requests. It supports a centralized security gate through which all requests must pass.

- *Metering.* A data server is able to monitor and record server usage for billing purposes.

- *Business rules.* A data server can enforce business rules on the data that it manages. Often these business rules are specific to the enterprise and must be specified by a data-base administrator.

- *Location transparency.* Some data servers can reside on the same computer as the client or on a different computer connected to the client by a communication network. The location of the server may be transparent to the client in the sense that programmers do not need to modify client software when server data are moved. However, a systems programmer must update directory tables in the communication system so that requests from the client can be routed to the server at its current location.

- *Horizontal scalability.* It is possible to add or remove client workstations that access data on the server.

- *Vertical scalability.* It is possible to migrate the service to a larger and faster server machine, that responds faster, handles more data accesses, or manages a larger database.

7.10 Clients Support User Interfaces to Server

Users frequently use PCs for word processing and spread-sheet manipulation, but can not access the data on the mainframe. From the PC user's point of view, the mainframe is another island of unreachability, albeit a large island. Recently, there has been a trend toward downsizing business applications from mainframes to local-area networks supporting a range of clients and servers. In some cases, the mainframe acts as a data server. In other cases, the data from the mainframe are downloaded to a different data server. In both cases, the application needs to be broken into two parts, the client part and the data-server part.

7.10.1 Common Applications Act as Clients for Data Servers

Most applications support commands to save and retrieve files. For example, word processing, presentation, drawing, and project management application systems all save and retrieve files. Each of these applications acts as a client. The files may be stored on a traditional file system on the computer where the application resides. Alternatively, the files may be stored in a file server residing either on the same computer or on another computer connected by a communication network.

7.10.2 Database Front Ends Act as Clients for Data Servers

Most database server venders also sell clients for accessing the database. These clients support easy-to-use mechanisms to formulate database queries. These mechanisms include fill-in form, by-example query formulation, visual programming, and natural language processing and translation. These clients enable novice computer users to formulate queries easily and quickly.

7.10.3 User Interface Generators Create Clients for Data Servers

Tools such as Visual Basic®, and PowerBuilder® enable programmers to quickly generate user interfaces to new applications. These new user interfaces act as clients that access data in a data server.

7.11 Client-Server Architecture Presents Problems

When adopting the client-server architecture, database administrators must reformat data from existing databases and files and integrate the data into the database maintained by the server. Using the bottom-up strategy from Chapter 4, database administrators first integrate the schemas describing data in the multiple databases and files and then convert and migrate data from each of the databases and files into the centralized database server.

Migrating Data to the Server. Database administrators and programmers may need to modify existing applications to access tne server rather than a local file or database. During this phase, programmers may elect to change the user interface of older applications from keyword-oriented, text-based user interfaces to graphical user interfaces. The database administrators and programmers must also decide which type of data server to employ. If a transaction server is chosen, the database administrators and programmers must factor transactions out of the existing application code and incorporate the transactions into the transaction server. They must also modify each application to formulate transaction commands that can be processed by the transaction server.

Dealing with Multiple Servers. Figure 7.7 illustrates how multiple clients and multiple data servers can be used to implement a distributed DBMS. Each client may contain modules for request construction, user interface translation, distributed query optimization, and distributed transaction management. Each data server may contain a local transaction manager, gateway, local optimizer, and runtime support processor. The communication system enables clients and servers to exchange messages.

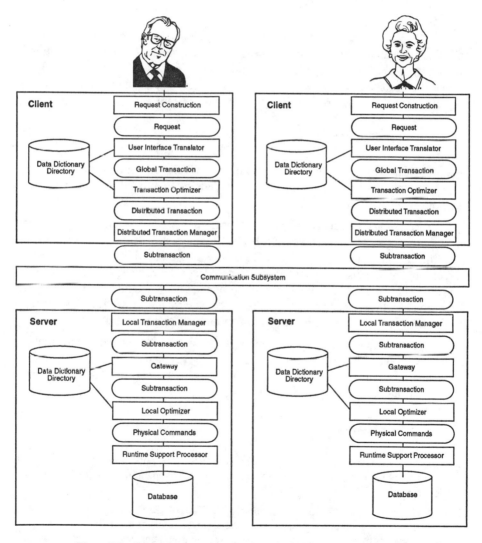

Figure 7.7 Using client-server computing to complement a distributed DBMS

In many client-server-based distributed DBMSs, several of these components may be missing. If there is no distributed transaction optimization module, then the programmer must carefully construct the distributed transaction. If there is no distributed transaction manager, then the application must take over the task of coordinating the execution of subtransactions on multiple component DBMSs. If there is no local transaction manager on the data client, then the application is responsible for both distributed concurrency control and distributed backup and recovery.

The transaction optimizer and distributed transaction manager may be factored out of the clients and placed into a server responsible for distributed transaction processing. This server may be integrated with the database server or may itself be an entirely separate server.

Multiple servers have many of the same problems as multiple, independent database management systems. Despite these problems, the client-server architecture is frequently used to solve the IOU problem. Perhaps, in the long term, each multiple server will become a component of a federated system, which in turn will eventually migrate into a tightly-coupled distributed database system.

Chapter Summary

Users access data using a variety of clients; GUI and fill-in form interfaces are popular with novice users, and keyword-oriented and command-oriented interfaces are popular with experienced users.

Servers manage data accessed by multiple clients. Several major types of servers support access to various types of databases. File servers support access to complete files. Database servers support SQL access to data within files. Transaction servers support a transactional interface to shared data. Document servers provide access to an electronic file cabinet containing documents created by application software. Bulletin board servers enable users to post and review messages. News servers examine and collect interesting news items broadcast by a news service.

Data servers are basically centralized databases with remote access by multiple clients. Multiple data servers introduce many of the problems of distributed databases, including location transparency, distributed transaction processing, and enforcement of business rules that span multiple sites.

Further Reading

Berson, Alex, *Client/Server Architecture*, McGraw-Hill, New York, 1992. Describes client-server development tools, operating systems, GUIs, LAN operating systems, and transaction managers.

Dewire, Dawna Travis, *Client/Server Computing*, McGraw-Hill, New York, 1993. Evolution of distributed systems and the place of the client-server architecture in distributed environments, open systems and standards, client-server environments, and distributed relational database management systems for mainframes and local-area networks.

Khoshafian, Setrag, Arvola Chan, Anna Wong, and Harry K. T. Wong, *A Guide to Developing Client/Server SQL Applications*, Morgan Kaufmann, San Francisco, CA, 1992. A thorough description of SQL relational databases, transaction processing, and application programming interfaces. Includes descriptions of IBM OS/2 Extended Edition Database Manager, Oracle Server, DEC Rdb/VMS, and Microsoft SQL Server as case studies.

Text-based Database Systems

This chapter discusses the following:

- How relational DBMSs support textual documents.
- How information retrieval systems manage textual documents.
- How to hoover and retrieve distributed documents.
- How to filter a stream of textual data.
- How a content server supports information retrieval, hoovering, and filtering.
- How to support updates to textual documents.
- How to collect payment for the use of textual information.

8.1 Documents Contain Content and Structure

Most commercially available database management systems are designed to manage structured data. Structured data consist of ordered sets of typed values organized into fields within records. Each field contains values from a predefined domain, such as integers within a prescribed range, floating-point values with a prescribed range and number of significant digits, or a character string of prescribed length. Many database management systems support business rules that database administrators use to prescribe valid values that can be placed into fields. Much of the information used by business enterprises falls into the category of structured data, including financial data, inventory data, production statistics, simulation results, and scientific data.

However, not all the information used by business enterprises consists of small, discrete, homogeneous units that fit nicely into the fields of records. This chapter deals with one such type of information: text. Chapter 9 will deal with other media types, including image, voice, and video.

Many of the activities of an enterprise revolve around paper documents such as letters, reports, memorandum, written messages, and instructions. Scanning and optical character recognition have advanced to the state where paper documents can be scanned and converted to text represented as ASCII files. With the advent of word processors, more and more information is in the form of electronic text. We will use the term *textual document* to refer to a sequence of sentences and paragraphs of textual information in electronic form. Using cut, copy, and paste operations, users readily create new documents from old. Using communication technology, textual documents are transmitted to other users. Today, users face a flood of textual documents. Just as users need a database to manage structured data, they need a document management system to manage textual documents.

Content and structure make up every document. *Content* is the information contained in the document, while *structure* is the arrangement and layout of the document that make it easy for users to scan and read the content. Examples of document structures include the arrangement of chapters, sections, paragraphs, lists, tables, and the like. Just as proofreaders used *proofreading marks* to convey instructions to the typesetter, document authors use a *markup language* to convey instructions to the document-rendering software about what the document structures are and how they should be laid out.

Several languages are used for marking documents with instructions for their rendering. Many word processors have their own file formats containing special language commands for displaying the document's content. TeX® is a powerful language for formatting mathematical formulas. Some painting programs create TIFF files (tagged image file format), and some drawing programs create object-oriented graphics in special file formats. With so many file formats, incompatibility problems may occur when documents are transferred among computer systems.

Adobe's Postscript™ is the most commonly used language for describing how a document should be rendered on a display device or printer. The document author can specify fonts, mathematical symbols, diagrams, and photographs. However, not all rendering devices use the same version of Postscript, resulting in documents that are printable on one device and not on another. Adobe has introduced a new Portable Document Format and an Acrobat® family of products for creating and displaying these files.

The Standard Generalized Markup Language (SGML) is being promoted by the Department of Defense's CALS (Computer-aided Acquisition and Logistics Support) program. SGML is a language for identifying the elements of a document and describing how they should be rendered. Tags are inserted into the document content to indicate the beginning and end of each structural element. For example <PARA> identifies the beginning of a paragraph and </PARA> identifies the end of a paragraph. The authors of a document may insert tags directly into their text, or the tags may be inserted automatically by the editor used by the document authors to create the text.

When the rendering software displays a document, it examines the document for tags and lays out each tagged element according to instructions contained in a Document Type Definition (DTD). For example, the DTD for <PARA> may instruct the rendering software to skip a line and indent the first word of the paragraph element. SGML is used to define the DTD for each tag. In order for the rendering software to display a document, each tag in the document must have a DTD. In some situations, users may select from among alternative DTDs for the same element. For example, by setting parameters in a style sheet, users may select between alternative DTDs for laying out a paragraph, with one DTD indenting the first word of a paragraph and another DTD not indenting the first word of a paragraph. Different views of the same document can be displayed by changing DTDs.

In addition to being used to identify document elements for layout and rendering, tags can also be used to identify elements for special processing. For example, chapter and section headings can be located and extracted to construct a table of contents. Tagged keywords can be extracted and referenced in an index. In Chapter 9 we will see how tags can be used to identify nontextual elements such as graphics, audio, and video, which require special software modules to be rendered to the user.

Documents containing SGML tags may have bugs. A author may misspell the type of tag or forget to indicate the end of a tagged element. Editors that automatically insert tags minimize these bugs. A rendering module needs a DTD for each tag in order to rendering the document appropriately. Problems may occur if two documents are merged with different DTDs for the same tag. Perhaps the biggest problem occurs when an author defines a new tag and associated DTD that either is not available to the rendering program or the rendering program is unable to process. When this occurs, either the rendering program fails or the rendered document contains "holes."

Languages like SGML and its variations enable information in a document to be located and used outside the document. Documents no longer need be forgotten in some file cabinet filled with stuff no one will ever read. And users will be able to selectively access the specific information they need, avoiding the glut of unorganized information facing users today.

8.2 Relational DBMSs Support Textual Documents

Relational database practitioners have tried to use relational DBMSs in three ways to manage textual documents:

1. *BLOBs*. A special data type contains a complete textual document. This data type is sometimes called a *binary large object*, or *BLOB*. A relational database management system must be specially designed to support BLOBs. The underlying storage structures of a relational database must be extended to handle large strings of text as a field within a database record. Because of its size, a BLOB cannot always be displayed in a column of a table; instead, the DBMS displays each BLOB as a separate document.

2. *Document fragmentation*. The textual document is partitioned into several fragments that are placed into fields within different records. Special database management system modules read several records to obtain all the fragments and then reconstruct the textual document for presentation to the user.

3. *Document properties*. Each textual document is stored as a file by the file system. Properties of the textual document are stored in a relational database. To retrieve and present textual documents to the user, the document management system first accesses the relational database to retrieve the document location within the file system and then retrieves the textual document itself from the file system. In addition to the location of the textual document within the file system, the database may also contain document properties such as the following:

   • The application used to create and/or edit the textual document.
   • Attributes of the textual document, including its size, length, date created, author, and so on.
   • Keywords and descriptors that characterize the contents of the textual document.
   • Relationships to other textual documents and/or other database records.

While a general-purpose relational database management system can be extended to manage textual documents, a special type of database management system called an information retrieval system is frequently used for this purpose

8.3 Information Retrieval Systems Manage Textual Documents

An *information retrieval system* is a collection of textual documents and their properties managed by a database management system specially designed for textual document storage, organization, and retrieval.

Users may access information in a collection of documents using several techniques:

   • *Browse documents*. Users examine the contents of documents, much like a library patron selects books from a bookshelf and pages through them.

- *Examine table of contents.* Users examine the document's table of contents to determine if it contains information of interest.

- *Chase links.* Users retrieve and access other documents referenced by the current document. Links relating documents may be either generated automatically by the information retrieval system or explicitly created by users as "see also" pointers. Documents related by interdocument links are called hypertext databases and are described in Chapter 10.

- *Search full text.* The information retrieval system examines each document to determine if it contains the words specified in the user's query.

- *Search keywords in an index.* User's formulate queries containing keywords from a thesaurus of keywords known to the information retrieval system. The information retrieval system examines an index of keywords to identify documents to present to the user.

Two data structures are useful in facilitating key word searching:

1. A thesaurus that contains keywords describing document contents. Figure 8.1 illustrates the contents of a very small hierarchically structured thesaurus. Users need a thesaurus when a restricted set of words is used to describe document contents. Users must use these words to describe documents that they wish to retrieve. Some information retrieval systems do not support a thesaurus. In these cases, all words in the English, Spanish, Russian, or other natural language used by the authors of the documents are considered to be the thesaurus.

2. An index that relates keywords from the thesaurus to the textual documents. Figure 8.2(a) illustrates the contents of such an index.

Indexing. One problem facing users of information retrieval systems is how to determine which keywords characterize a document. The process of assigning keywords from the thesaurus to textual documents is called *indexing*. Approaches to indexing include the following:

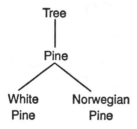

(a) Graph representation

Thesaurus	
General Term	Specific Term
Tree	Pine
Pine	White Pine
Pine	Norwegian Pine

(b) Table representation

Figure 8.1 Example thesaurus

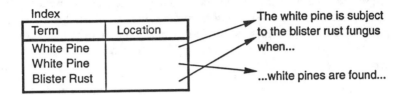

(a) Thesaurus terms indexing textual documents

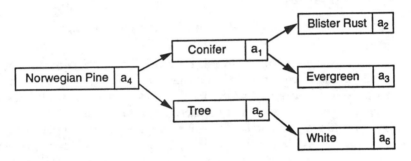

(b) Thesaurus represented as a binary tree—an "a" represents address of each document

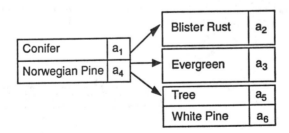

(c) Thesaurus represented as a B-tree

Figure 8.2   Index implementation techniques

- Manual assignment. A person familiar with the contents of a textual document selects keywords from the thesaurus that characterize the document. Usually, individuals inserting documents into the information retrieval system perform this task.
- Software compares each word from the textual document with words in the thesaurus. Matching words are used as keywords to characterize the textual document.
- As a variation of the previous approach, software compares each root word from the document with root words in the thesaurus. A *root word* is a word with all prefixes and suffixes removed.

Example Word	Root Word
going	go
helpful	help
houses	house

- All words in the document (except very common words such as *and*, *of*, *the*, and *a*) are considered to be keywords. A document is said to be *inverted*

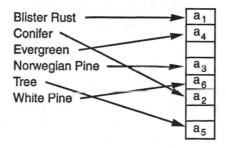

(d) Addresses located by using hashing techniques

	d1	d2	d3	d4	d5
Blister Rust	0	1	0	1	0
Conifer	1	1	1	1	0
Norwegian Pine	0	0	1	0	0
Evergreen	1	0	1	0	1
Tree	0	0	0	1	1
White Pine	0	0	1	0	1

(e) Document signatures—a "1" indicates that the keyword indexes the document

Figure 8.2 (cont.)　　Index implementation techniques

when all its words are keywords. This approach is frequently used when the information retrieval system has no explicit thesaurus.

Index Implementation. The index may be implemented using any of a large variety of data-structure techniques, including the following:

- *Binary tree structure* [Figure 8.2(b)]. Traversing the index for a key word yields the address of documents containing the key word. However, the hierarchical structure of a binary tree may become distorted when keywords are inserted, resulting in long searches to retrieve some document addresses.

- *B-tree index* [Figure 8.2(c)]. Traversing the index for a key word yields the address of documents containing the key word. The hierarchical B-tree index is self-organizing because it adjusts itself when keywords are inserted so that all of the leaves are the same distance from the root. This structure guarantees an upper bound on the time necessary to retrieve the addresses of documents associated with any key word.

- Table hashing [Figure 8.2(d)]. A hashing transformation transforms each key word into a one of several slots where the addresses of the document are stored. Each key word of a query is transformed by the same hashing function into a slot that yields the addresses of documents indexed by the query key word. Because hashing may transform two different keywords into the same slot, retrieved documents should be verified to contain the specified key word before they are presented to the user.

After obtaining the sets of addresses of documents for each key word, the information retrieval system manipulates the addresses as follows: If the query is the "and" of two keywords, then only documents in both address sets need to be retrieved, so the information retrieval system intersects the two address sets before retrieving the documents. If the query is the "or" of two keywords, then the documents in each of the address sets need to be retrieved, so the information retrieval system unions the two address sets (and removes any duplicate addresses) before retrieving the documents. If the query involves a "not," then addresses associated with the "not" key word are removed from the address set before documents are retrieved.

Another form of hashing can be used to retrieve documents containing a set of keywords:

- *Signature hashing* [Figure 8.2(e)]. A hashing transformation transforms the keywords associated with a document into a *signature* bit string associated the document. The query is hashed to another signature bit string. If the query's signature bit string is contained within the document's signature bit string, then the document may contain the same keywords as the query. This technique requires that the query signature be compared with the signature of each document. Because a hashing function may transform two different sets of keywords to the same signature, this technique may yield some addresses of documents not indexed by the specified keywords. All documents should be verified as being indexed by the specified keywords before they are presented to the user.

Information retrieval systems differ in the technique they use to implement indexes. Information retrieval systems also differ in the format and content of queries that users may formulate.

Formulating Queries. The user must formulate a query before the information retrieval system can retrieve documents containing information desired by the user. A query may consist of one or more of the following:

- One or more keywords from the thesaurus. Documents containing the specified keywords are retrieved and displayed to the user.

- Multiple keywords in a Boolean expression, for example;

  green and (red or blue)

  In this example, documents containing both the keywords green and red or both the keywords green and blue are retrieved and presented to the user.

- A natural language request that is converted into a Boolean expression. For example, the natural language request

  Retrieve things that are green and red and retrieve things that are green and blue

  might be converted into the Boolean expression

  green and (red or blue)

- Weighted requests, for example,

  green (2), red (1), blue (1)

  which indicates that green is very important, while red and blue are both desirable. Documents are ranked by how close their keywords match the weighted request and presented to the user in ranked order.

Relevance. After the user has formulated his or her request, the information retrieval system uses the index to locate documents that match the request, ranks the documents with respect to the degree that they match the user's request, and then presents the retrieved documents to the user in ranked order. Some documents will contain information relevant to the user's needs and some will not. Practitioners use two criteria to measure the relevance of retrieved documents to user needs:

$$\text{recall} \;=\; \frac{\text{retrieved relevant documents}}{\text{relevant documents in the database}}$$

$$\text{precision} \;=\; \frac{(\text{retrieved relevant documents}) - (\text{retrieved nonrelevant documents})}{\text{relevant documents in the database}}$$

Precision measures the usefulness of retrieved documents to the user, while recall measures how many of the relevant documents from the database were retrieved. It is desirable to have both recall and precision measures as close to 1.0 as possible.

Relevance Feedback. After the user retrieves documents, the user may want to modify the query to retrieve additional relevant documents. If the user initially retrieved many documents, the user may "and" additional keywords to the query or replace a general key word by a more specific key word in order to make the query more precise and retrieve fewer documents. If the user retrieved too few documents, the user may "or" additional keywords or replace a specific key word by a more general key word in order to generalize the query and retrieve more documents. Sometimes the user does not attempt to modify the existing query, but instead formulates an entirely new query. Users may iterate this process, modifying their queries several times. Some information retrieval systems automatically modify the user's previous query based on which documents the user declares relevant and nonrelevant.

8.4 Distributed DBMSs Hoover, Filter, and Retrieve Distributed Documents

Each approach to distributed DBMS described in Chapter 1 can be applied to information retrieval systems.

8.4.1 Data Extraction for Information Retrieval Systems

In Chapters 1 through 6 we used the term *query processing* to refer to the process of applying a query against the contents of a database. We will use the terms *hoovering* and *filtering* to refer to the process of capturing documents from a remote source and placing them into a local database for later use. Hoovering refers to copying documents from a remote database into a local database, while filtering refers to capturing documents from a stream of documents arriving via a communication channel into a local database. News feeds are examples of document streams that arrive via a communication channel. Both hoovering and filtering are data-extraction processes that provide additional documents containing information relevant for users.

Hoovering. Data extraction refers to the copying of data from a source database and placing it into a target database. In information retrieval systems we will call this process *hoovering*, appealing to the metaphor of a vacuum cleaner sucking up objects that are then placed into a common receptacle. Figure 8.3 illustrates the hoovering of documents from a remote database. These documents are automatically transferred and inserted into a local database. As each document is placed into the target database, two tasks should be performed:

1. If the document's keywords are not all found in the thesaurus of the local information retrieval system, then adjust its set of keywords so that only keywords from the local thesaurus are used.

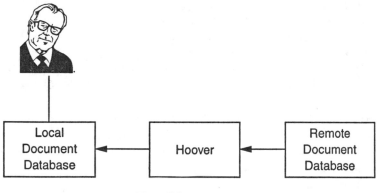

Figure 8.3   Hoovering

2. Verify that the document does not already exist in the local database. Several approaches for determining if a document is already in the local database are possible:

• The user detects duplicate documents. Generally, users do not appreciate performing this task.

• Automatically compare each hoovered document with each document in the local database letter by letter. This approach may be time consuming, especially if large number of documents are hoovered.

The next two approaches assume that documents in both databases are indexed using keywords from the same thesaurus.

• Automatically compare the keywords of each hoovered document with the keywords of each document in the local database. Pairs of documents that have the same or nearly the same keywords are considered to be candidate duplicate documents. Compare pairs of candidate documents letter by letter to determine if they are really duplicates. If the hoovered document already exists in the database, then do not insert it again into the database.

• Automatically compare the keywords of each hoovered document with the keywords of each document in the local database. Do not insert a hoovered document into the database if its keywords match the keywords of a document already in the database. It is possible that with this approach some relevant documents would not be transferred from the remote database to the local database. As an example, two documents are both characterized by the keywords "stock market" and "crash." One document announces that "the stock market has crashed." while the other document declares that "the stock market has not crashed," The two documents clearly contain different information, but appear similar when considering only the keywords. Sometimes small articles such as "not" are important; without them two very different articles may appear to contain duplicated information.

Filtering. As illustrated in Figure 8.3, hoovering is a process in which documents from one database are selected and inserted into a second database. However some information publishers broadcast information in the form of a stream of textual documents and articles. International and national news wire services such as the Associated Press, Reuters, and United Press International fall into this category. Electronic mail also falls into this category in the sense that new documents arrive over time.

Most users find it time consuming and tedious to examine each document as it arrives. To solve this problem, we take an approach similar to that used in information retrieval systems: assign keywords to each document. Many of the approaches for indexing documents for information retrieval are useful to index documents as they are delivered via a communication channel.

Users specify criteria to select arriving documents and place them into a database or in box for later examination by the user. The criteria used to select documents and articles is called a *filter*. The system used to filter a stream of documents is called an *information filtering system*. Figure 8.4 illustrates an information filtering system.

The primary difference between hoovering and filtering is the source of information. Information filtering is typically applied to streams of incoming data, while in information hoovering it is applied to the contents of a remote database. Filtering involves capturing information from a stream, while information hoovering involves searching and copying information from a remote database.

The primary difference between retrieval from a local database and retrieval via hoovering or filtering is the length of time in which user requests are processed. User preferences for information filtering or information hoovering usually represent long-term interests, while queries in information retrieval systems represent short-term interests that can be satisfied by performing the retrieval. Criteria used by hoovering systems are usually expressed in terms of a *user's interest profile*, which describes topics of general interest to the user over an extended period of time. Criteria used by information retrieval systems are usually expressed as a query to be processed immediately.

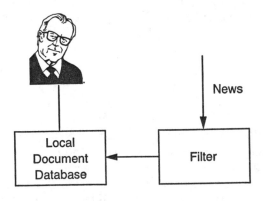

Figure 8.4   Filtering

Just as relevance feedback is useful in information retrieval systems, users may modify and refine their profiles to improve the recall and precision of filtered and hoovered textual documents. Users may modify their interest profile directly. Some information filtering systems and hoovering systems automatically refine the user's interest profile based on filtered or hoovered documents that the user declares to be relevant or nonrelevant.

8.4.2 Remote Access to Information Retrieval Systems

Whereas data extraction hoovers and filters documents from news feeds and remote information retrieval systems for integration into a local database or inbox for later review by the user, remote access enables the user to immediately review the results of hoovering as soon as they are available. However, unlike the data-extraction approach, the user does not need to assign keywords to hoovered documents because they are not placed into a local database.

8.4.3 Gateway to Remote Information Retrieval Systems and News Feeds

A gateway hides the user interface of an information retrieval system or news feed from the user. It translates the user's query or user profile into the format and thesaurus terms required by the remote information retrieval system. Retrieved documents are presented to the user, who must sort and prioritize them and remove any duplicate documents.

Currently, gateways are an appealing technique to gain remote access to information. The disadvantage, however, is that gateways are a "point solution." Each gateway provides remote access to a specific retrieval system or news feeds. Most gateways do not provide interfaces to multiple systems.

8.4.4 Loosely-coupled Information Retrieval Systems

In a loosely-coupled system, the thesauri of each local information retrieval system are integrated to form a global thesaurus. Each word in a local thesaurus is placed into the global thesaurus. Users may formulate three types of queries.

1. *Local query*, using a local thesaurus for execution by their local information retrieval system.

2. *Remote query*, using a remote thesaurus for execution by the corresponding remote information retrieval system.

3. *Global query*, using the global thesaurus for execution by multiple foreign information retrieval systems. Keywords in a global query that are not in a local thesaurus are ignored by the local information system. Thus some documents retrieved from local databases may not satisfy the original request. Users are expected to perform two tasks

a. Verify that each retrieved document satisfies the original query.

b. Identify and remove duplicate documents retrieved from different local information retrieval systems.

8.4.5 Tightly-coupled Information Retrieval Systems

Two information retrieval systems are said to be tightly-coupled if the user uses a single thesaurus and formulates queries using a single user interface. A copy of the query is translated to the format required by each information retrieval system. Query keywords not in the local thesaurus are ignored by the information retrieval system. Documents returned by the local system may therefore not satisfy the original request. The tightly-coupled information retrieval system (and not the user) examines each document returned by a local information retrieval system and performs the following:

- Verifies that the document satisfies the original query.

- Identifies and removes duplicate documents retrieved from different information retrieval systems.

8.4.6 Information Retrieval Servers

Information Retrieval Server. Document property information and the documents themselves may be placed into a server. Users may then submit requests to access documents maintained by the server. If there is a large collection of documents, they may be stored on a second server especially designed to store documents, as illustrated in Figure 8.5. The index server contains document property information, including keywords for each document, and the document server contains the

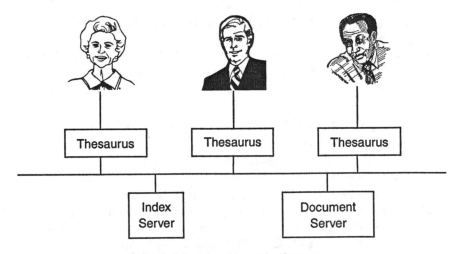

Figure 8.5   Information-retrieval servers

documents themselves. Because they can store large number of documents, optical disks are often used in document servers.

The thesaurus may be replicated and placed at sites where users make requests. This enables users to browse the thesaurus without incurring any communication expense. Because the thesaurus is seldom updated, keeping replicated copies of the thesaurus up to date is not a major problem.

Filter Server. Because of the time constraints to examine each document as it arrives and to determine if it matches a user's profile, the process of filtering news feeds is often placed onto a server, allowing the client to be used for a variety of other activities without being interrupted each time a new document arrives.

The filter server can serve multiple users by comparing each document against multiple filters, one for each user whose workstation or PC is connected to the filter server via a local-area network. Whenever a document matches a filter, it is placed into the corresponding user's database or in box. If requested to do so, the server also notifies the user of the document's arrival.

A filter server may use a combination of a group filter and router. The *group filter* extracts documents of interest to any of its users from the incoming information stream. The *router* then transmits selected documents to interested users. To accomplish this, the individual user filters must be integrated into the group filter and rules must be specified to the router for sending filtered documents to the appropriate users. Changes in individual user filters must be reflected in corresponding changes in both the group filter and router.

Content Server. Information retrieval, hoovering, and filtering systems attempt to connect users to documents in which they may be interested. It is natural to consider a server that supports information retrieval, filtering, and hoovering. We will call this server a *content server.* A content server provides users with information available from several sources, including the following:

- Information on optical and magnetic disks delivered to the user via parcel delivery services.
- Information delivered via a direct connection or LAN from a mainframe database.
- Public databases such as American Online®, Prodigy®, and Compuserve®.
- News feeds containing news stories and financial and stock information.

A combined information filter, hoover, and retrieval system is illustrated in Figure 8.6. In addition to private document databases for each user, a combined system may include the following:

- Group database of textual documents. Large numbers of documents can be easily and inexpensively distributed on optical or magnetic disks. Information administrators integrate these documents with other documents by running a utility that integrates document property information with the property information of documents already in the group database. A wide variety of documents can be made available to a group of users, including the following:

General reference works, such as dictionaries, writing style guides, and general encyclopedias.

Domain-specific information of interest to users. Examples of domains include legal, financial, medical, engineering, and scientific books and document collections.

Catalogue information, including product and service descriptions, information, and costs.

- Updates and corrections to static information made available from the authors and publishers of the original information. This information can be made available by using a wide-area network to download the updates and corrections to the group database.

- Augment group and private document collections by filtering documents from news services delivered via a wide area network. The filtering system selects documents from the stream of documents that may be of interest to one or more users. Selected documents are placed into the document databases of individual users, with the appropriate users notified of their availability.

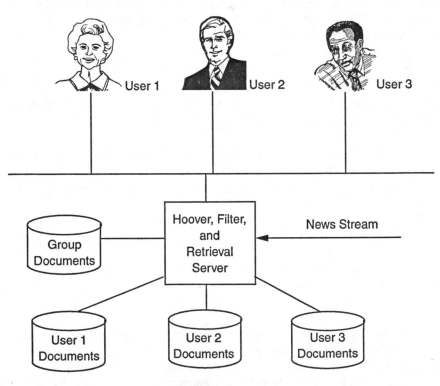

Figure 8.6   Content server

The server enables users to access a wide collection of textual documents from their workstations and PCs. Such a server might also support limited types of transactions, such as the following:

- Requesting additional information about goods and services for sale or rent. The server transmits requests to the vendor and receives responses from the vendor.

- Placing orders for goods and services. The server transmits orders to the vendor and receives order conformations from the vendor.

- Making hotel, airline, car rental, restaurant, and other travel reservations. The server transmits reservation requests to the vendor and receives reservation confirmations from the vendor.

The content server acts as an electronic clearinghouse, providing textual documents from several sources to several users. Users could subscribe to special topics, with the server hoovering and filtering for documents about those topics. Users could query for additional information from alternative sources. The content server brings entire libraries of information literally to the user's fingertips.

8.5 Concurrency Control Prevents Lost Modifications to Documents

Generally, information retrieval systems are used for document retrieval and not document update. This is always the case for archival systems in which the user is explicitly prohibited from modifying archived documents. However, some applications require users to modify the contents of documents. We know from Chapter 6 that, if two or more users attempt to modify the contents of the same document at the same time, modifications can be lost. Some form of concurrency control is necessary to prohibit multiple users from attempting to modify the same document at the same time.

The same techniques used in relational DBMS, two-phase locking, time stamps, and optimistic methods, may be used for concurrency control for updating documents in information retrieval systems. Generally, a locking approach is used. Users may lock a document by "checking it out" and unlock a document after they are finished modifying it by "checking it in."

Occasionally, a document has multiple authors who wish to modify different parts of the document at the same time. This can be accomplished by either partitioning or copying the document into two documents. When both authors are finished, the authors merge the two documents back into a single document. The authors need to negotiate with each other to figure out how to merge copied documents that each has modified.

8.6 Users Pay for Information

Many information consumers are conditioned to receiving information for free (via broadcast media) or for a minor subscription fee (via print media such as newspapers and magazines). Information providers cover their expenses and make a profit from income earned by broadcasting and distributing advertisements. Authors and publishers of electronic information also need to pay their expenses and make a profit. As in the printed and broadcast media, the electronic media will be funded by both advertisers and subscription fees.

Some textual documents will have embedded advertisements. For example, a document may contain a product review, a catalog may contain product specifications, and news articles may contain announcements of new products.

Some users will subscribe to information services. For example, users may pay connect charges to access an on-line database. Users may subscribe to electronic magazines delivered either electronically via a wide-area network or on optical or magnetic disks via package delivery services.

The above strategies reflect a coarse granularity for user fee assessment. The user pays a lump sum for a collection of textual documents. The user pays the same irrespective of how frequently he or she accesses the documents. The user pays the same irrespective of whether he or she access a single document or all the documents. A finer granularity for user fee assessment may be needed.

A more sophisticated strategy for monitoring information usage and accessing usage fees is possible. One strategy involves the use of a module that we will call a *gatekeeper*. The gatekeeper controls access to documents. Each time the user accesses a document, the gatekeeper performs the following tasks:

- Verifies that the user has permission to access the document.
- Decrypts the document into a the textual form understandable by the user.
- Adds an entry to a usage log describing the time, date, and amount of information delivered to the user.

Periodically, the gatekeeper transmits the log to the information publisher, who calculates a usage fee to the user. After the user pays the fee to the publisher, the publisher transmits a new password to the user. This password is required by the gatekeeper before the user can access additional information.

The gatekeeper supports safeguards so that devious users are prohibited from doing the following:

- Bypassing the gatekeeper to access the data directly.
- Modifying the information usage log.
- Directly changing the gatekeeper code in any way.
- Forging passwords and otherwise tricking the gatekeeper into providing information.

Some users will feel that their user profiles and usage logs are confidential. Publishers will want to use this information to tailor information content and delivery. Socially acceptable policies for using user profiles and usage logs for purposes other than calculating fees will need to be established.

Chapter Summary

Information retrieval systems are special DBMSs for maintaining and accessing textual documents. Information filtering systems select documents of interest to users from an incoming stream of documents. Information hoovering systems select documents from a remote information retrieval system. A document server may support information retrieval, filtering, and hoovering. Such a server may provide a clearinghouse for textual information from several sources, in effect acting like a distributed DBMS for textual information. A strategy for billing users for document use will be necessary to encourage publishers to distribute information electronically.

Further Reading

Salton, G., and M. McGill, *Introduction to Modern Information Retrieval*, McGraw-Hill, New York, 1983. Overview of information retrieval techniques and strategies.

9

Multimedia Databases

This chapter discusses the following:

- The multimedia database.
- How to compress and decompress multimedia data.
- How to use relational DBMSs to store media documents.
- The hypermedia system and how it supports multimedia browsing.
- How a multimedia document is organized.
- How multimedia will affect distributed DBMSs.

9.1 Databases Contain Media Documents

In previous chapters we examined DBMSs for both structured data and textual documents. However, much useful information is neither structured nor textual. Information is often represented in several additional types of data which we will call *media* data types. Graphics, images, audio, and full-motion video are examples of media data types. We will use the term *media document* to refer to information represented using one of these media data types. Examples of media documents include the following:

- Charts, graphs, illustrations, and line figures.

- Images consisting of an array of black and white, gray, or color pixels that the human eye perceives as a picture.

- Digitized voice messages, announcements, speeches, discussions, and recorded music.

- Digitized videos of scenes and activities.

- Animation consisting of sequences of line drawings, each slightly different from the preceding drawing.

Several applications can benefit from multimedia databases, including the following:

- *Office information systems.* Much of the information in today's offices is on paper, which could be scanned and stored in an image database. Telephone messages, verbal instructions, and recorded video presentations and instructions could also be managed by a multimedia database. Photos of insured items are especially useful for insurance companies.

- *Medical information systems.* Medical databases contain medical imaging (X-ray, CAT scan), monitoring information (EKG recordings), as well as photographs of characteristic physical symptoms.

- *Engineering information systems*, including both manually generated and computer-generated blueprints, sketches, diagrams and illustrations. Photos documenting construction stages are also useful.

- *Library information systems.* Information on paper can be scanned and stored in an image database. Nonpaper objects can be photographed or video taped and stored in a multimedia database.

- *Geographic databases.* Maps of all kinds, as well as aerial and satellite photographs, can be stored, coordinated, and analyzed by geographic database systems.

- *Consumer catalogues.* These databases not only contain pictures and textual descriptions, but may also contain verbal commentary and video demonstrations of goods and services.

- *Training and education.* Databases can contain video clips demonstrating how things work, how to repair things, and how to assemble things.

- *Reference works*, including encyclopedias containing news clips, audio clips, and digitized photographs.

In a *multimedia document*, information is represented using two or more media types. A *multimedia database* contains multimedia documents. Sound, animation, and video media data types are sometimes called *temporal data types* because of their time dimension. We will use the term *title* to refer to presentations, programs, shows, and guides involving one or more temporal data types. Because of their time dimension, we say that titles are *presented* or *replayed* (rather than displayed) to the user.

Compression and Decompression. Media documents require much more space for storage than traditional data types. For example, 24 hours of color television requires 10^{12} bytes of storage without compression. Practitioners use data-compression techniques to significantly reduce the amount of storage required. Compressed data are also less expensive and faster to communicate from site to site than uncompressed data. However, each site that displays or prints media documents will need to support decompression algorithms to convert compressed data into the form needed for presentation to users.

A wide variety of compression-decompression algorithms are possible. Different algorithms are used for each media type. Compression techniques for text include the following:

- Replace long sequences of the same character by a single instance of the character and the length of the sequence. Decompression consists of detection of the replacement and replicating the character the required number of times. This simple technique is used to remove sequences of blank spaces, which often occur in text.

- Replace reoccurring character sequences by preassigned codes. For example, frequently occurring words such as *the, and, often, Mr., but,* and *not* are replaced by shorter binary strings. Decompression consists of replacing the short binary strings with the corresponding character sequences. With this technique, both the compression and decompression algorithms must use the same table of word-binary string correspondences.

- Dynamically detect frequently occurring character sequences, assign short binary representations to each sequence, and replace the character sequences by the binary representations. With this technique, the compression algorithm includes the assignment of binary strings to character sequences as part of the compressed text. As the decompression algorithm examines compressed text, it extracts the mappings between character sequences and binary representations, constructs a table of word-binary string mappings, and replaces the short binary strings by the corresponding character sequences.

Compression-decompression algorithms for text are said to be *lossless* because the complete text can be reconstructed from the compressed format. Compression algorithms for images, audio, and video are usually *lossy,* because some information is lost during compression that cannot be reconstructed during decompression. Lossy compression algorithms result in compressed information that is more compact and requires less space than lossless algorithms. Depending on the amount of information that is lost during compression, users may not notice the missing information.

Lossy techniques include the following:

* Scanned text is converted to strings of ASCII characters by optical character-recognition technology. In addition, shrinking the size of the document, this technique also produces textual documents that can be automatically indexed for information retrieval. However, the font type, size, and layout of the text may be lost and cannot be reproduced when the ASCII characters are displayed to the user.
* Audio is captured by periodically sampling and digitizing audio waves. The digitized audio can be compressed by removing some of the sound samples.

Similar reoccurring sound samples such as a repeating tone or period of silence may be replaced by a single sample and the length of the original sound. Because similar sound samples are replaced by a single sound sample, the sound reproduced during replay is not precisely the same as the sound compressed by the compression algorithm.

Periodic sound samples are eliminated. For example, every other sound sample is removed. To reconstruct the sound, each of the remaining sound samples is replayed twice as long.

* Two types of compression are used for video:

1. *Intraframe compression.* (This technique is also used for compression and decompression of still images.) Regions of similar color are replaced by a code representing the color. However, the user may notice jagged edges between colored shapes within a frame. The user may also notice image fuzziness as the shape, size, and position of images change from frame to frame.
2. *Interframe compression.* Sequences of similar regions in successive frames are detected and replaced by a single region and the number of frames in which it appears. The decompression algorithm detects repeating regions and reinserts the color into the successive frames. Disadvantages of this approach are that (a) the replay of video must start with the frame that contains all the regions, (b) video cannot be replayed in reverse, and (c) if a frame with a region is lost, the following frames may have "holes" with the wrong color left over from earlier frames.

Special hardware may be necessary to decompress media documents in the time frame suitable for humans, especially for titles. Intel has recently introduced Indeo®, a software-only algorithm for decompressing compressed video.

Relational DBMSs Store Media Documents. Section 8.2 described how practitioners have used three approaches for extending relational database management to support textual documents. These same approaches can be used to manage media documents:

1. A special field holds a complete media document. These fields are called binary large objects, or BLOBs.

2. The media document is partitioned into several fragments and placed into separate fields in different records. A database application reads several records to obtain all the fragments and then reconstructs the media document.

3. Each media document is stored as a file. The location of the file and other information about the media document are stored in a database. To retrieve and present a media document to the user, the DBMS first gets its location from the database and then retrieves the media document from the file system. In addition to the location of the media document in the file system, the database may also contain the following:

- The media type and the name of the application used to create and/or edit the media document.

- Attributes of the media document, including its size, length, date created, author, and so on.

- Keywords and descriptors that characterize the content of the media document. While it is possible to use optical character-recognition technology to convert scanned paper documents into ASCII text and then use automatic techniques to assign keywords to the text, in general is it not yet possible to automatically index media documents.

Presenting Media Documents. Each media document has a visual presentation that is displayed on a computer screen so that users can observe it. Even a voice document has a visual presentation, usually consisting of the name of the voice document, perhaps some of its attributes, and an indication of what portion of the voice document is currently being presented (or replayed) to the user. The media DBMS locates and retrieves the media document, decompressing it if necessary. A rendering component accepts the multimedia document and prepares it for presentation to the user.

Multimedia document authors may use SGML (described in Chapter 8) or one of its variations to instruct the rendering component on how to lay out the multimedia document in both space (screen layout) and time (replaying). Hypermedia/Time-based (HyTime) provides a standard way to tag nontext objects so that they can be rendered as a complete document or processed as independent objects. HyperText Markup Language (HTML) is widely used on the World Wide Web. HTML has a special tag called an anchor, which identifies a section of a document to which another document can link. The rendering software presents this section as a hypertext link. When the user clicks the hypertext link, the linked document is retrieved and presented to the user. The next section describes how users browse among documents in a media DBMS.

9.2 Hypertext and Hypermedia Manage Links among Media Documents

Hypertext Systems. A hypertext system is a collection of interrelated textual documents. A relationship (Figure 9.1) between two documents consists of the following:

1. *An anchor in each of the documents participating in the relationship.* An anchor is a subset of the document that participates in the relationship. An anchor may be a word or phrase of a text document. For example, in Figure 9.1, the anchor "white pine" in the one document is linked to the anchor "white pines" in the second document. Anchors are marked so that users can differentiate them from the nonanchor parts of a document.

2. *Links that connect the anchors involved with the relationship.* Links may be unidirectional or bidirectional. Links may connect exactly two anchors or connect two or more anchors.

3. *Rules about how to display the documents when the user traverses an link.* For example, a rule may specify that, when the user traverses a link from document A to document B, document A is removed from the screen and replaced by document B. Another rule may specify that document B is placed on a stack of documents in such a way that the user can see the edge of each document in the stack.

Users browse among documents by traversing links connecting anchors located within documents. Figure 9.2 illustrates sets of documents and the links among the documents. Anchors are not illustrated in Figure 9.2 in order to emphasize the following navigational structures: Figure 9.2(a) illustrates a linear set of documents. Users are restricted to browsing the documents in sequential order, either forward or backward (similar to a slide show). Figure 9.2(b) illustrates a circular arrangement of documents (similar to a Rolodex). Users may browse these documents in a circular fashion. Figure 9.2(c) illustrates a hierarchy of documents. If the nonleaf documents contain only anchors, then this structure can be thought of as an electronic filing cabinet. The root document represents a filing cabinet and their children represent folders, which in turn contain documents. Figure 9.2(d) represents a collection of documents with a complex collection of links among documents.

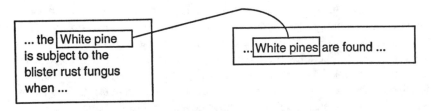

Figure 9.1   Links and anchors in a hypertext system

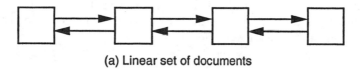

(a) Linear set of documents

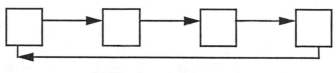

(b) Circular set of documents

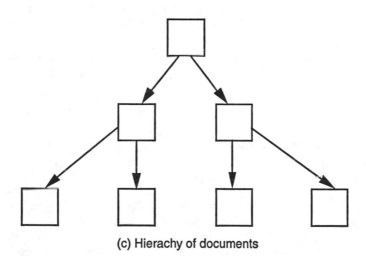

(c) Hierachy of documents

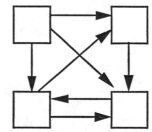

(d) Complex collection of documents

Figure 9.2   Links among documents

The Microsoft Help System is a hypertext system used by several Windows applications. The user selects highlighted words from a list of help topics by clicking them, causing the current page to disappear and a new page to appear that gives additional information about the selected word.

Hypermedia Systems. A hypermedia system is like a hypertext system in which any document may be a media document. A media document may contain an anchor and thus participate in relationships with any other media document. Anchors may be physically embedded within a document or may be displayed externally to the document's presentation. The latter is useful for temporal documents in which anchors are presented outside a video's presentation or simply appear as icons on the screen in the case of an audio document.

A user browses a hypermedia system as follows. The user enters the hypermedia system by viewing a special multimedia document called the *home document*. The user examines the document and selects an anchor. This causes the home document to disappear and the media document to which it is linked to be presented to the user. If the media document is nontemporal, it is presented to the user. If the media document is temporal, the document is replayed to the user. Anchors associated with the media document are displayed to the user, who may select one of them and view yet another media document.

The hypermedia designer may associate rules with links. These rules describe the following:

- Under what conditions the *linked-to* document may be presented or replayed to the user.
- Whether the *linked-from* document remains visible to the user.
- Other computations and side effects that take place when the user selects the anchor associated with the link.

If the hypermedia designer requires that for all links the *linked-from* document be always removed and the *linked-to* document be immediately presented to the user, then the hypermedia database becomes a *slide show* if the documents are textual or graphical, a *sound track title* if the documents are audio, or a *movie title* if the documents are video. If the hypertext designer enables the user to select from among two or more anchors associated with a media document, then the slide show, sound track title, or movie title is said to be *interactive*. Interactive titles are useful for training, educational, and sales applications, as well as entertainment.

Some hypermedia systems are designed so that the links among anchors are stored within the media documents. This presents two major problems:

1. The document cannot be moved without adjusting all the other documents that contain links to it.
2. Link information about neighboring documents (and their neighbors, and so on) cannot be presented to a user without retrieving the entire document, an expensive operation considering the size of some media documents.

A preferred approach is to store the link information external to the media documents. This enables the link information to be accessed and transmitted to the site of the user without accessing and transmitting all the large media documents. Users browse through the link information until they select one or more media documents to access.

Here are some popular hypermedia systems. The ever popular HyperCard® system, which comes bundled with most Macintosh computers, has spawned a cottage industry of implementing and selling hyperstacks, the HyperCard equivalent of a database. HyperCard users trade or purchase hyperstacks. Each hyperstack consists of several cards containing one or more buttons that act as anchors. When the user clicks a button icon, the current card disappears and the card linked to the clicked button is displayed. Both HyperCard and ToolBook® (probably the most popular Windows hypertext system) have scripting languages that designers use to specify actions performed when users manipulate objects within a card. Both HyperCard and Tool-Book have been extended to include graphics and audio and video data types and can thus be called hypermedia systems. Because both HyperCard and ToolBook embed links within cards, link information cannot be presented without retrieving and displaying cards.

Both PowerPoint® and MicroMind Director® are examples of presentation tools that have several aspects of hypermedia systems. PowerPoint is a presentation tool in which users construct and display visual *foils* for presentation. Foils may contain text, graphics, and images. By using Microsoft's Object Linking and Embedding, audio and video can also be linked and embedded into PowerPoint foils. Generally, foils are linked sequentially. Users may move to the next, previous, or *n*th foil of a sequence. In the most recent version of PowerPoint, users may link to "backup foils" which fall outside the linear list of presentation foils.

MicroMind's Director is a presentation package that sequences and replays graphics, animation, and audio. Users glue together audio and animation clips using a "musical script" metaphor by arranging icons onto several "tracks" of a "time line." A MicroMind presentation has breakpoints during which users can jump to another point elsewhere in the time line.

The World Wide Web (WWW) is a collection of documents linked together via the Internet. Mosaic™ and Netscape are software clients that renders a HTML document and enables users to select and retrieve linked documents in any World Wide Web server (subject to security constraints). Gopher, developed at the University of Minnesota, provides a hierarchical menu interface to locate and deliver documents, lists of documents, and indexes.

Visual Content Abstractions. A *visual content abstraction* is a visual representation that captures significant aspects of a media document. Visual content abstractions help users browse large collections of media documents. Several visual content abstractions may be presented to the user at the same time so that the user can concentrate more on interesting abstractions and quickly skip through the uninteresting ones.

- *Text.* Several types of content abstractions are used for text documents. A *keyword* represents a major topic of a document. An *abstract* summarizes the key points of the document. A *table of contents* outlines the major chapters, sections, and headings. Users can quickly browse keywords, abstract, and table of contents without having to access the complete text.

- *Images.* A *thumbnail* is a small illustration preserving the major features of an image document but omitting much of the detail. Users may browse through several thumbnails, quickly searching for major features, without having to access the complete illustration or scanned image.

- *Video.* A *story board* contains a sequence of thumbnails extracted from frames of a video document. Users may examine multiple story boards to select a single video title for replay. Users may also examine the story board to select scenes from a video title for replay. In another approach, frames are periodically extracted from the video and arranged as a skewed stack so that the user can see the edge of each frame. The user is thus able to see major changes within the video clip.

- *Audio.* An *audio story board* contains a sequence of short audio clips extracted from an audio recording. Users listen to the audio story board to determine if it is of interest and to locate segments of an audio document for replay. Some sound systems also display characteristics of the short clips, such as volume, tempo, and waveform diagrams that may be useful in recognizing interesting audio segments.

Hypermedia and Information Retrieval System. Figure 9.3 illustrates a combined hypermedia and information retrieval system. One database table contains link information. Another table contains property information. Note that the link and property information is stored separately from the documents themselves. Of course, the link and property information should be stored on a readily accessible and updatable medium, while the media documents themselves may be stored on less expensive (and slower) medium.

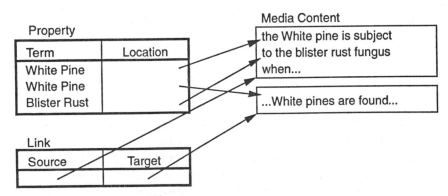

Figure 9.3   Hyperlinks and properties are separate from media content

9.3 Multimedia Documents Contain Structure and Multiple-media Documents

Figure 9.4 illustrates a multimedia document containing several media documents organized as a hierarchy. The leaves contain media documents and the internal nodes contain relationship information about the media documents. The relationship information is used to construct the layout and presentation of the multimedia document when it is presented to the user. Relationship information may include the following:

- *Geographical relationships of media documents*, for example, the relative positions of two media documents on a screen.

- *Temporal relationships of media documents*. For example, an audio clip should be synchronized with a video clip; one video clip should complete before a second video clip is started.

- *Visibility of two documents*. For example, one line chart superimposed on top of another line chart should transparently reveal the underlying chart.

Two approaches are used to represent multimedia documents:

1. Store each leaf node as a media document in a file system and store the internal nodes in a separate database [Figure 9.4(a)]. To present a multimedia document, the multimedia DBMS retrieves the document structure and the locations of media documents from the database and then retrieves the media documents from the file system. The multimedia DBMS then constructs the multimedia document and presents it to the user [Figure 9.4(c)].

2. Store all the internal nodes and media documents together as a file in a file system [Figure 9.4(b)]. Each internal node and media document will be preceded by an information tag that describes its data type and length. Multimedia DBMS software must then reconstruct the multimedia document [Figure 9.4(c)] from this representation for presentation to the user.

With the first approach, the DBMS can easily construct only part of a multimedia document without having to access all the internal nodes and media documents. This approach also enables a media document to belong to multiple documents and only be stored once. However, it is more work to retrieve all the pieces of a multimedia document if it needs to be transmitted to another site.

With the second approach, it is easy to transmit a complete multimedia document to another DBMS and store it as a BLOB. However, it is more complicated to extract pieces from the representation if only a portion of the multimedia document is to be displayed or printed. Also, with this approach a media document needs to be replicated if it belongs to two different multimedia documents.

9.4 Distributed Multimedia DBMSs Are Coming

Media document structure and properties should be separated from document content for several reasons.

- Information can be distributed to storage devices based on its volatility. Information that does not change, such as images, audio, and videos, should be stored on optical disks. Information that is likely to change, such as indexes, synchronization points, and presentation relationships, should be stored on updatable storage.

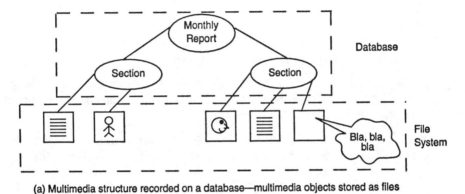

(a) Multimedia structure recorded on a database—multimedia objects stored as files

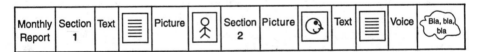

(b) Objects and structure stored in a file

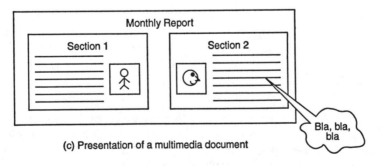

(c) Presentation of a multimedia document

Figure 9.4   Compound document

- Information may be distributed and replicated to locations where it is frequently accessed. Information that is frequently accessed, such as the thesaurus and document properties, may be replicated.

There are few experimental distributed multimedia DBMSs and even fewer commercial distributed multimedia DBMSs. Extending a distributed DBMS to support media documents will require several enhancements.

- The fragmentation and allocation procedures must be modified to consider not only the size of media documents, but also the temporal and synchronization constraints of media documents.

- The request optimization algorithms must be modified to consider the following:

    Location of media documents and minimizing their movement.

    Continuous nature of temporal clips. If some temporal information arrives too late, then the presentation contains gaps. If it arrives too early, it may overflow the local buffer space, causing missing gaps to appear during presentation replay.

    Synchronization and coordination of multiple temporal clips. Sound tracks must be kept synchronized with video tracks. Multiple sound tracks must be synchronized with each other.

    Format of the multimedia information and whether it must be decompressed before presentation to the user.

- The user interface must be modified to present media documents to the user.

- The communication system may need to be extended to support the transfer of large media documents in a timely fashion.

9.5 Future Distributed Multimedia DBMSs Will Provide Useful Features

Because there are so few distributed multimedia systems, we must look elsewhere for examples of distributed systems. The following examples from radio and television broadcasting illustrate the various approaches to distributed multimedia databases outlined in Chapter 1. Future distributed multimedia DBMSs will provide entertainment titles as well as reference and training titles, enabling users to access multimedia information from the office or home.

9.5.1 Data Extraction for Multimedia Systems

Just as textual documents may be hoovered from remote databases and filtered from news feeds, media documents, titles, and programs can be hoovered from media libraries and filtered from radio and TV broadcasts.

Today, hoovering is a manual process of visiting a video rental store and selecting one or more video tapes or computer games for rental or purchase or visiting a music store and purchasing CDs or cassette tapes. Customers may review title abstracts (on the title cover) and, in some stores, preview a clip before purchase.

Today, filtering consists of programming a VCR to record a video from a specific channel or station, beginning at a specific time and recording for a specified length of time. Because so few people are able to program their VCRs, television stations now broadcast a unique number at the beginning of each program (title). VCR owners can now enter the unique number of the program that they wish their VCRs to record.

Most consumer libraries of multimedia titles are manually maintained by stacking and organizing tapes and CD disks in cabinets and boxes. Legal constraints attempt to discourage consumers from copying titles for uses other than replay at home.

In the future, multimedia data will be hoovered, filtered, and organized electronically. Users will filter streams of multimedia delivered via cable or radio transmission. Users will hoover on-line databases of multimedia data. Users will organize and structure captured multimedia using the electronic equivalent of cabinets and boxes.

9.5.2 Remote Access

Consumers with cable service and hotel visitors can rent titles on a pay-per-view bases. The titles are replayed to the user, who pays a rental fee to the cable service or hotel management. In the future, pay-per-view will be more widely available, and the titles and topics that can be viewed will be much broader.

9.5.3 Gateways

Adapters attached to TV sets that unscramble signals or adapt one broadcast format to another can be thought of as multimedia gateways. Gateways may also be used as a billing mechanism so that title producers and distributors can charge consumers for titles.

9.5.4 Loosely-coupled and Tightly-coupled Media Systems

Our television and radio receivers are a type of loosely-coupled system in which users select one from among several different channels or stations. Some television receivers provide a more tightly-coupled system in which the video from two channels is displayed at the same time, often with the video from one channel embedded as a small picture within the picture from the other channel. This enables users watching one program to eavesdrop on another program broadcast at the same time.

9.5.5 Multimedia Servers

Today, most multimedia databases are manual, consisting of magnetic tapes and CDs stacked into cabinets and boxes. However, servers like the content server described in Chapter 7 will be constructed and extended to support documents of various media types.

One popular type of document server is an *image document server*, which manages scanned paper images, ASCII text generated by optical character recognition of scanned text, and document properties automatically extracted from the ASCII text.

Another useful type of document server is an *electronic document server*, which manages not only text and images, but a variety of electronic documents as well, including word-processing documents, spread sheets, and business presentation graphics and "slide shows." Whenever the user retrieves an electronic document, the application that created the document is automatically invoked so that the user can view and possibly modify the document.

A useful server for creators of compound documents and multimedia titles would be a *media clip library server.* Just as graphic clip art is widely used in desktop publishing, authors may reuse clips from libraries of images, audio, and video clips for creating multimedia business presentations, sales presentations, and educational and training films.

From a consumer's point of view, modular home entertainment systems will replay multiple coordinated audio and video clips. Video games and virtual reality "experiences" will provide interactive entertainment to the home consumer.

Chapter Summary

Media data types include graphics, images, audio, and video. Information retrieval systems enable users to quickly locate and present information represented as either traditional or media data types. Hypermedia systems enable users to browse among media data types. A compound document integrates several media data types into a multimedia document. There are currently few distributed multimedia DBMSs. Future distributed multimedia will enable office workers and home consumers to access multimedia titles and programs.

Further Readings

Berra, P. B., C. Y. R. Chen, A. Ghafoor, C. C. Lin, T. D. C. Little, and D. Shin, "Architecture for Distributed Multimedia Database Systems," *Computer Communications*, Vol. 13, No. 4, May 1990, 217–231. Uses Petri nets to describe the synchronization of multiple-media clips for replay.

Christodoulakis, S., M. Theodoridou, F. Ho, M. Papa, and A. Pathria, "Multimedia Document Presentation, Information Extraction, and Document Formation in MINOS: A Model and a System," *ACM Transactions on Office Information Systems,* Vol. 4, No. 4, Oct. 1986, 345–383. Describes MINOS, an object-oriented multimedia information system for creating and managing complex multimedia objects.

10

Object-oriented DBMSs

This chapter discusses the following:

- What an object is.

- An object-oriented DBMS and how it manages objects.

- How to support object versions and configurations.

- How object orientation affects distributed DBMSs.

Object-oriented techniques are becoming popular for designing and implementing user interfaces, applications, and systems. It is natural to apply object-oriented techniques to databases. Whereas relational databases are record oriented in that data are viewed as a collection of record types (or relations), objects in object-oriented databases represent real-world objects and entities. Although information about complex real-world objects may be scattered among relational tables (especially after table normalization), the goal of the object-oriented database is to maintain a direct correspondence between real-world and database objects. Users can easily identify objects and perform operations on them that are similar to the operations users perform on their real-world counterparts.

10.1   Database Objects Represent Real-life Objects

An object-oriented database contains several object classes; each class consists of zero or more object instances. An *object class* can be thought of as a template or blueprint from which several object instances can be made. An object class describes several attributes (sometimes called value holders or slots). A class also describes operations that may be applied to object instances.

An *object instance* (sometimes just called an *object*) represents a single real-world object or entity. Each object instance conforms to its description within its object class. An object instance may have a value for each attribute of its object class. Operations from the object class may be applied to the object instance, causing the values of its attributes to change.

An object class is like a relational table in that it describes a set of homogeneous objects. An object class is unlike a table in that an object class may describe special operations that apply only to instances of that class.

Figure 10.1 illustrates two object classes, PERSON and EMPLOYEE. The Person class contains three attributes, Name, Birthdate, and Dependents. The Employee class contains three attributes, Department, WorksOn, and Salary, and a method, GiveRaise, for operating on the Salary attribute. Figure 10.1 also illustrates four object instances, two for the PERSON class and two for the EMPLOYEE class. Also shown are the values for each attribute for each of the four instances.

Each object has an identifier that is independent of its attribute values. No two objects in the object-oriented database may have the same *object identifier*. While

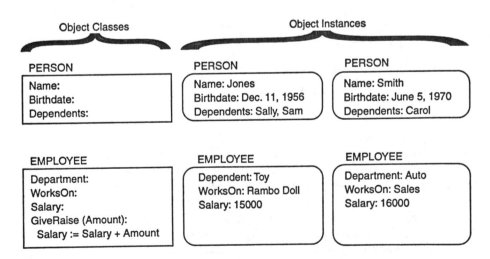

Figure 10.1   Object classes and instances

values of attributes may be changed, the object identifier is permanent. It is not dependent on the object's name, key, or location. The object identifier is automatically generated by the object-oriented database system whenever an object instance is created. An object identifier is not the same as a primary key in relational databases. A primary key consists of the values of one or more attributes, whereas an object identifier is independent of the values of the object's other attributes.

Object identifiers are convenient for associating objects. Accessing related objects using object identifiers is faster than using foreign keys in relational DBMSs. Objects can be directly accessed via their object identifiers, avoiding indexed lookups or the time-consuming joins necessary in relational databases. However, because object identifiers are computer generated, they have no semantics in the real world, making it difficult for users to remember and use object identifiers.

Each object class has procedures called *methods*, which are invoked when the object receives a message. Unlike relational databases, which describe only the representation of data, object-oriented databases support a behavioral model, describing both the representation and manipulation of data within the database. Attributes describe the data representation, and methods describe the behavior of objects.

There are two types of methods, private and public. *Public methods* can be seen by other objects as well as by users. The public methods contain application logic and business rules. *Private methods* enforce referential integrity, security, and other housekeeping functions normally associated with a DBMS. Private methods cannot be seen or directly invoked by users.

Objects communicate via messages. A *message* consists of the name of an object or several objects followed by the name of a method to be applied to the objects. For example, the message <Jones, Amount, GiveRaise> means that the Jones object is to be given a raise of the specified amount.

Object-oriented programming languages are popular because they support encapsulation, inheritance, aggregation, and polymorphism. These properties are not directly supported in nonobject-oriented programming languages.

Encapsulation of an object is the hiding of the implementation of its data structure and methods from the object class's interface. For example, in Figure 10.2 the EMPLOYEE class contains a method for the GiveRaise command. Users may send the GiveRaise message to instances of the EMPLOYEE class. When this occurs, the method from the EMPLOYEE class is invoked, causing the value of the salary attribute to be increased by the value specified for Amount. A programmer may change the method, perhaps to calculate the new salary as 110% of the old salary plus the value specified for Amount, without changing the name or format of the GiveRaise command. Encapsulation enables programmers to change how a method is executed without changing the command for invoking the method. This enables programming changes to be localized to an object class. Encapsulation is naturally attractive from a user's point of view. The user issues commands meaningful to himself or herself and doesn't need to worry about how those commands are carried out.

EMPLOYEE

EMPLOYEE
Department: WorksOn: Salary: GiveRaise (Amount):   Salary := Salary + Amount

EMPLOYEE

Dependent: Toy
WorksOn: Rambo Doll
Salary: 15000

GiveRaise (100);

EMPLOYEE

Dependent: Toy
WorksOn: Rambo Doll
Salary: 15100

Figure 10.2   Object method

Programmers frequently write methods to enforce business rules. While the relational data model is quite restricted in the business rules that database administrators can specify, in object-oriented databases methods can be used to specify a wide variety of business rules. This is possible because the language used to write methods is a general-purpose language such as C++.

Inheritance is the ability of one object class to reuse the data structures and methods of another object class without reimplementing them. For example, EMPLOYEE inherits attributes and values for Name, Birthdate, and Dependents from their PERSON instances. This is illustrated in Figure 10.3. The double-lined arrow of Figure 10.3 indicates that EMPLOYEE is a special case of PERSON that inherits all of PERSON's attributes.

Object classes are often placed into a hierarchy. Each subordinate class is a specialization of the superior class and inherits attributes and methods from its superior class. This inheritance hierarchy of classes is sometimes called an *IS-A hierarchy* because each subordinate class is a specialization of its superior class. Inheritance allows programmers to take advantage of methods that already exist in other object classes. Programmers implement only the differences between a new class and the existing classes from which the new class inherits attributes and methods.

Aggregation is the grouping of parts into a whole. Attributes are aggregated into objects, and objects are aggregated into composite objects. For example, several words are aggregated into a sentence and several sentences are aggregated into a paragraph. Several paragraphs are aggregated into a section. Sections are aggregated into chapters. Chapters are aggregated into a book. Books are aggregated into libraries, and so on. One advantage of object-oriented databases is that one object may be *part of* or an aggregate of another object. An object may be an aggregate of several other objects. An aggregation of object-oriented classes is sometimes called a *part-of hierarchy*. Aggregation is important because it enables users to construct new, complex objects from existing objects.

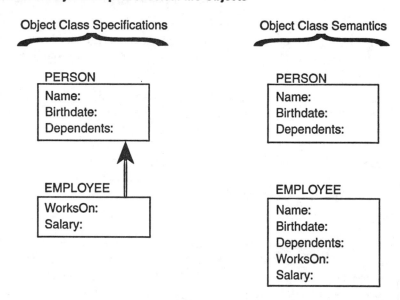

Object Class Specifications   Object Class Semantics

Figure 10.3 Inheritance

Polymorphism means two different objects may respond to the same message with different methods. For example, when they receive the GiveRaise message, instances of the EMPLOYEE class may add the Amount to the Salary field, while instances of the SUPERVISOR class may add Amount*1.1 to the Salary field. In this way, new object classes, each containing their own methods, can be added to a system without having to add any new message types.

Object-oriented DBMSs support many of the features of nonobject-oriented DBMSs, but often with some interesting enhancements.

- *Durability.* Data remain in a database after applications that create or modify the data terminate. Objects may be transient and persistent. *Transient objects* reside in a program's work space and are lost when the program terminates. *Persistent objects* are stored in the object-oriented database and exist after the application that created them terminates. While users of relational databases must often construct transient objects from multiple tables from a relational database and then reconstruct the tables from the transient object before they are returned to the database, user's of object-oriented databases only need to move objects between the program's work space and the DBMS. No translation is necessary between transient and persistent objects.

- *Sharing and Isolation.* Data in a database can be accessed by multiple applications and users. Wherever there is sharing, some type of concurrency control is required to provide isolation when objects users update objects. Many object-oriented DBMSs handle concurrency using a check-in/check-out approach. A user checks out an object before using it and checks it in after using it. Checking out is similar to locking, and checking in is similar to unlocking. When a user checks out an object, it is copied to the user's private work space, and when a user checks in an object, it is moved back to the database.

Some object-oriented databases allow users to check out objects for several days or even weeks. These are called *long-lasting transactions*. Object-oriented databases also enable users to check out several objects at the same time. Because long lasting transactions and multiple-object check outs may decrease the concurrency of objects, some object-oriented DBMSs support optimistic approaches for concurrency control. Under an optimistic policy, two conflicting transactions are compared and then their serial ordering is determined. As long as the database is able to serialize them, the transactions can continue.

- **Constraints.** Business rules and security constraints can be enforced on data in the database. In an object-oriented database, private methods enforce business rules and security constraints. Because methods may be written in a general-purpose programming language, constraints of arbitrary complexity can be specified.
- **Backup and Recovery.** Data in the database are backed up and can be restored if necessary.

Many object-oriented DBMSs also support SQL so that users can access objects just as if they were relational tables. Object-oriented DBMSs also support operations specific to object classes, something that traditional relational databases cannot do.

10.2   Object-oriented Design Encourages Reuse

When developing new applications, programmers using traditional programming languages such as C or Pascal typically begin with a clean sheet of paper, develop a design, and then implement the code. Object-oriented programmers, on the other hand, typically search through existing object-class libraries, looking for object classes that perform functions similar to those in the new application, and then copy and modify those object classes. One major goal of object-oriented design is reuse. Programmers are also encouraged to reuse objects through the use of the inheritance property of object-oriented programming languages. Because object classes can inherit both structure and methods, programmers are able to reuse parts of existing object classes and incrementally add additional structure and methods.

However, some designers suffer from the "lose sight of the forest for the trees" syndrome by concentrating on the individual object classes and losing sight of the overall application. Modifying and debugging applications can be difficult because of the distributed nature of the application; making a minor change to one object class may affect other object classes in unsuspected ways.

Other disadvantages of switching to object-oriented programming languages and DBMSs include the lack of international standards, the cost of retraining existing programmers, and conversion costs from existing relational DBMS technology.

Despite these drawbacks, application developers are beginning to use object-oriented databases to implement new databases, especially in areas requiring complex data structures, such as engineering design, expert systems, and multimedia applications. However, traditional database applications, especially those involving financial data, remain implemented using relational databases.

10.3 A Standard Object-oriented Data Model Is Emerging

The Object-oriented Database System Manifesto, published in 1989 by a group of experts in object-oriented DBMSs, describes a set of features desirable in an object-oriented DBMS. These features include the following:

1. *Complex objects.* Basic objects can be combined into complex objects.

2. *Object identity.* Each data object must have a unique identifier.

3. *Encapsulation.* The data and the implementation of its operations are hidden from the user.

4. *Classes.* The common features of a set of objects with the same characteristics are specified.

5. *Inheritance.* A subclass will inherit attributes and methods from its superclass.

6. *Polymorphism.* The implementation of the operation depends on the object to which it is applied.

7. *Computationally complete.* Any computational function can be expressed in the data-manipulation language.

8. *Extensibility.* New classes can be added to the system-supplied classes.

9. *Data persistence.* Data must remain available after the application that created them has terminated.

10. *Very large databases.* Store data on secondary storage in such a way that large databases can be supported.

11. *Concurrency.* Multiple users can use the database at the same time.

12. *Recovery.* Recovery mechanisms enable the database to be restored in the event of software or hardware failures.

13. *Ad hoc queries.* Users may specify requests in a high-level, application-independent form.

In 1990 the Object Management Group (OMG), an international software in-dustry consortium, published architecture and interface specifications for object-oriented languages, systems, databases, and application frameworks. In 1993, the Object Database Management Group published a standard consisting of an object model, object definition language, object query language, and two language bind-ings (C++ and SMALLTALK™). However, today a database implemented in one commercially available object-oriented DBMS cannot be easily ported to another object-oriented DBMS. Each object-oriented database management system uses different approaches for representing objects and organizing data.

Several approaches for object-oriented data-manipulation languages have been used by various object-oriented DBMSs:

- *Extend a programming language.* An object-oriented programming lan-guage is extended to describe data in an object-oriented database. Any objects in the program space can be made persistent by placing them into the database. Any operation that could be applied to a nonpersistent object can be applied to the object after it becomes persistent. For example, the Servio Corporation has extended Smalltalk into their proprietary language called OPAL for the GemStone object-oriented DBMS.

- *Extend a data model.* An existing data model (such as the relational data model or the entity-relationship data model) is extended with object-ori-ented features, including inheritance, polymorphism, and encapsulation. A DBMS is designed and implemented that supports the extended data model and the corresponding object-oriented features. For example, SQL has been extended into a new form called Object SQL.

- *Provide extendible object-oriented DBMS libraries.* Add class libraries to existing object-oriented programming languages to support aggregation, transactions, concurrency, security, and the like. For example, Ontos, Inc., provides a library of classes for C++ that programmers use to access the Ontos® object-oriented DBMS

Most object-oriented DBMS vendors have used the third approach. When us-ing libraries, the class descriptions of an object's attributes and methods are stored in a class library that is separate from the database, not stored in the database itself. Us-ers must always use the class library to access data in these object-oriented DBMSs.

To be classified as object-oriented, a DBMS must support the creation of new classes of objects. Any DBMS that supports only built-in objects is not really object oriented, but instead is said to be *object based*. Object-based DBMSs are not as flex-ible as object oriented databases because they are limited to the types of object class-es that they support. However, object-based DBMSs may be very efficient because they are carefully designed and implemented to optimize object classes for a specific domain. Object-based databases are sometimes sold as specialized tools in areas such as CASE (computer-aided software engineering), CAD (computer-aided design), and expert systems.

Commercially available object-oriented DBMSs include the following:

- GemStone® from Servio Corporation is based on SMALLTALK.
- Ontos® from Ontos, Inc., is based on C++.
- O2® from O2 Technology is based on O2C.
- ObjectStore from Object Design is based on C++.
- Objectivity/DB™ from Objectivity, Inc., is based on C++.
- Versant® from Versant Object Technology is based on C++.

10.4 Object-oriented DBMSs Support Versions and Configurations

Each time a user modifies an object, a new *version* of the object is created. A version history is a set of versions of an object, with each version linked to its preceding version. Some version histories are sequential, in which one or more users sequentially modify an object. Occasionally, a branching version occurs, in which two users update the same object at about the same time, resulting in a branch in the version history. Branching versions are useful when two or more users must work independently on revisions that involve some of the same objects. However, eventually the users must merge their work and create a single new version of the object that supersedes their separate, branched versions. Version histories may contain both branch and merge points.

Versions may be implemented by either of the following approaches:

- *Chaining each new version of an object to its old version.*
- *Appending a time stamp to the object identifier.* A fully specified reference to an object must then consist of both an object identifier and a time stamp. (If branching is permitted, then additional ancestral path information is needed for a fully specified reference.)

A *configuration* is a collection of versions of the objects in the database that are mutually consistent. Configurations are themselves special objects, with an object identifier, name, and other attributes. When the user opens a database, the user may open any of several existing configurations, such as the *previously released*, the *most recently released*, or any of several *working* configurations.

Object-oriented DBMSs differ in their management of versions and configurations. Some leave it to the user to name and maintain versions and configurations. Others manage configurations and versions on behalf of users.

10.5 Distributed Object-oriented DBMSs Provide Flexibility

Each approach to distributed DBMS described in Chapter 1 can be applied to object-oriented DBMS.

10.5.1 Data Extraction

The data-extraction process consists of the following two steps:

1. Copy the object classes from the source database to the target database.

2. Copy the object instances from the source database to the target database. The target object-oriented DBMS will assign a new, unique identifier to each object instance.

10.5.2 Remote Access and Gateways

In object-oriented DBMS, remote access consists of sending a message to a remote object-oriented DBMS and receiving messages from that remote object-oriented DBMS. This implies that the message system for each object-oriented DBMS must be able to support messages to and from foreign systems. A gateway may be needed to modify messages to reflect differences in the unique identifiers, message format, and data types of the respective DBMSs.

10.5.3 Loosely-coupled and Tightly-coupled Object-oriented DBMSs

Both loosely-coupled and tightly-coupled object-oriented DBMSs have an integrated class hierarchy that describes objects in each local DBMS. The loosely-coupled DBMS allows users and objects to use either a local class hierarchy or an integrated class hierarchy. In a tightly-coupled DBMS, users and objects use the integrated class hierarchy.

Constructing an integrated class hierarchy is similar to integrating the relational schemas described in Section 4.4. The database administrator determines the relationship between each pair of classes:

- *One class is logically contained in the other.* Both object classes are placed in the integrated class hierarchy, with the "contained" class a subclass of the "containing" class.

- *The two classes are equivalent.* The two classes are integrated into a single class and placed into the appropriate position in the class hierarchy.

- *The two classes overlap.* Three classes are integrated into the class hierarchy: one class contains the common attributes and methods of the two classes, and the other two classes contain the leftover attributes and methods of each of the two classes.

- *The two classes are disjoint.* Both classes are inserted into the hierarchy without modification.

The final class hierarchy should be examined and minor adjustments made. For example, if all the subclasses of a class contain a common attribute or a common method, that attribute or method should be factored out of the subclasses and placed into the containing class.

Unfortunately, some major problems occur when objects themselves are distributed.

- Object allocation and replication is difficult because complex objects may need to be partitioned across sites.

- Automatic query optimization is possible for distributed relational systems because the optimizer takes advantage of the semantics of the standardized SQL language. Without a standard language, the optimizer may be unable, for example, to, replace a single operation by two equivalent operations for execution on different sites. Automatic query optimization may be impossible for distributed object-oriented DBMS unless the object classes reveal their methods to the optimizer for analysis.

10.5.4 Object-oriented Database Servers

Database administrators may integrate the class hierarchies of multiple object-oriented DBMSs and construct a single integrated class hierarchy that is placed onto a server. All the object instances are migrated to the object-oriented database on the server. Many of the problems that plague distributed object-oriented DBMSs are avoided. There is no allocation of objects that span computers, and there is no need for distributed optimization. If the object-oriented server supports concurrency control, versions, and configurations, several users and applications can share the objects.

10.6 Distributed Objects Support Distributed Computation

In object-oriented programming, an application consist of several objects. In theory, objects can be placed on different computers, resulting in a distributed application. We can envision multiple objects on different computers, each executing their individual methods and sending messages to each other. Object distribution enables parallel computations by objects on different computers, resulting in faster executing applications.

We can conceive of objects migrating from a computer with several active objects to another computer with fewer active objects. The application periodically reorganizes itself to take advantage of available computing resources.

To date, little work has been done on distributed computation within distributed object-oriented DBMSs. This promising area of research may one day result in powerful processing of complex objects.

Chapter Summary

Object-oriented database management systems support an approach for describing and managing data that is compatible with recent object-oriented design methodologies and programming languages. Object-oriented databases include object classes and instances. Distributed object-oriented database management systems provide the advantages of object-oriented programming, but lack automatic techniques for data allocation and query optimization.

Further Reading

Cattell, R. G. G., *Object Data Management: Object-oriented and Extended Relational Database Systems*, Addison-Wesley, Reading, MA, 1991. Describes database systems that manipulate objects, including object-oriented and extended relational database systems. This book compares object-oriented systems with conventional systems and shows the range of applications object-oriented database systems now make possible.

Cattell, R. G. G., *The Object Database Standard: ODMG-93 Release 1.1,* Morgan Kaufmann, San Francisco, CA, 1993. Describes the object model, object definition language, object query language, and bindings to C++ and Smalltalk. More chapters may be added at a future date for other language bindings. Suggests a unified object model for sharing data programming languages as well as a common query language.

Zdonik, S. B., and D. Maier, eds., *Readings in Object-oriented Database Systems*, Morgan Kaufmann, San Francisco, CA, 1989. Collection of important papers in the area of advanced database systems. The editors provide good summaries of the important issues for each group of papers.

Communication Subsystem

This appendix discusses the following:

- Wide-area networks
- Local-area networks
- How the communication system affects distributed DBMSs

The type of communication systems and their characteristics, such as delay time, cost, and reliability, need to be considered when designing distributed transactions. If there is no query optimizer, then the programmer must carefully design the distributed transaction to minimize the communication costs and delay times. If a query optimizer is available, then it generates the distributed transaction that minimizes the communication costs and delay times.

In Figure A.1, the communication subsystem is highlighted. A distributed DBMS uses the communication subsystem to transfer requests and data among the distributed transaction execution manager and one or more local transaction managers located at different sites. Communication systems are often classified as either of two types: (1) *local-area networks,* which connect computers in the same building or computers in multiple buildings geographically close to each other and (2) *wide-area networks* (also called long-haul networks), which connect computers located in different cities, states, and countries.

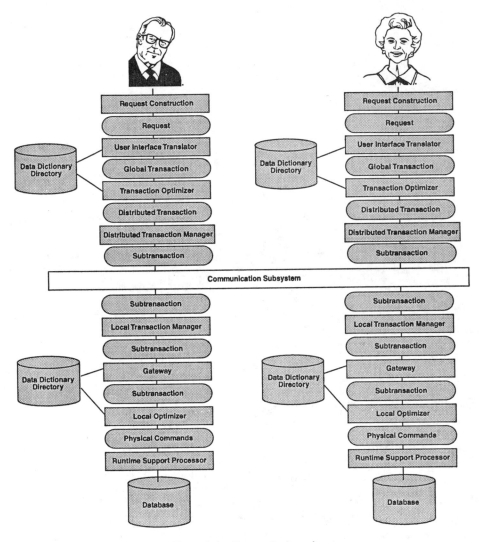

Figure A.1   Communication subsystem

A.1   Wide-area Networks Support Communication

Wide-area networks support either point-to-point or broadcast topologies.

Broadcast Topologies. Radio, satellite, and microwave broadcasting channels are the basis for broadcast topologies. In this design, a single communication channel is shared by all sites. Every site broadcasts messages directly to every other site. Each site examines each received message to determine if the message is addressed to itself.

Point-to-point Topologies. Wire or cable are the basis for point-to-point or store-and-forward topologies . Examples of point-to-point topologies are illustrated in Figure A.2. *Star networks* [Figure A.2(a)] are commonly used to connect several remote computers to a central headquarters computer. Local processing is performed at each remote computer, with results transmitted to the headquarters for final integration. However, if the central computer fails, then the entire network is disrupted. The central computer may also be a bottleneck to communication among multiple remote sites. *Tree networks* [Figure A.2(b)] are useful for connecting computers in field offices to computers in regional offices and regional office computers to the headquarters computer. The *meshed network* [Figure A.2(c)] provides the most reliability, but is also the costliest due to the large number of direct connections. The majority of topologies fall into the *irregular network* category [Figure A.2(d)], the category for topologies that don't fit into any of the first three categories.

Although some organizations can afford their own dedicated networks, most organizations rent or subscribe to public networks. Public telephone networks provide most of the long-distance data communication services. Because it is clearly impossible to provide a direct link between each pair of telephones in the world, a number of intermediate switches are used to provide the interconnection between two telephones. *Circuit switching* is frequently used for voice communication. In circuit switching, a path between the two telephones is established and dedicated during the

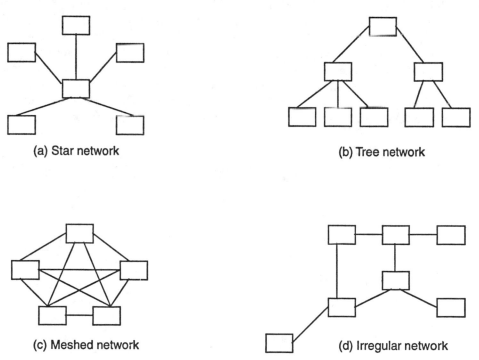

(a) Star network

(b) Tree network

(c) Meshed network

(d) Irregular network

Figure A.2   Point-to-point topologies

complete conversation. *Packet switching* is often used for data communications. A message is broken into several packets that are transmitted separately, possibly over different paths. Software at the destination reassembles the complete message from the received packets. Packet switching provides better channel utilization because each channel can be shared by multiple conversations. Packet switching may also permit parallel transmission of data and reduce the total data transmission time.

A wide-area communication system is built in a layered fashion with well-defined set of interfaces between adjacent layers and protocols among corresponding layers at different sites. An understanding of the concepts of *layers*, *interfaces*, and *protocols* is necessary to understand communication systems. We will illustrate these concepts with the familiar paradigm of sending a letter. When John wishes to send a letter to Sally, he first writes the letter and gives it to his secretary. John's secretary then places the letter into an envelope, writes Sally's address on the outside of the envelope, and drops the letter into a postbox. Post office employees physically move the envelope from John's postbox to Sally's postbox. Sally's secretary removes the envelope from Sally's postbox, removes the letter from the envelope, and passes the letter to Sally, who reads the letter. Figure A.3 illustrates the three *layers* involved: John and Sally at the top level, their secretaries at the middle level, and their respective mailboxes at the lower level.

Between each pair of adjacent levels there is an *interface*. The interface between John and his secretary is sheet of paper with the message to Sally written on it. The interface between John's secretary and John's postbox is an envelope with Sally's address on it. In general, each level accepts information from an adjacent level in some prespecified format. Information at one layer is encapsulated within information at a lower level. In Figure A.3, the letter is written on sheets of paper that are in turn placed into an envelope. (An individual writes a letter on paper; paper is the data unit passed between an individual and his or her secretary. Secretaries place paper into envelopes; the envelope is the data unit passed between secretaries and postboxes.)

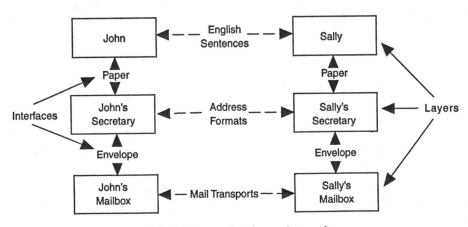

Figure A.3   Layers, interface, and protocols

Entities at the same level interact with each other using agreed-upon *protocols*. John writes his message in English, a language he knows that Sally understands. John's secretary writes Sally's name and address and John's name and address on the envelop in a standard format. Sally's secretary verifies that the letter is intended for Sally before opening the envelope and giving its contents to Sally. At the lowest level the protocol describes how the envelope is moved between mailboxes.

By the late 1970s, it was generally recognized that a common model of distributed data communications would be necessary for the development of distributed systems. In 1977, the International Organization Standardization (ISO) Technical Committee 97 (Computers and Information Processing) created Subcommittee 16 to define protocols for Open Systems Interconnection (OSI). The Subcommittee ISO/TC97/SC16 proposed the "Reference Model of Open Systems Interconnection" in 1978. From this proposal, the Draft International Standard 7498 "Data Processing Open Systems Interconnection Basic Reference Model" was produced in 1981.

The ISO/OSI architecture specifies that a network is to be built in a layered fashion similar in style to the above example of John sending mail to Sally. However, the basic reference model consists of seven layers, not three. At the top resides the application layer, which is part of the information processing system. In a distributed DBMS, the application layer at one site is the distributed transaction manager, and the application layer at another site is the local transaction manager. At the bottom of the reference model is the physical layer, which is concerned with the physical interconnection. The other five layers—the presentation, session, transport, network, and datalink control layers—bridge the gap between the physical media and the application process.

Between each layer is an interface. This allows for the design of each layer as a separate subsystem, which only has to meet the interface characteristics. Each layer may pass data upward to the layer above it and downward to the layer below it. Between the corresponding layers at different sites, protocols are defined to specify how the two layers at different sites present messages to each other.

Figure A.4 illustrates the ISO/OSI layer architecture for a distributed execution manager that exchanges messages between a distributed execution manager and a local execution manager. Suppose that the distributed execution manager sends messages to the local execution manager. The distributed transaction manager passes the messages to the presentation layer at its site. As the message moves downward, it is modified by adding headers and trailers, as well as redundant bits for error detection and correction. At the lowest level, the messages are transported to the other site. As the message moves upward toward the local execution manager, the added bits and fields are stripped off. The original message is passed to the local transaction manager. Responses from local transaction managers are similarly passed to lower levels, transported to the site of the distributed execution manager, passed upward, and delivered to the distributed execution manager.

Each layer of the ISO/OSI provides services for the layer above it.

Layer 1: The *physical layer* maintains a transparent flow of raw bits across a communication channel. This layer addresses physical problems such as the type of transmission channel to use (twisted wire, coaxial cable, or other) and the operation mode (simplex, half-duplex, or full duplex). The design issues deal with electrical, mechanical, and procedural interfacing to the communication channel. This layer protocol establishes, maintains, and releases the physical means of bit transmission for layer 2 (data-link) entities. It does not make any difference how the bits are grouped or what they mean at this level. Perhaps the best known physical layer protocols are RS-232 and RS-499.

Layer 2: The *data-link layer* provides functional and procedural means to establish, maintain, and release data-link connections among layer 3 (network) entities.

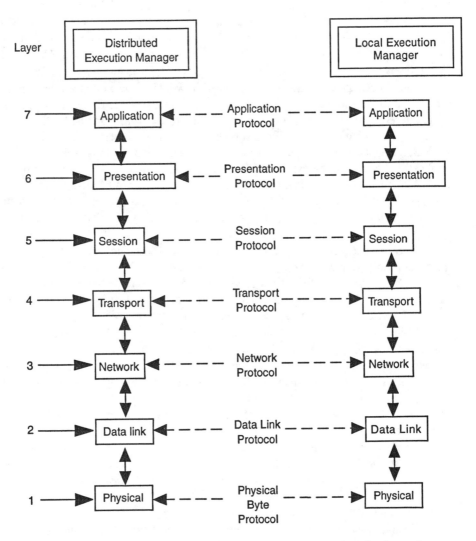

Figure A.4   ISO/OSI architecture for a distributed execution manager and two local execution managers

It transforms streams of bits into logical blocks or frames that are delineated by a start-frame and an end-frame delimiter (bit stuffing), transmits the frames, and then reconstructs the bit streams. The data-link layer protocol detects and corrects errors that may occur during transmission. When an error is detected, either (1) error-correcting codes are used to correct the error or (2) the source can be asked to retransmit the message. One of the most widely used data-link protocols is the high-level data-link control or HDLC. Other examples of data-link layer protocols are IBM's SDLC, the X.25 LAPB, and ANSI's ADCCP.

Layer 3: The *network layer* establishes, maintains, and terminates network connections among the layer 4 (transport) entities. This set of protocols also provides for network connections between the systems containing communicating applications. This layer is responsible for intra- or internetwork data routing and switching. Perhaps the best know network layer protocol is CCITT's IP and X.25.

Layer 4: The *transport layer* provides network-independent and reliable transport services to the layer 5 (session layer) entities. As such, a protocol at this layer logically connects two session entities and relieves them of any details concerning the detection of lost or out of order session data. Examples of transport layer protocols are the Department of Defense's TCP and Xerox's ITP.

Layer 5: The *session layer* provides services to cooperating layer 6 (presentation) entities to establish a session connection for a dialog and for data exchange. A session connection is a logical relationship between two presentation entities for the duration of the session. In many networks, the transport layer connects the hosts, while the session layer connects the processes. A session might be used to transfer a file between two computers or to log into a remote time-sharing system. Complex protocols may be implemented to guarantee that each participant is properly authenticated and to agree on whether the communication is to be half-duplex or full duplex.

Layer 6: The *presentation layer* services allow the information to be transformed for presentation to the layer 7 (application) entities. This layer also makes some transformations, such as text compression and encryption, before information is sent to the session layer. Conversion between character codes, such as EBCDIC to ASCII, and conversion of file formats may occur at this level.

Layer 7: The *application layer* provides a set of services that enables users of the communications system to communicate. For distributed DBMS, this layer contains the distributed transaction manager at one site and several local transaction managers at other sites. Protocols at this level include distributed execution, concurrency control, and commitment protocols.

A.2   Local-area Networks Support Communication

Local-area networks are used to provide high-bandwidth communication over coaxial cables, twisted-wire pairs, or optical fibers. Local-area networks fall into two basic topologies, ring networks and bus networks.

Ring Networks. Figure A.5 illustrates a ring network. Each site is connected to the ring network via a ring interface. Each ring interface receives messages from one of its neighbors and retransmits the message to its other neighboring ring interface. If a ring interface detects that a message header contains the address for its site, it copies the message for delivery to the distributed execution manager or local execution manager. When a ring interface receives a message that it originally sent, it does not retransmit the message; instead, it reports to the distributed transaction manager or local transaction manager at its site that the message was received.

Bus Networks. Figure A.6 illustrates a network bus in which a common channel is used to transmit data among computers. In *carrier sense multiple access* (CSMA), each site listens to the bus for messages to itself. If it wants to transmit, it waits until it detects no activity on the bus and then places its message on the network. In *carrier sense multiple access with collision detection* (CSMA/CD), a site keeps listening to the bus to determine if two sites are trying to transmit messages concurrently. If this occurs, both sites stop transmitting; each waits a random amount of time before retransmitting.

Recently, the use of radio and infrared light for transmissions among sites located in the same building has lead to a wireless local-area network. While these networks are not able to support the same bandwidth as hardwired networks, they are less expensive to install.

The Institute of Electrical and Electronics Engineers (IEEE) Committee No. 802 is leading the standardization effort for local-area networks. The three layers of the IEEE 802 local-area network standard are the physical layer, the medium access control layer, and the logical link control layer. The latter two layers correspond to the data-link layer of the ISO/OSI architecture.

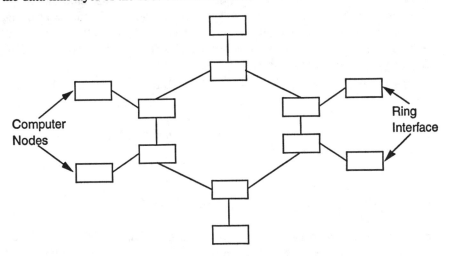

Figure A.5   Ring network

A.3 The Communication System Affects Distributed DBMSs

Three aspects of the communication system affect the execution of the distributed execution plan:

1. *Delay time*. This is the time between when a message is sent from its source site and the time it is delivered at its target site. Delay time estimates are used by the transaction optimizer when it generates a distributed transaction.

2. *Communication costs*. The expense of leasing, renting, or buying the communication channels should be factored into the cost of executing distributed queries.

3. *Reliability*. Designers should consider the disruption to an enterprise of not being able to use the distributed database management system in the event that the communication system is not usable for long periods of time. Short periods of nonreliability can be tolerated by requesting source sites to retransmit messages that are not received correctly or not received at all.

Three components in a distributed database management system are directly affected by the communication system.

Transaction Optimizer. Because communication expenses are greater in a wide-area network, the query optimizer needs to minimize the number, size and distance of transmissions in the distributed transaction. If the transmission costs between pairs of sites are different, the transaction optimizer should also choose sites for local processing that are connected by inexpensive paths, as well as choose paths with minimal expense. In general, the transaction optimizer should take advantage of the network topology when generating distributed transactions.

Distributed Transaction Manager and Local Transaction Managers. These two components must be able to send and receive messages using the communication subsystems. These two components should be designed to interact with the highest levels of the communication system. It may be desirable to implement the

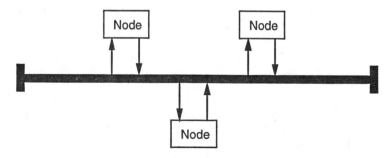

Figure A.6   Bus network

concurrency control and commit protocols to take advantage of characteristics of the communication subsystem.

One technique to minimize the number of messages is to transmit multiple types of messages in the same transmission. For example, the "Ready to commit" message from the local transaction manager can be concatenated with the data obtained from a component database by its runtime support processor. Another technique used to shorten messages is to compress data before transmission and decompress data after they are received.

Further Readings

Ceri, Stefano, and Giuseppe Pelagatti, *Distributed Databases Principles and Systems*, McGraw-Hill, New York, 1984. Chapter 3 deals with computer networks.

Ozsu, M. Tamer, and Patrick Valduriez, *Principles of Distributed Database Systems*, Prentice Hall, Upper Saddle River, NJ, 1991. Theory, algorithms, and methods that underlie distributed database management systems.

Tannenbaum, Andrew S., *Computer Networks*, Prentice Hall, Upper Saddle River, NJ, 1981. Standard text for computer networks.

B

Selecting a Commercial Distributed DBMS

This appendix presents checklists for the following:

- The basic concepts a DBA should understand
- The DBA's objectives
- The specific data requirements for each component of a distributed DBMS
- How to evaluate commercially available distributed DBMS

B.1 DBAs Should Understand Basic Concepts

After reading this book, you should have a basic understanding of federated and distributed database management systems. However, no book can contain the latest trends and information about distributed DBMSs. Sources of current information about commercially available distributed DBMSs are available in the form of seminars from both vendors of distributed DBMSs and noted experts in the distributed DBMS field. Software review services, such as Datapro, Auerbach, and Software Digest, provide information. Database publications such as *Data Based Advisor*,

Database Newsletter, and *Database Programming and Design,* in addition to the more general computer magazines such as *PC World,* and *Byte,* contain up-to-date information about commercially available distributed DBMSs. User-group meetings and visits with other organizations who use distributed DBMSs will also be useful.

This appendix presents a recipe for choosing a distributed DBMS. Choosing a distributed DBMS is much like choosing any type of software system. The basic stages are as follows:

1. Set objectives.
2. Specify requirements.
3. Evaluate commercially available systems.
4. Make final recommendation, purchase, and install the system.

These four tasks are discussed in detail with respect to distributed databases in the remainder of this appendix.

B.2   DBAs Set Objectives

B.2.1 Identify the Problem to Be Solved

Distributed databases are used to solve either or both of two very different problems:

- Does your organization have islands of unreachable information that need to be logically integrated into a continent of shared information?
- Does your organization have a centralized database that needs to be distributed across multiple computers?

If the integration of multiple islands of unreachable information is the problem to be solved, then use a bottom-up development process similar to that described in Section 3.3.1. If you need to distribute an existing centralized database, then use a top-down approach similar to that described in Section 3.3.2.

B.2.2 Determine Objectives

How will the distributed DBMS be used? Keep in mind, the more objectives that must be satisfied, the fewer are the commercially available systems that will meet all the objectives. In general, the more objectives that must be satisfied, the more expensive the resulting system will be. In Chapter 1 we identified the following potential objectives of distributed DBMSs. Determine which of the following objectives must be satisfied by a DBMS to be installed in your enterprise. These objects may apply to a centralized DBMS as well as to a distributed DBMS.

- Multiple interfaces
What human interfaces are needed?
Is an API needed?

- Security enforcement policies and mechanisms

- Business rule enforcement policies and mechanisms

- Concurrency transparency

- Transaction processing

- Backup and recovery of data

B.3   DBAs Identify Specific Requirements

Armed with a subset of the above objectives, determine which of the following requirements for sharing data (discussed in Section 1.3) are applicable to your enterprise?

- Users can access data from multiple databases.

- Users must obtain up-to-date results.

- The distributed DBMS hides data location and replication from users.

- The distributed DBMS translates queries on behalf of users.

- The distributed DBMS merges data from multiple databases.

- Transactions enforce business rules involving multiple databases.

- The distributed DBMS supports coordinated commitment and recovery.

Choose a general approach for sharing data: data extraction, remote access, gateway, loosely-coupled DBMS, or tightly-coupled DBMS. Select the corresponding architectures in Figures 2-10 and 2-12 through 2-14. You will want to select a distributed DBMS that supports the features of each component of the architecture you selected.

For each component required by your distributed DBMS, develop answers to the set of questions outlined in the following corresponding subsections.

B.3.1 Request Constructor and User Interface Translator

Which of the following user interface styles will your users need?

- API for use by programmers to write applications

- SQL for experienced users to enter keyword-oriented commands

- Fill-in forms for novice users to enter data and formulate simple patterns for retrieval commands

- Natural language interface for knowledgeable domain users to formulate commands
- Direct manipulation and window interfaces for novice or occasional users
- Voice recognition and voice synthesizer for visually impaired or for users whose hands and/or eyes are busy with other tasks
- Report generators and fourth generation languages for generating commonly used business applications

What is the form of the global transaction it produces?

- SQL
- SQL extended to describe transactions in which a transaction may involve one or more SQL commands against multiple databases
- SQL extended to support input and output of data for user
- Nonprocedural language other than SQL
- Procedural language

What types of business rules can it enforce?

- Range checks
- Enumerated value checks
- Type checks
- Entity constraint (unique value of primary key)
- Referential integrity constraints (foreign key constraint)
- Null values permitted or prohibited
- Cardinality constraints (maximum number of rows in a table)
- Permission constraints (grant and revoke authority to other users)
- Other

Does the system support standard SQL?
Does the system support an API?

- Into which programming languages is SQL embedded (and does the programming language require the use of a precompiler to process the SQL requests)?
- Is there a call level interface and what programming languages can use the call level interface?
- Does the system support cursors (objects that enable the application program to access and manipulate sets of records one at a time)?
- Does the DBMS support stored procedures (SQL requests that can be executed on demand)?

Does the DBMS support recursive queries? (A recursive query involves a single table in which the foreign key references the primary key of the same table, for example, a query against a *ReportTo* table to generate an organization chart.)

B.3.2 Transaction optimizer

What is the goal of the transaction optimizer?
• Minimize response time
• Maximize throughput
• Minimize the cost of processing at one or more sites
• Minimize the number of communication transmissions
• Minimize the amount of data transmitted

Which types of optimization are performed?
• Heuristic based
• Cost based

How may the optimization algorithm be extended?
• User may specify parameters that affect how the optimization may behave.
• Programmers may modify or extend algorithms by writing code.

Does the distributed query optimizer consider differences in capabilities of different component DBMSs?

When does optimization occur?
• Runtime
• Compile time
• Both

Can only selected transactions be optimized?
• Which classes of transactions are optimized?
• Can the DBA turn the optimizer on and off?

What types of transparency are supported?
• Location
• Replication
• Fragmentation
• Data model used by the local DBMS

Does the optimizer support distributed updates?

• No updates in a distributed request
• Update only a single component database
• Update data in multiple component databases
• Distributed joins

B.3.3 Distributed Transaction Manager

To what communication subsystem does the distributed transaction manager interface?
What control model does it use?

• Master–slave
• Triangular
• Hierarchical
• Other

What type of distributed concurrency control does it support?

• Locking with deadlock prevention
• Locking with deadlock detection
• Time stamps
• Optimistic
• Other

What is the locking level of granularity?

• Data block or page
• Table
• Record or tuple
• Field within a record or tuple

What type of commit protocols does it support?

• None
• One phase
• Two phase
• Other

Does it support data replication? How is data captured at the primary copy and applied to the secondary copy?

• Data driven
• Timer Driven
• Application driven

What type of distributed backup and recovery does it support?

- None
- Transaction log
- Transaction log with quiet points
- Transaction log with checkpoints
- Other

What type of replication control does it enforce?

- Locking
- Time stamping

B.3.4 Local Transaction Manager

Is it compatible with the global execution manager?
Is it compatible with each of your existing component DBMSs?

B.3.5 Gateway (One for Each Type of Component DBMS)

Can it translate each subtransaction to a form executable by the component DBMS?

Does it support updates as well as retrievals?

Can it translate data and error messages from the component DBMS into the format needed by other modules higher in the architecture?

B.3.6 Local Optimizer

How effectively does it hide the access methods of the database from higher-level modules?

Can it generate physical commands for the range of access structures supported by the runtime support processor?

B.3.7 Runtime Support Processor

Can it support multiple users?

Are its concurrency control mechanisms compatible with those of the distributed transaction manager?

Are its backup and recovery mechanisms compatible with those of the distributed transaction manager?

Can it support temporary tables (needed in some cases for distributed queries)?

Does it support a variety of file structures and access methods?

- Hashed indexes
- Clustered indexes

- Clustered storage of multiple tables

Does it support performance monitoring tools?

B.3.8 Vendor Support

Is there a local representative who can answer your questions?

Is there a technical support group you can reach by telephone, fax, or electronic mail who is able to answer your questions? What is the cost of this support? Is it available 24-hours a day?

Is documentation available and easy to read and understand?

Will the vendor continue to enhance and evolve the product? Will the vendor provide upgrades?

For how long is free support available and is there an option for purchasing support after the end of the free support?

What is the product quality warranty?

B.3.9 Training

Are training classes readily available?
Are on-line tutorials available?
Are workbooks, video tutorials, and hands-on tutorials available?

B.3.10 DBA Tools

Which of the following DBA tasks are supported by tools?
- Schema translation
- Schema integration
- Data fragmentation
- Data allocation and replication
- Data dictionary directory management
- Backup and recovery
- Monitoring
- Journaling and auditing
- Performance analysis
- Utilities for recovery from workstation failures
- Utilities for recovery from server failures
- Utilities for automated backups

- Utilities for establishing user groups and granting them privileges
- Auditing and journaling user actions
- Other

B.3.11 Efficiency

How does this system compare with others using standard benchmarks?

How does this system compare with others when executing your critical applications?

What is the mean time between failure of the system?

How much effort is required to install the system?

B.4 DBAs Evaluate Commercially Available Distributed DBMSs

Armed with the above set of questions, you now have a set of criteria for evaluating alternative distributed DBMSs. A three-phase approach seems reasonable.

- *Phase 1*. Identify likely candidate distributed DBMSs. Use mandatory criteria to filter out distributed DBMSs that clearly will not satisfy your needs. For example, consider only distributed DBMSs that can execute on your current hardware with your current operating systems and communication systems.
- *Phase 2*. Perform a detailed evaluation, matching your requirements to the capabilities of each candidate distributed DBMS. Because some criteria are more important than others, assign a weight to each criterion.

For each set of questions, try to obtain answers by one or more of the following methods:

- Review literature supplied by the vendor of a candidate DBMS.
- Review articles and summaries in the trade press.
- Ask questions of the sales representatives of the candidate DBMS vendor.
- Ask actual users of the candidate DBMS.

Score each candidate with respect to each criterion. Sum the products of the criterion weight times the criterion score. Only the candidates with the highest grand totals advance to phase 3.

- *Phase 3*. Perform a hands-on evaluation of the final candidates. Nothing tells the true capabilities (and drawbacks) like taking a "test drive." Actually convert some of your exiting databases and port some of your critical applications to the candidate distributed DBMS and see how it works. Keep track of the effort to do this evaluation. Extrapolate this information to estimate the expense of converting all your databases and applications to the candidate distributed DBMS.

B.5   DBAs Follow Pragmatic Device

Now the real work begins. After purchasing, the distributed DBMS must be installed and the data migrated to the distributed DBMS. The distributed DBMS is then placed into production and continually fine-tuned so that it works efficiently. A wise DBA carefully plans these activities well in advance, with plenty of time reserved to handle the unexpected.

The initial purchase cost of the distributed DBMS is probably the least important factor. The cost of conversion will likely be greater than the initial purchase cost. The objective is to select a distributed DBMS that you can live with for a long time. You will likely get locked in to the distributed DBMS as applications are set in place and people get used to it. Change will not be easy.

There is no best distributed DBMS for all applications. There may be a best one for your set of applications. Choose carefully, because you and your enterprise will need to live with your choice for a long time.

Appendix Summary

The process of selecting a distributed DBMS is similar to selecting other software systems. You should set objectives, specify requirements, evaluate commercially available systems, and make final recommendations. The evaluation step should occur in three phases: Identify likely candidate distributed DBMSs. Perform a detailed evaluation, matching your requirements to the capabilities of each candidate distributed DBMS. Perform a hands-on evaluation of the final candidates. Effort is necessary to make a good choice that will last for a long time.

Glossary

after images   Value of a data item after updating. Used by database recovery mechanism algorithms to restore lost data.

aggregation   Grouping several data items into a composite data item. For example, the birth year, birth month, and birth day can be aggregated into birth date.

allocation   The assignment of files or file fragments for storage in a local DBMS.

anchor   A subset of a document that participates in a relationship with another document. Hyperlinks connect two or more anchors within documents.

application programmer interface (API)   Function names, parameters, and return codes used by a programmer to write applications that invoke the functions provided by a computer system.

atomicity   A property of a transaction that guarantees that either the transaction is entirely processed or none of its processing is reflected in the database.

backup and recovery mechanisms   Facilities that enable users to make copies of their databases and database changes and to restore a database from the copied data if the database is damaged or lost.

before images   Value of a data item before updating. Used by database recovery algorithms to restore lost data.

binary large object (BLOB)   A data type that contains a large string of binary bits, possibly representing a textual document, bit map image, audio or video clip.

bulletin board server   A server containing a database with messages about general announcements and news.

business rules   Rules about the values of data that the database must satisfy.

call level interface   A collection of data structures and functions that a programmer may embed into a program in order to access the database.

centralized database   A database that resides on a single computer and is managed by a single DBMS.

checkpoint   A point in time when the identifiers of active transactions are stored for possible use during database recovery.

client   Hardware that consumes services provided by a server and provides the user interface for the end user.

client-server architecture   A cooperative processing environment that provides a single-system image to each user. The architecture consists of multiple servers which provide services upon request by one or more clients.

CODASYL (network) data model   A data model in which records are organized as a network structure.

command router A simplified transaction optimizer that routes a transaction to the DBMS and returns the response to the user.

commit protocol Protocols for exchange of messages among multiple processors to achieve a state in which all processors have made changes to the database permanent.

communication subsystem Software and hardware that transmit messages among the distributed transaction manager and one or more local managers.

compression Process for reducing the size of the representation of information.

concurrency transparency Concurrency transparency allows multiple users to use the DBMS at the same time and not worry about updating the same data item at the same time.

concurrent transactions Transactions whose executions overlap in time.

conflicting transactions Transactions whose executions overlap in time and in which one transaction needs to modify a data item that another transaction needs to reference.

consistency (1) A database satisfies business rules about database values. (2) A property of a transaction that converts the database from one consistent state to another.

content server A server that provides users with information from several sources, including broadcast news feeds, public databases, and optical and magnetic disks delivered via parcel delivery services.

control model General approach for coordinating the execution of component DBMSs within a distributed DBMS.

cost-based query optimization Query optimization algorithm based on the query syntax, availability of indexes and access paths to data objects, and statistics about data in the database.

cursor   A SQL object associated with a specific SELECT operation that enables a program to access a set of selected records and process them one at a time.

data control language   Language for controlling user's access to data.

data definition language   Language for defining and describing data.

data dictionary   A repository that contains the names and descriptions of data elements, their uses, and possibly the individuals responsible for keeping them up to date. Often the data dictionary is integrated with the data directory.

data directory   A repository that contains the names of data elements and their locations within one or more databases and files. Often the data directory is integrated with the data dictionary.

data extraction   An approach for sharing data in which data is copied form the source database and inserted into the target database.

data item   A data type and a value. A database management system stores only the value in the database. For example, the data item (integer, 5) is represented by binary '00000101'.

data manipulation language   Language for manipulating data.

data-manipulation language transparency   The distributed DBMS supports data-manipulation transparency if the data-manipulation languages of the underlying DBMS are hidden from the user and the user formulates all requests in using a single data-manipulation language.

data model   (1) Style of describing, manipulating, and describing business rules. (2) A schema of a specific database.

data replicator   Software that maintains a copy of a file or database.

data type   Set of values with an implied physical representation. Widely used data types include integers, floating-point numbers, and character strings. Additional data types are coming into use, including graphics, images, audio, and video.

database A collection of interrelated data managed by a database management system.

database administration The role filled by individuals who design and manage databases.

database administrator (DBA) The individual who designs and manages a database.

database engine Software that performs requests to access the database. The database engine contains components that accept requests to access the database, determines if the user may perform the request, locates and accesses the desired data, records all changes made to the database, and prohibits multiple users from updating the same data at the same time.

database link A pointer from a record in one database to a record in another database.

database machine Special hardware designed for use as a DBMS.

database management system (DBMS) Software for storing and accessing databases.

database server A server with a DBMS.

deadlock A situation in which multiple transactions wait for each other to unlock shared data.

deadlock detection An algorithm for detecting the existence of deadlocks.

deadlock prevention A strategy for assigning locks in such a fashion that a deadlock can never occur.

decompression Process of reconstituting or reconstructing compressed information to its original size and format.

deferred updates Process of executing transactions but not writing the results to the database until the commit point.

derived fragmentation   Partitioning or fragmentating the rows of a table based on the fragmentation of another table.

deviant transaction   Improperly written transaction that violates a business rule.

distributed DBMS dimensions   Classes of features of a distributed DBMS.

distributed transaction manager   Software component of a distributed DBMS that sends commands to the appropriate local transaction managers via the communication subsystem. The distributed transaction manager also executes the synchronization aspects of the distributed transaction causing temporary files to be transmitted among local managers. The distributed transaction manager is also responsible for distributed concurrency control and commitment.

distributed transaction optimizer   Software component of a distributed DBMS that converts a user query into a distributed transaction that may involve accesses to multiple component databases. The distributed query optimizer isolates users from the data structures used by the underlying database management system.

distribution path   The process of fragmenting a centralized database and migrating the data to a distributed DBMS.

document server   Database management system for documents.

document type definition (DTD)   Rules for interpreting the tags and laying out document content.

downsizing   Replacing expensive systems with cheaper, smaller systems.

durability   A property of a transaction that guarantees that, once the transaction has committed, the changes it made will be reflected in the database for future transactions.

embedded SQL   A programming language that has been extended to also support SQL commands.

encapsulation   Hiding the implementation from the use of an object.

encryption   Transformation of data into a form that cannot be understood without the decryption algorithm.

entity integrity   A business rule that requires each record to have a unique identifier.

federated database   Integrated view of parts of data from multiple databases in which data may join and leave.

file   An ordered set of homogeneous records.

file server   Server which manages one or more files on behalf of multiple users.

file system   Hardware for storing files and software for accessing those files by file name and location within a hierarchical directory. Popular file systems include the UNIX and MS-DOS file systems.

filter server   Server which selects data from data streams that satisfies filtering rules.

foreign key   A column of a table that must either be null or must contain the value of a primary key of some table.

fragmentation transparency   A distributed DBMS supports fragmentation transparency if the user is not aware that a table has been fragmented by the DBA.

gatekeeper   Software that verifies users have the right to access data.

gateway   Software component that translates a user request into the format of the target DBMS and translates the resulting data to the form required by the user.

gopher   A hierarchical menu system for delivering documents over the Internet.

global transaction   Specification of data in one or more databases to be accessed. A global transaction may be a query in which data are retrieved from one or more databases, or it may update one or more databases.

heuristic-based query optimization   Query optimization algorithm based on the query syntax and the availability of indexes and access paths to data objects.

hierarchical data model   Data model in which the records form a hierarchy. IBM's IMS is an example of a DBMS conforming to the hierarchical data model.

hoovering   Process of selecting data from multiple remote databases.

horizontal fragmentation   Partitioning or fragmenting a table into subtables for storage at different sites in a distributed DBMS.

HTML   Hypertext Markup Language used to describe documents on the world wide web. HTML allows a document to contain links to other documents, giving the world wide web its hypertext (and hypermedia) capabilities.

hypertext   A scheme for supporting embedded links within documents. While browsing a document with hypertext links, a user can select one of those links and quickly move to the document it points to.

hypermedia   A multimedia system that incorporates hypertext-style links embedded within documents.

immediate updates   Process of executing transactions and updating the database prior to the transaction commit point.

incremental backup   A backup that is made while the database is being updated. Changes made to the portion of the database already backed up are also recorded so that, if the database needs to be restored from the backed-up copy, the changes made during the backup are also restored.

index   (verb) To identify keywords that characterize a document; (noun) Access path to data characterized by keywords.

information retrieval system Text-based database management system.

inheritance Implied inclusion of information from one data object within another.

integration path The process of integrating data from separate databases into a distributed DBMS.

islands of unreachability (IOUs) Data files residing on different computers that users find difficult to locate and access.

isolation A property of transactions that guarantees that the changes made by one transaction cannot be seen by other transactions until the transaction commits.

local optimizer Component of a DBMS that determines an optimal or near optimal strategy for processing each data request.

local transaction manager Software component of a distributed DBMS that accepts subtransactions from one or more distributed transaction managers via the communication subsystem. It accepts results from the local database engine and places them on the communication subsystem for delivery to other local transaction managers or to the distributed transaction manager. The local transaction manager also executes local synchronization aspects of a distributed transaction.

location transparency Distributed DBMS supports location transparency if the user is not aware of the location or site of the data being accessed.

lock Mechanism to prohibit access to a data item by multiple users at the same time.

logically distributed data The DBA assigns data to reside within one of several databases. The databases may be on the same computer or different computers.

loosely-coupled distributed DBMS Data sharing approach in which users may access any of several databases using the components of a distributed DBMS or may access their own local database directly.

lossey compression   Compression in which information is lost and can not be recovered. Lossy compression is frequently used for images, audio and video.

lossless compression   Compression in which information is not lost.

metering   Process of measuring the use of information by a user.

method   Object-oriented term for function or operation.

middleware   Software that provides transparent linkage between client application and server data that makes the server data appear local to the application on the client.

Mosaic   A client program supporting a distributed hypermedia system based on the world wide web.

multimedia server   Server managing drawings, images, voice, video, or animation data types.

multiversioning   A transaction manager maintains multiple versions of data being accessed by multiple transactions. Some DBMSs use multiversioning instead of locking to provide isolation without serialization.

natural language   User interface consisting of words structured according to the rules of a national language such as English, German, or Spanish.

Netscape   A client program supporting a distributed hypermedia system based on the world wide web.

object based   System that supports only build-in object classes and can not support the creation of new object classes.

object-oriented database server   Server that supports an object-oriented database.

one-phase commit protocol A commit protocol consisting of one phase of message exchange to determine if all sites updated by a distributed query should be committed or rolled back.

optimistic concurrency control algorithms Concurrency control algorithms in which transactions are allowed to execute before serializability is validated.

physically distribute data The DBA assigns data to reside within one of several databases, each database residing on a different computer.

primary key Unique identifier for each row of a relational table.

public key encryption algorithm Widely used algorithm for encryption and decryption. The algorithm uses a parameter called key.

quiet point A point in time during which a database management system accepts no new transactions while waiting for all currently executing transactions to commit.

query A request to access data from a database.

record A set of data items. For example, a record might contain the data items (integer, 5), (character string, 'John Doe'), and (integer, 1989).

recovery Restoration of a database to a previously consistent state.

referential integrity A database rule that guarantees that the value of a column either is null or is the value of a primary key of a foreign table.

relation A set of records or relationships in a relational database; often called a table.

remote access An approach to sharing data in which one user extracts data directly from the database of another user.

replication transparency A distributed DBMS supports replication transparency if the user is not aware that more than one copy of the data exists.

request constructor DBMS component that provides an interface used by human users. A request constructor helps a user formulate requests by accepting and examining the commands and parameters entered by the user and validating them for syntactical correctness. Some request constructors assist users in formulating database transactions by displaying menus of currently valid options. Some request constructors display error messages describing syntactically incorrect portions of the request and enable users to easily enter corrections. Several request constructors are possible, one for each type of user interface supported by a DBMS.

rightsizing Using a processor that fits the task at hand. The new processor may be bigger or smaller than the old processor.

rollback The end of a transaction that aborts, and any changes it has made to the database are undone.

row See tuple.

runtime support processor Component of a DBMS that is responsible for accessing the database in response to the commands passed to it from the user. It schedules and performs these requests. The runtime support processor also enforces local concurrency control, ensuring that two concurrently executing requests do not try to update the same data at the same time. It also creates a journal log of changes made to the database.

schema Description of a specific database expressed using the data description language of a data model.

serial transactions Transactions whose executions do not overlap in time.

serializability Test for determining if concurrent transactions conflict.

server Hardware that provides services consumed by a server.

SGML   Standard Generalized Markup Language is an ISO standard for describing structural information embedded within a document. SGML provides multiple views of a document and fosters document reuse.

single-site update   A transaction that updates data at a single site within a distribute DBMS.

smartsizing   Re-engineering the business process in addition to changing the physical processor.

software architecture   Software components organized and integrated together to support a predefined collection of features.

software component   Software module that performs a specific task.

stored procedure   An SQL request that is stored as part of database.

structured query language (SQL)   Standard query language for relational databases.

table   See relation.

thesaurus   A collection of terms that may be used to formulate a query against a textual database.

three-phase commitment   A commit protocol consisting of three phases of message exchange to determine if all sites updated by a distributed query should be committed or rolled back.

tightly-coupled distributed DBMS   Data-sharing approach in which users may access any of several databases using the components of a distributed DBMS, but may not access any component database directly.

timestamp ordering   A concurrency control strategy in which transactions are serialized based on when they were initiated

transaction   A sequence of database operations that must be executed as a unit.

transaction management Ensuring that transactions satisfy the ACID properties of atomicity, consistency, isolation, and durability.

transaction optimizer Software component of a distributed DBMS that converts a user transaction into a distributed transaction that may involve accesses to several component databases. The distributed query optimizer isolates users from the data structures used by the underlying DBMS.

tree-structured query Query that involves a single table in which the foreign key references the primary key of the same table. For example, a query against a "report to" table to generate an organization chart.

tuple An individual record or relationship in a relation or table; often called a row of a table.

two-phase commitment A commit protocol consisting of two phases of message exchange to determine if all sites updated by a distributed query should be committed or rolled back.

two-phase locking A locking scheme in which all locks are acquired before any locks are released.

upsizing Evolving a system to bigger hardware to support increased processing needs.

user A human or an application program that accesses a database.

user interface The set of commands and responses by which a user accesses a database. A user interface is a front end to the database engine that (1) aids users in formulating requests to access the database and (2) formats and displays the results in a useful form for the user.

user interface translator Software component of a DBMS that converts the request constructed by its corresponding constructor into a standard form used by the other components of the DBMS. Each user interface translator hides the user interface from the other DBMS components.

wait-for graphs Data structure constructed during the detection of deadlocks.

world wide web A network-based hypertext document system that supports links among different documents.

Index

union operation 84
Unland, R. 153
upsizing 158
user 4
user interface 25-27
user interface component 25, 30-31
user interface translator 31, 40, 41, 92,
  95, 119
user profile 88
user's interest profile 182

V

Valduriez, Patrick 20, 95, 118, 153
validity constraints 93
versions 207, 215
vertical fragmentation 84-85, 106
vertical scalability 165
visual content abstraction 199

W

wait-die protocol 128
wait-for graph 129-132
wide-area network 219-225
Wong, Anna 118, 152
Wong, Harry K. T. 152, 118
World Wide Web 195, 199
wound-wait protocol 128

Y

Yannakakis, M. 153

Z

Zdonik, S. B. 218